MW00512738

LEADING
FROM THE
INSIDE OUT

**Hard-Earned Lessons
from Education, Government
and ... Baseball**

CHARLES E. PASCAL

First published in 2020 by Onyx Publishing, an imprint of Notebook Publishing of Notebook Group Limited, 20–22 Wenlock Road, London, N1 7GU.

www.notebookpublishing.co

ISBN: 9781913206444

A CIP catalogue record for this book is available from the British Library.

Typeset by Onyx Publishing of Notebook Group Limited.

For Roger and all his jazz

CONTENTS

What They're Saying About
Leading from the Inside Out

Charles Pascal was a brilliant deputy minister, college president, and more. He remains today, a wonderful teacher and mentor. His Inside Out lessons are invaluable for anyone who aspires to be a more effective leader whether in education, government or the broader community.

—Hon Bob Rae
Canadian Ambassador to the United Nations & Former Premier of Ontario

Charles has been an invaluable mentor to us and trusted leader. He has taught us that his lesson about "Evidence-Based Storytelling" can impact policy change and transform lives.

—Julia Davison
CEO of Australia's Goodstart Early Learning

'Knowledge comes, but wisdom lingers'. Tennyson's well-known adage perfectly captures the experience of reading Charles' latest work. An exquisite balance of reflection, evidence and insight from a global leader.

—Sir Kevan Collins
Visiting Professor
Institute of Education
University College London

If he hadn't chosen education and government to ply his superb ability to lead, Pascal would have made an excellent contribution to baseball. Love the way this true guru of the game weaves in baseball analogies.

—Paul Beeston
Former President & Chief Operating Officer of Major League Baseball and
President Emeritus of Toronto Blue Jays

Inside Out deconstructs bias through the lens of this pioneer in equity and inclusion. Informed by strong moral purpose, Charles Pascal deftly articulates some hard-earned lessons that aim to ignite enduring systemic change for "the many, rather than the elite few."

—Dr. Avis E. Glaze
Global Education Advisor
Former, Ontario Education Commissioner

Charles' reciprocal mentorship approach with me generates sharing of our respective lived experience evidenced by his genuine desire to be an effective ally in support of Indigenous fairness. He is a true leader-learner.

—Sean Monteith
(Anenonkawenans: The Little Paddle That Stirs)
Director of Education
Hastings and Prince Edward School Board (Ontario)

What a valuable resource for both emerging and experienced leaders! Inside Out *will greatly benefit educational leadership scholars, students and professionals.*

—Dr. Ann E. Lopez
Director, Centre for Leadership and Diversity, OISE/University of Toronto
Co-Editor-In-Chief, Journal of School Leadership

Inside Out *is a testimony to Charles Pascal's knowledge and experience about how government works and how it can benefit from the leadership lessons he offers up in this important memoir. A must read for public servants at all levels.*

—**Hon. Roy J. Romanow**
Former Premier of Saskatchewan
Royal Commissioner on the Future of Health Care in Canada
Chancellor, University of Saskatchewan

Inside Out *offers important lessons and wonderful human insights. Pascal makes it clear that when we're on a mission to "change the world" it is vital to understand that leaders and leadership doesn't always come from the top down, but instead comes from a range of perspectives and positions.*

—**Annie Kidder**
Executive Director & Founder
People for Education (Canada)

Foreword
by
Michael Fullan

WHAT HAPPENS WHEN YOU get a chomping at the bit champion leader anxious to let loose on the latest challenge? What if each opportunity deepens the desire mediated by a combination of both greater wisdom and insight—and the voice that cautions: "look before you leap". What if you string together 40 years of such action in a variety of complex settings? And what if you take notes and feed forward reflections as you encounter each problem?

Well, you get Charles Pascal, a renaissance leader for all seasons: once upon a time baseball catcher, University Professor, Community College President, Deputy Minister to several governments in Ontario, a CEO of a major Foundation, early childhood commissioner, international consultant, and political commentator for various media outlets.

Collaborating with Charles is always a joy. On some days he takes the role of the 'man who would be blunt'—euphemistically calling this trait 'authenticity'. The next day he empathizes his way into and out of complexity. He has an uncanny ability to accumulate wisdom and insights while approaching each new situation as a novel phenomenon. He is a divergent thinker, a dot connector and a natural animator that is key to creating shared vision with others that drives things forward.

What we get in *Leading from the Inside Out* is a dozen major leadership lessons that seem both unique and generalizable. Each one is richly contextualized across multiple situations. And each lesson is bolstered by other related ideas about creative change-making. While these lessons need to be read and understood carefully in context, you get a sense of their playful validity by their labels: *feedback is the breakfast of champions, being right is not a strategy, the power of evidence–based story-telling, the graceful power of apology,* and *improvement is the enemy of change* and so on. He also dedicates a chapter to important lessons from the Pandemic.

Chapter One is called "The Rear-View Mirror as Compass". This is only partly true. Yes, the cumulative insights that come from where you have been can be very instructive—especially if you deliberately learn from them and the lessons are embedded in your emotional and rational psyche. But you also have to treat each new situation as having its unique history and culture. Charles is a master of combining his studied intuition and appreciation of the situation he is facing. He always builds fresh and meaningful rapport with whatever group is working with.

When I was adviser to Ontario Premier Dalton McGuinty in 2007, Charles approached me about getting "early childhood" learning on the Premier's action agenda. I had a front row seat when Charles was appointed as commissioner to develop a comprehensive plan to implement full-day universal learning for all of Ontario's four- and five-year-olds. The program development and political complexity of genuinely respecting and sorting out the diverse input from thousands of people and organizations was a showcase for Pascal's ability to mobilize what's required for sustainable change. He has a visceral understanding regarding the cardinal change principal that the people who will ultimately be key to implementing any complex change, must be involved from the start.

To be sure, Charles Pascal is a thoughtful, reflective practitioner who has provided his lessons learned for leaders in any public or private space. Take time to learn and appreciate each. You will find them individually valuable, but especially, you will learn to appreciate the links across the lessons. The big bonus is that the stories vary, real people are named and featured, and it's a damn interesting read.

Michael Fullan
Professor Emeritus, OISE/University of Toronto
Global Director, New Pedagogies for Deep Learning

Chapter One
The Rear-View Mirror as Compass

SINCE I WAS TWELVE, it seems like leading others has come naturally to me. Of course, at that age, it was all about the sense I felt as a catcher on my baseball team and how my peers responded to my shenanigans in school. It's been a while since then, however, but the leadership thing seems to have maintained its hold along the way. For me, the time has come to share with the next generation of change-makers the lessons learned, to confess what I learned the hard way and what came naturally.

My three-quarters-of-a-century mark is now in the rear-view mirror. Yikes. It's hard to imagine, especially given the fact I feel at least twenty years younger. The notion of me publicly recognizing that 76 is the new 55 simply won't cut it; at best, it's a sign of insecurity—a sign that dusk is that much closer than dawn. *Insecurity*? Yep—I recently referred to myself as a "middle-aged White guy", which is kind of right if reaching a century and a half is possible.

Naturally, my early years have had an indelible impact on the person I am. In terms of politics, I grew up in a "broken home" in Chicago. My father, a liberal Democrat, was the son of a carpenter who built soda fountains for my mother's father, an owner of several drugstores and a conservative Republican.

That's how my parents met.

Growing up, the dinner table was often a battlefield of political banter, my parents attacking each others' preferences. I vividly remember watching the very first television broadcasts of American political conventions on our brand-new black-and-white Philco in 1952. I was drawn to my dad's side and was a fervent eight-year-old supporter of Adlai Stevenson. He looked at the world through a progressive, albeit intellectual, lens, drawing the nickname "Egghead"—in stark contrast to the grandfatherly "I'll take care of you" Dwight Eisenhower. As history notes, Mom won that one, as well as the rematch in 1956.

For me, my development as a leader—that urge to "step up"—began, as it so often does during those early years. It started with my parents, Sam and Harriett, and my paternal grandparents, Rose and Dave, who lived upstairs in our somewhat non-descript duplex on the North side of Chicago. Notwithstanding my parents' political fisticuffs, these four adults placed me on top of a pedestal. I have no doubt that their unconditional love imbued in me both a sense of confidence and a challenging need for recurrent affirmation for performing good, silly, and stupid things. I deeply recognize the privilege that accrued from this early environment. Although none of them had attended university, the emphasis on education was clear. My late brother, Roger, was the first in our large, extended family to pave the way regarding the value of high-quality educational opportunity.

It was through sports—recognizing that the difference

between resources available to both my peers and competitors was often a function of skin colour—that I began to develop an early sense of the inequity. It was this that fueled my feelings surrounding the importance of social justice. These were the earliest hints that Black lives didn't seem to matter as much as White lives when it came to real fairness. In plain sight, there were noticeable differences, such as the quality of equipment, uniforms, and baseball diamonds of the "other" teams.

It was also through sports that my natural interest in leading others evolved. As a quarterback in football and baseball catcher—during which time I called the "shots"—I learned that the success of a moment-by-moment notion of what's next, would only be successful if others on the team did their part. Essentially, the essence of the importance of genuine collaboration was sewn into the very fabric of my being from day one.

For a good chunk of my professional life, I was used to being perceived as young for my accomplishments: I was the youngest player on our town's competitive baseball teams; I'd completed a doctorate and became an assistant professor at 25; I'd achieved full professorship at age 32; I'd become a college president at 37... The list goes on. Now, still feeling full of energy despite usually being the oldest in the room at this point in the journey, I still aim to make a difference in one way or another, however small that may be. That said, at this point, my major professional purpose—or obligation—is to mentor the next generation of agents of change in any way I can—and quickly get out of the way! This modest literary effort holds that notion at its absolute core.

Indeed, this three-quarters-of-a-century temporal benchmark reinforces the natural tendency within us to spend time reflecting on our lives—often with a very selective and self-aggrandizing lens. For me, there is some truth to that: I find that my lifetime batting average from my ballplayer days admittedly goes up a few percentage points with each passing year. Is this a function of a faulty memory, or a rose-coloured rear-view mirror masking the insecurity of not having moved up to The BIGS? Totally guilty on the second count.

Despite all of this, however, I have attempted to be an effective reflective practitioner for a long time, paying close attention to the lessons learned each day concerning how to be a better leader at home, in the workplace, and in the community. The key, of course, is not merely writing these lessons down: *behavior* is ultimately what counts. Learning from these lessons in an effort to improve what I actually *do* is where the gold of reflective practice lies. Given the fact that no one is perfect, my view is that effective leaders are active and reflective learners, constantly striving for honesty with self in pursuit of knowing what we don't know, as well as what and where we are in relation to an aspiring zest to be better tomorrow than we were yesterday.

This reflective practice began as an organized process when I had one of my many "going away" parties—this one at the Ontario Institute for Studies in Education, back in the dawning days of 1981, on the eve of my presidency of a community college in Ontario, Canada. One of my mentors, Professor Dave Hunt, gave me a book on journaling with the inscription, *You are one of the few professors who is going to actually apply theory to practice. Use this book as a guide to your daily learning about how to be a better leader. Imagine how much more authentic your teaching will be when you come back to the academy!*

What a wise and wonderful gift that was. I have been journaling ever since.

Dave passed away recently at the age of 93. He was inspiring to his last moments, going to the gym twice a week and continuing to be an active observer and commentator regarding all things important, including our shared love of baseball.

The impact of my reflective practice is the basis for this book. Thanks to Dave's encouragement, I have been completing a diary entry reflecting on what transpired the day before for a grand total of 39 years. These reflections have been informed by several core values and the behaviors I associate with each one, and present an attempt at holding myself accountable. For many years, this was a daily practice; now, it is down to an average of three times per week. In my view, effective leaders are *reflective learners*; those who pause to take stock as part of an ongoing, intentional commitment to be better. Whether one holds a major position of authority in an organization or is a parent or teacher, I encourage all to consider this kind of reflective practice.

It is this regular journaling, focusing on our core values and associated behaviours, that gives rise to the title of this book. The notion of *Leading from the Inside Out* is about ensuring that we lead from within. Driven by these explicit core values, we learn through experience from the various spheres of our lives how to be more intentional leaders. Importantly, I have found that this process of reflective practice provides remarkable grist for an ongoing journey of learning, and adapting leadership lessons that improve our ability to bring about change, first to ourselves, and, in turn, how to better collaborate with others to improve the "worlds" around us. In my case, as the book's subtitle suggests, the leadership lessons that follow derive from my experience in education, government, and yes, baseball.

And speaking of *the* game, before we go on, here's a baseball tangent (I simply can't help it). While *Leading from the Inside Out* is indeed designed to connote the importance of reflective practice as key to both leading in one's outside environment and learning from all that the external world has to offer, my love of baseball naturally has references to the concept. As a former catcher, inside/out can be taken as an approach to keeping a batter off balance by varying pitches inside or out (and up and down). As a former batter, if I am batting (as a right-handed batter) against a right-handed pitcher with no outs and a runner on second, I am going to try to hit the ball to the right side to advance the runner. How? With an inside/out swing. Yep, I couldn't help it. I can use baseball to explain anything. More to come.

So, regarding my reflective practice, I once used it as the basis for a convocation address I gave upon my son Jesse's graduation from college. At that time, I held four core values: vision, example, passion, and dignity. The reflection exercise was simple: each morning, I would pose the following questions:

1. The Vision Question: What did I do yesterday that was a good or bad example of thinking and acting strategically?

2. The Setting an Example Question: What did I do that modeled my beliefs? Did I walk the talk?

3. The Passion Question: Did I have fun and remain engaged, or did I sabotage my own ability to have fun and to remain effectively passionate about my role as a partner, father, or colleague?

4. The Dignity Question: What did I do or not do to reinforce the dignity of those with whom I live and work?

More recently, I have condensed my four-values-driven personal review questions into two. I haven't reduced the size of the mirror; I have simply made the process of taking a hard look in the glass a little simpler. Now, *authenticity* and *equity* drive my reflective practice; elements that encompass the essence and related behaviours of the original four. In today's deeply divided world, it is hard to imagine there is a more important value than the notion of equity.

While equity does not mean "sameness", it deals with issues of human dignity, fairness, and doing both big and small things to support those who are disadvantaged through no fault of their own. In my view, inequity is the most challenging, deleterious, and insidious issue of our time. Whether it flows from a simple moral imperative or the principle of enlightened self-interest, the gap between the haves and the have-nots, both domestically and globally, inflicts harm on us all. While my early years afforded me some baby steps toward understanding inequity through my experience in sports and school environment, two major forces in our current zeitgeist have laid bare the have/have-not unfairness that has long harmed our worlds: the COVID-19 pandemic and Black Lives Matter. The virus crisis has pulled back the curtain on education and health chasms that clearly show significant and shameful differences when it comes to race, culture, and other "identities" that define humankind. The Black Lives Matter movement seems to have stunned millions for whom White lives have mattered more... much more.

You will note throughout these pages that I make some reference to all or part of what I consider to be my vision statement about the future. I guess it's a world view kind of thing. The value of equity sits at its core. In my view, simply put, *the future needs to be healthier, safer, more just, and prosperous for the many rather than the elite few.* This underscores the devastating differences between the lives of racialized people, Indigenous peoples, and others who are grossly disadvantaged through no fault of their own. If you are uncomfortable with this, you might want to ask for your money back. If you are uncomfortable with Black Lives Matter, you might, indeed, want to return this book. If you think too much is made of the devastating and recurring consequences of hundreds of years of ignorant oppression of Indigenous peoples, perhaps re-gift this book to someone with whom you've argued with about all of this. But if your discomfort is tolerable, if it stems from feeling embarrassed about needing to learn things we should have known, or if your discomfort, like mine, stems from knowing we have to change some fundamental assumptions and alter our behaviour accordingly, hey, stay with it, join me on the journey, please. I definitely need the comfort of company in dealing with the discomfort of being too far from "perfect." Great leadership is all about how we handle these challenges, not how we avoid them. It is out of more than a measure of that discomfort in various circumstances that has propelled my own leadership into a better place.

So, of course it is hard for me to imagine that any of us who aspire to be more effective leaders could possibly ignore the indelible lessons arising from what surrounds us today. Without question, genuinely reflective practice *will* make many of us uncomfortable. And that's a good thing. Resolving this unease will require guidance from others. A dose of self-doubt and humility can actually help. Recently, a colleague of mine, Kate Graham, interviewed[1] the wonderful Mary

[1] Podcast: "Is COVID Reshaping Gender Roles? Interview with Mary Robinson", 2020.

Robinson, former president of Ireland, and noted: *women leaders have a quality that you don't see as much in men who lead, and that is a quality of self-doubt. Now, that might surprise you, but I think that's a valuable quality in a leader— to doubt your own ability in a way that makes you open, makes you want to listen more to the advice of others and the wisdom of others in order to do better.* Interesting! For me, this has meant my need to be guided and mentored by those with genuine lived experience to be authentic about what I know and be clear that I cannot possibly and fully understand full-throttle discrimination. Yes, a heavy dose of humility and a bit of self-doubt will open up our hearts and minds.

Regarding authenticity as a values driver, in my view, it is simply a sweeter word for "bluntness"—a kind of transparency that leaves little room for doubt concerning where my thinking lies at any particular moment. A strength of mine— and, naturally, a weakness—is my bluntness; being *too* blunt. I have had to apologize on many occasions for not tempering the manner in which I convey a point of view. Notably, striving to be authentic doesn't mean striving to be stubborn: for me, it creates opportunities for dialogue with the huge potential to change the course of one's thinking and subsequent actions. It allows others to either showcase support or not; to provide feedback that results in human progress rather than a kind of defensiveness that keeps us trudging through the status quo. Being authentic with myself is of the highest importance; it is at the very core of self-improvement, and what a wonderful and liberating but scary gift it is to have that "don't kid yourself" refrain ringing in your ears on a regular basis. Yes, *being blunt with self is key,* as it opens me up for following people who can guide me, learning things I thought I knew or things about which I had no clue.

Authenticity and equity, as well as all the behavioral expectations I have for myself that naturally follow these values, are what I choose to use as my compass. When I conduct leadership development workshops, I make it very clear that these values work for *me*; the key message for you is to be explicit about what *you* care about. In other words, what is central to *your* aspirations for being a little more effective tomorrow than today through personal accountability. What do *you* care about?

So, I have actively and consciously built and incorporated into my life this incredibly powerful habit of reflection and learning from my leadership efforts. This regular meditative process provides continuous revelations regarding the good, the bad, and the ugly of my actions, in turn providing countless opportunities to turn hard-earned lessons into improvements, giving way to occasions for necessary and timely apologies to others as a result of my own self-reflection. A continuous *Inside Out* process!

This practice has additionally increased my empathy and sympathy for other leaders in the public eye who do amazing, stupid, and even hurtful things; for the latter category of achievement, I am an ardent learner, as I am always challenging myself on how to do better at something. When it comes to evaluating those who are ridiculed for big mistakes, while I recognize it is tempting to join the cat-caller parade, reflective practice, when taken seriously, means asking oneself, "Could I ever, or *would* I ever, do that?" Often, the answer for me is a slightly jarring *yes*.

The lessons learned by observing others and the ways in which they lead and learn are invaluable and form part of my reflective routine. In sum, every leader should give some real thought to, and thus align themselves with, very clear core values and a way of holding themselves accountable for progress in applying the behaviours associated with each value. So, to be clear, I am not selling mine; there are many ways to create accountability. Everyone already has values concerning what constitutes good leadership; the problem lies in the fact that far too many of these are buried, implicit notions. Later, I will provide a simple exercise that may assist you in shifting your values from implicit to explicit, along with ideas for gaining self-knowledge concerning the gaps between your leadership aspirations and the reality of your behaviour.

So, I have considered myself a leader for a long long time; it's hard not to, given my early years as a catcher in baseball and a high school quarterback and high school class president. To me, these clearly indicate that I wanted to be "out front" and that I was ambitious to do things that made a difference. As senior class president, my main campaign promise, fulfilled after election, was centred on organizing my peers in service of doing chores for senior citizens in our neighbourhoods. We mobilized about 75% of us. With authenticity in mind, regarding the only election I have ever stood for, I was actually unopposed, and, as I like to tell it, with a soupcon of false humility and myth-making, I still only received 10 votes. Regardless, my drive for making a difference has never felt altruistic; it was just something inside me that sought to guide others; to learn from them as part of a reciprocal engagement to get stuff done. Naturally, I like to think that a good deal of what I have tried to do is driven by moral purpose.

When people discuss leadership, conversation often revolves around the more visible, extroverted version—and, while this is a grossly superficial way of looking at leadership, my friends and colleagues would certainly classify me as "up front" and "out there" when it comes to my general style. It's easy for me to understand why I consistently arrive at a mid-range score on the extroversion scale. As I noted, I was one of the fortunate ones with loving parents and devoted grandparents who put me on that proverbial pedestal as a kid. So did Miss Pond, my Third Grade teacher in Chicago's Clinton Public School.

Miss Pond was a key difference-maker for me in the classroom and beyond; she may have even saved my life. She cared enough about my own journey to take an interest in seeing me through some rougher patches in my life, showing me that getting through a day in the classroom while being creative and having fun was not a contradictory idea. The problem was that, as a student, I was totally bored, I didn't feel challenged, and, as an overly energetic student, I did a fair bit of over-the-top playful acting out that wasn't always seen by others as "playful". Before Miss Pond, I spent more time listening to vice principals sermonize me for not using my "leadership talent for good rather than evil". On more than one occasion, I was sent home, where I was able to do as I pleased; reading books that interested me or going to nearby Wrigley Field with my grandfather to watch a Cubs day game.

It was in third grade that Miss Pond lit a fire in my soul—something that probably prevented me from lighting a fire to the many other things for which I had little time or interest. She allowed me to use my love of baseball as the backbone for my work in English, math, social studies, and science. I completed a paper on the physics of hitting a baseball, noting that the bat's force on the ball was a function of mass—the weight of the bat—and acceleration—more popularly known as "bat speed." I correctly concluded that when selecting a bat, one should select one heavy enough to secure good mass, but not so heavy that it will slow down the swing. So, in the third grade, I learned that $F = m \times a$! It was then that I learned the power of adapting your individual differences to the tasks presented by any given context—whether that is home, school, the community, or the workplace.

Importantly, Miss Pond tapped into what she perceived to be my interest in helping others to improve. She saw the leader in me and went about using me as a peer tutor for three other kids. I'm pretty sure that peer tutoring didn't become common practice until many decades later, but Miss

Pond was a superb leader—always ahead of the game.

Years later, during my time as a professor at Montreal's McGill University, I wrote a speech for a conference in New York City regarding the characteristics of effective teaching and learning. Flying from Montreal to New York gave me the opportunity to review my remarks, which I found to be way too long and technical: it was a good read but made for a boring speech. So, rather than read a speech likely to clear the room after a few pages, I took out a barf bag, listed the three teachers who had the biggest impact on my life, then noted what made them impactful regarding my development. I challenged the audience to do the same: How about you? Who is the best teacher you've had? Why? The process will reveal what you value in a leader; what your values are. My revised approach received a very positive response from those gathered at that conference.

Over the years, I have become very comfortable at the podium, trying new things to ensure I keep the audience engaged—or at least awake. Now, my biggest worry is that *I* might be the one to fall asleep listening to myself expound.

During the Q&A session at that particular conference, someone asked if I had ever thanked each of the three educators for their contributions to my journey to date. Nope, I confessed, but I pledged to do so when I returned to Montreal. I received two of three responses relatively quickly. But given that Miss Pond would have been well into her eighties at the time, I had sent my letter to Clinton Public School in Chicago, requesting that the Principal pass it on to

Miss Pond if she was still alive. Six months later, I received a short and curt response. *Of course I remember you, Charlie. You terrorized your Second Grade teacher, and my job was to set you straight. No big deal.* Each of the three great educators I chose were different in how they went about their leadership, but each held a common commitment to treat each student with passion, integrity, and a respect for their differences. Have you thanked the key educators who have made a difference to your development? Because it's never too late—as I discovered.

This brings me to an important lesson for me, and likely for you, too: leadership has many faces and styles. The concept of leadership is associated far too often with those who have what is known as "Position Power"—people who hold management positions. For me, while many managers are, indeed, effective leaders, true leadership exists on its own terms, independent of any formal power. Regardless of government policy or a school board's decision-making, in the field of education, teachers are the ultimate and most important leaders in bringing out the best in students. Effective parenting is also an example of great leadership. In the corporate world, the most successful leader has the ability to think and act strategically, communicate effectively and honestly, and possesses a heavy dose of emotional intelligence—regardless of whether that leader hangs around the boardroom or the shop floor. In an organizational sense, as many have pointed out, *leadership is doing the right things, and management is doing things right*; groups large or small, formal or informal, thrive when the right things are done well. (Although this lesson is usually attributed to Peter Drucker, I first came across it as part of the works of one of my favourite leadership gurus, Warren Bennis[2].)

In this regard, it is my view that the *best leaders who carry formal position power are those who spare their use of it in favor of leading through reciprocal communications, clarity of ideas, and good old-fashioned respectful relationships.*

Effective relationships are indeed respectful and reciprocal, and when those who work under the management of great leaders have ample opportunity to offer guidance to their "boss," they, too, are leaders, facilitating the development of those "above" them on the traditional organizational chart. Furthermore, the descriptive language that characterizes this relationship in turn shifts from working *for* to working *with* the official manager/leader. In this way, everyone is learning from everyone—something that serves as a fairly good motto for a healthy organization or family.

The majority of my professional life has been in what we refer to as the "public sector"—although I have also spent 15 years heading up a private foundation. Foundations are given special charitable status in Canada, and the very best foundations operate with a public trust mentality. My journey to date has been filled with an abundance of opportunities to develop as a leader and to learn from my own mistakes—not

[2] Bennis, W., On Becoming a Leader, 1989.

only those successes that are usually due to the contributions of so many others in my work in education, government, and within various "communities." For me, the most effective leaders, whether in the public or private sector, are passionate, lifelong learners. In a book that I co-authored with my daughter, Tai, when she was 17, *Too Far from Perfect*, she describes her best teachers as those who "continue to be learners who are more excited about what they don't know as they teach us what they do know"[3]. Tai's sentiments convey the simple but, nonetheless, very challenging notion that I am not through with me; that I am, indeed, too far from perfect in the contexts of my family life, my professional worlds, and the communities in which I live. Indeed, great leaders are life-long learners who also know about the importance of testing old assumptions and casting away some that no longer work in a changing world. Futurist Alvin Toffler has often noted that *the illiterate of the 21st century will not be those who cannot read and write, but those who cannot learn, unlearn and relearn*[4].

What follows, then, are the lessons learned through my ongoing leadership journey—many of which have been easily learned, while many have been learned the hard way: through trial-and-error, through successes and failures.

The *Inside Out* process of reflective practice is key to

[3] WildElement: T. Notar & C. Pascal, *Too Far from Perfect: A Father-Daughter Conversation about Public Education*.
[4] Oxford Essential Quotes, 2016.

advancing self-knowledge that drives improvement. Having a life partner like Tassie Notar and children like Blaise, Jesse and Tai, who all understand that love includes honest feedback as they see it, is also of great help; each has had a huge impact on all I do. As a successful current affairs journalist, Tassie's understanding of the media has informed my commitment to respond in a timely fashion to any requests. I will also share later the lessons I have learned regarding how best to deal with the media.

Tassie is a talented editor, as well as someone who ensures that my many pursuits have a clear, compelling lead. My eldest, Blaise—notable for her off-the-charts creativity—is likely responsible for my commitment to feminism: she provided my early chance of seeing life's opportunities through the lens of a newborn baby girl, as well as of witnessing her own incredible journey as one committed to equity in all its forms. Jesse is a monument to integrity and kindness in all he does—a role model for me to be gentler in my relationships. He has shown incredible kindness and forgiveness for my imperfections. Meanwhile, Tai, my youngest, is a poster-person for millennials and post-millennials rejecting a 9–5 life in favour of a freer and more fulfilling one for her entrepreneurial drive.

For me, also ensuring you have a handful of genuinely good friends and constructive colleagues goes a long way in avoiding "kidding yourself." There are lessons to be derived from those seemingly ugly but promising moments. I am fortunate to have such people in my life. As an example, former Ontario Finance Minister Greg Sorbara is someone I can always count on to provide the straight goods, whether I ask for them or not! And he knows how to give feedback in a clear but constructive manner. Absolute gold.

The leadership lessons that follow—as well as the stories that hopefully bring them to life for you—come largely from the opportunities I have been fortunate enough to have as a university professor at McGill and the University of Toronto (at the Ontario Institute for Studies in Education [OISE]), as President of Sir Sandford Fleming College in Eastern Ontario, as an Ontario deputy minister (non-partisan unelected head of each government department) in very diverse fields, as head of the Atkinson Charitable Foundation, from my work in various community settings, and my time in and around sports, especially baseball. Although many of the lessons learned are embedded in my Canadian context, they are also universal—many being informed by international experiences, including consultancies and professional relationships with a wide variety of people and organizations in the U.S., Australia, the U.K., China, and South Africa. Indeed, my living obituary clearly showcases the challenges of my holding a job.

I have thought of other books to write relating to each of these contexts. When I first became a university professor, the lessons I was learning led me to outline a book I titled *The Not-So-Ivory Tower*. Upon leaving government as a Senior Public Servant, I wrote the first chapter of *Government Lost: Why Government Doesn't Work and How it Could*. I have also imagined a book on strategic philanthropy entitled *Farewell to Alms*. Maybe I will dedicate my next tome to one of these areas of focus; however, the leadership lessons I have learned to date are generic, cutting across all contexts—those I have worked in, and those I haven't, but which I have witnessed both up-close and from a distance. I have concluded, at least for the time being, that one book will do—at least one effort at a non-fiction. Besides this book, I am working on a novel loosely based on my poker group—a gathering of great friends now in its 27th year. The working title of this murder mystery? *Let the Chips Fall.*

For this true tale, however, each of the following chapters is dedicated to one overriding lesson, along with other related lessons, most of them original, meaning I have never heard them "voiced" before. Some of the lessons, however, were authored by others, but nevertheless are ones I wholeheartedly embrace.

You may notice I present two or more versions of a lesson throughout, as well as my repeated underscoring of the same lesson/principle, which I choose to do for emphasis. This is because I'm a serial repeater—and because I want these lessons to hit home for you and, one may hope, ingrain themselves within your very fibre one way or another. You may also notice that I will offer up the same meaning in different forms in order to provide diverse, and short- and long-form examples of the same concept—another form of emphasis.

Naturally, my role as a son, brother, father, grandfather,

and partner are inseparable from who I am, from what I believe to be true at my core, and from my aspirations to get closer to a perfect leader across all facets of my life—and, again, I want to emphasize that these are *my* lessons and *my* values. With that said, I hope they stimulate your own thinking and actions.

Upon completing the penultimate draft of this book, COVID-19 became the most challenging global crisis witnessed in my lifetime—and, likely, this has been the case for most, if not all, who are reading this. The notion of a book on leadership that fails to consider the lessons learned during the darkest hours of this pandemic, or, as I suggested earlier, fails to use this crisis to reinforce other lessons already learned, would have rendered this manuscript dead on arrival, ergo "Chapter Eleven: Lessons Learned from World War III."

One other note in advance of your journey through these pages: I will often refer to the importance of clear *policy* priorities as key to transformational leadership. While *policy* is usually associated with the vernacular of government, I use the notion broadly with full recognition that non-governmental organizations—both public and private—also develop policies that encapsulate priorities to guide their futures.

Finally, importantly, I want this experience for you to be more than a somewhat passive exchange from me to you. I want to engage with you. I want to learn with and from you. So, at the conclusion of each chapter, I will encourage you to answer a few questions about how you already apply, or how you might possibly start to apply, the key takeaway lessons. And, in the concluding chapter, I will direct you to my website, where you can post an idea, ask a question, and interact with me and other peers on their leadership journeys. I encourage you to take notes, to record your answers, raise questions, and provide great examples of how you apply my leadership lessons—and also share some of your own.

Chapter One Takeaways

- **The critical importance of having explicit core values:**
  Ensure your leadership is informed by clear values and principles that drive commitment to related behaviours that matter.
- **The power of reflective practice:**
  Use your core values and related behaviours to hold yourself accountable through regular self-reflection about how you are measuring up to advance your progress as a leader.

EXERCISE #1:

As I have emphasized, those who aspire to be better leaders should start by being both explicit about their core values and associated behaviours and have a mechanism to hold themselves accountable. Here's an exercise that will take you five minutes. Please consider completing this before you read further. This simple exercise carries with it high-impact potential. So:

Who are the leaders you respect—living or dead, well-known or personally connected—and why, in specific terms, do you respect them?

When you are clear about why you admire other leaders, you are taking implicit notions you harbor within and making them explicit. Write the results of this simple task down and use your list of values and characteristics of great leadership to audit what you are about to read. See how we match up.

I look forward to your feedback on all that follows, given that Chapter Two conveys my first big lesson: that feedback is the breakfast of champions.

Your Notes

Chapter Two
Feedback is the Breakfast of Champions

I HAVE ALREADY NOTED that reflective practice—regularly standing back and quietly and honestly appraising one's lived experience—is key in identifying lessons worth noting and acting upon. I still engage in journaling as a way of trying to hold myself accountable for what I may do differently tomorrow as I reflect today about yesterday's experience. It is useful to note what went well and why, what requires a follow-up phone call or perhaps an apology for something that was said or that was not recognised or acknowledged, and what elements of leadership practice require alteration or modification.

With full paraphrasing credit to the Wheaties cereal boxes that depicted some of the favorite sports heroes of my youth, feedback is truly the breakfast of champions—and while holding oneself accountable through this kind of reflective practice is extremely valuable, it is also essential to seek and receive feedback from others in order to increase the *essential engine of personal and professional growth: self-knowledge.*

After a few years of journaling during my tenure as a college president, I decided it was time to invent a new feedback system. I had always sought feedback as a teacher, constructing safe ways of having students assess my skills as a teacher/leader; I even co-authored a book concerning the importance of student feedback in an effort to change the almost impenetrable culture of the academy[5].

As a newly minted college president in 1982, I had a healthy dose of self-doubt when it came to doing a job with much more scope than I had previously experienced. Being authentic about what I did not know and frequently seeking feedback from those I perceived to be able to mentor me on my weak areas (or, more importantly, to identify my blind spots) was essential to survival as step one. So, in 1983, after a year or so on the job, I developed a way of gathering feedback about my performance from many "surrounding" perspectives—a 360 approach. The key was working with others to develop a survey that focused on all the values and behaviors that were important to both the college and myself.

Next, I had to find someone who could select a random sample of professors, administrators, support staff, and student leaders who would receive and be asked to fill out the survey on my performance—all, of course, in a strictly anonymous manner—and return it. It was critical to choose a person I trusted highly to coordinate this and to summarize and present the results back to me. It was also essential that this person was trusted by the organization to ensure safety in offering truthful feedback.

---

[5] Knapper, C. K., Geis, G. L., Pascal, C. E. & Shore, B. M: *If Teaching is Important: Evaluation of Instruction in Higher Education*. Toronto: Clarke, Irwin, 1977.

While I was already in the habit of seeking feedback in a variety of ways—including the simple evaluation of the meetings I led (for example, "So, how did we do today? What were three things that went well? How can we improve?")—this 360 approach totally captured my need to know how I was doing, as well as how I could improve through the use of a process that was "safe" for the assessors. My first 360 report was full of good ideas for doing some things differently and staying on-course with other things. However, the real big takeaway from this "safe" way of securing feedback dealt with the "expectations gap" between what I was saying publicly about my leadership intentions and values, and how the grassroots of the folks of the organization felt about my pronouncements.

For example, right at the beginning of my tenure as President, I made it clear that *participation breeds creativity and commitment*. This meant that there would be an increase in everyone's contribution to the key decisions made at all levels of the organization. There was a sort of initial honeymoon euphoria created that quickly began to dim as a result of the mixed styles of deans and department chairs, with some continuing on with their top–down command-and-control management approach. Meanwhile, others stepped up to the plate, enthusiastically embracing a new level of democratic leadership. Over time, too many in the organization felt I was "out of touch" with their reality—that things really hadn't changed.

Frankly, too many of my colleagues, while initially

hopeful, thought I was a hypocrite—and because the 360 worked, I became aware of my inconsistent application of a core principle of organizational change. My self-knowledge increased, and we did something about it, establishing an in-service professional development program for managers to develop more skills and comfort regarding how to more effectively involve "their people" in decision-making and communications. This process also made clear to some that the old adage of leopards and spots was at play, and several who simply could not get in sync with a more democratic approach were supported for early retirements and other opportunities. Only a few required a modest nudge and a bit of incentive to move on.

I have implemented this same 360 Feedback approach in other organizations, too. Frankly, it seems that assisting the development of others is at the very core of my DNA. For a number of years, I was asked by a large Australian organization to work with their entire senior team, collaboratively developing a tailor-made feedback survey with each one before distributing it to their team members and peers, and subsequently summarizing the results in an anonymous fashion. However, such a process does not and should not end with a report: while in today's world we have Survey Monkey and other e-methods for securing feedback, it is what we *do* with the information that counts. Hence, the work I continue to do in this space includes discussing the received feedback and developing a plan for change as appropriate. I continue to assist others in Canada with this method, and I am currently doing this for a colleague in the U.K. as a trusted coach.

The lesson is clear. It's *not just about securing useful feedback; it's what you do with it that counts.*

Naturally, we all want to live, work, and play in high-trust environments in which it is natural for everyone to give and receive effective feedback in direct ways; however, the world is not perfect, and people are often either too resistant to giving or seeking feedback, or require more training to know how to do so. Remember the last time you were served an awful meal at a restaurant, complaining to your meal partners before proceeding to tip 15–20%, responding that the meal was, "Fine, thank you" to the perfunctory, "How is your meal?" Is it our polite Canadian persona that makes us resistant to anything that could lead to conflict? This has been my restaurant experience in other parts of the world—except in places like Australia where tips are included in pricing a meal. In my view, far too many of us are too shy in dealing with any form of conflict. We naturally don't want to intentionally create conflict, but there is a need to recognize that conflict is inevitable when transformational leadership is in play. In addition, it is equally, if not more, important to acknowledge that *it's not the presence of conflict that is the problem, but how it is resolved that propels or prevents an organization or relationship from developing.*

I am convinced that the more people who keep it safe but constructive in seeking, receiving, and giving honest feedback, and living with the positive consequences of it all, the higher the trust and the closer we will get to not needing more formalized approaches.

When I worked at McGill University back in the day, my best friend was a wonderfully kind man. George Geis was our department chair, and, like so many, while he was a world leader in the field of applied learning, he was also a conflict-avoider. For several years, the majority of us in this small department complained about the lack of effectiveness of the department's administrative assistant—somebody else who was a wonderful person, but nonetheless mismatched in her position. With specific examples in hand, we constantly urged the Chair to do something about the chaos of inefficiency and serial mistakes. Finally, after a few years, the Chair—my friend George—called me on our office intercom and asked if I would visit his office to provide him with moral support for the "big event"—more specifically, feedback and notice to our administrative assistant.

I arrived in his office at the same time as the admin assistant, and, as we sat down, George said, "Charles has something he wants to say to you..." No joke!

Flabbergasted, I tried to maintain my composure and proceeded to communicate the "mismatch" message to the assistant. Her reply? "What took you guys so long?"

It took two weeks for us to work together to locate a job better suited to her skills and interests. George was, indeed, a classic conflict-avoider, but dealing directly with the issue at hand was actually an act of kindness for the individual and the organization. You can be nice and kind in effectively dealing with conflict.

After I had completed a few years as a college president, members of our board and I were participating at the annual colleges' conference where presidents and a selection of board members would come together. Some of the presidents dreaded these conferences; they were afraid their board chairs may get strange and creative ideas from other board chairs. These presidents were proxies for too many CEOs of public and private organizations who create a culture whereby their boards think they are in charge but are actually working for their CEO. This has been my experience in Canada and well beyond, from which I have obtained many examples of bad governance—but they will have to reside in another book.

Back to the college's conference of presidents and board members: one night, at around 2AM, there was a gestapo-like bang on my hotel room door. I dragged myself to the door and, upon opening it, found three seemingly tipsy peers, all demanding that they tell me how upset they were that their board chairs had spent time with my board chair. The crime? My chair had told them about my 360 Feedback System.

"Why the hell would you allow faculty and others to evaluate you, *and*, worse yet, share the results with your board's executive committee?" one demanded.

Gathering as much composure as I could as I faced them half-asleep and in my underwear, I responded, "Because I would never want to be the last to know how I could do better—and *I* decide whether to share the results with anyone else. It helps my chair and others guide me. I guess I'm too insecure to avoid knowing what others in the college think about how I can improve."

This led to my being called a "flaky asshole" by two of the three of them. Meanwhile, the third colleague hung behind, asking if I could spend some time the next day to explain the details of my feedback system. He subsequently adopted and implemented the same approach as me.

Creating a true learning organization requires a culture of helpful support and ideas that are exchanged in a trusting manner in every direction. The higher the trust, the easier it is to reduce the amount and frequency of more formal and "anonymous" systems of feedback.

As I have noted, my experience to date suggests that too many of the most seasoned managers are not very good at both soliciting and giving timely and helpful feedback. One of my stints as an Ontario deputy minister was in a large and complex department with 12,000 employees and a 12 billion dollar budget. As is my habit when going into a job from the "outside", I spent some quality time with the two previous deputies who had held my new post, each one of which asking on their own accord what I planned to do with "old so-and-so"—a senior-level individual who they stated clearly did not have the skillset and judgment to perform his job. I thanked them, trying to suspend judgment for a few months so that I could carry out my own observations and work with this individual. I quickly learned that, if anything, my colleagues had understated the problem. This led to me to check this person's file, only to discover that the performance reviews—

separately written by my two colleagues regarding the individual in question—were short and glowing, capped off with merit increases. I wish I could say that this kind of conflict avoidance is rare, but it is not.

Speaking of the culture of government: after assuming my first deputy ministerial assignment in the Ontario government—the one alluded to above—I decided to continue on with the implementation of my 360 process in my effort to garner feedback from colleagues with varying roles and perspectives in a large and complex organization. For this process, I engaged a respected senior civil servant who, on my behalf, sent out surveys to over 300 colleagues in the ministry, randomly selected according to gender, role, and level in the organization. A total of 12 of the 25 deputy ministers at the time were randomly chosen since there was a need for wraparound feedback that included peers. The return rate for the pool of those within my ministry was 96%—a return rate I was overjoyed with, since it suggested they trusted the third-party colleague who, in turn, provided a very useful summary report. It is my belief that my ministry colleagues trusted that their feedback would be held in confidence. I also believe that the respondents trusted me enough to believe that my interest in receiving feedback was sincere. On the other hand—both interestingly and disappointingly—was the fact that only one of the 12 of the selected deputy ministers returned their survey to the third-party 360 coordinator. Another sent me their survey, ripped into pieces, with a note: *It's not my job to give you feedback; that's the job of the*

Secretary of Cabinet [head of the public service], your minister and the Premier. So much for the culture of most of the governments with which I have worked in one way or another.

On the other hand, regarding that first 360 in government, this yielded a high return from the public servants within the ministry—something that was encouraging. Civil servants aren't used to being asked to rate their deputy in what is normally a very top–down culture, and the ideas I received about what to continue doing, do better, or stop doing, were fantastic and constructive. That is, with one confusing exception!

One of the survey's questions was, "How would you rate Charles on accessibility and approachability?" The result was a stunning 50/50 split from "Outstanding" to "Not at All", with no grey in-between. What to do? After all, it's not about seeking and getting feedback that's important; it's what you *do* with feedback that's the key. It's all about learning what to do differently so that one's quest to be closer to the ever-elusive goal of perfection can continue.

In this case, I did two things: first, because this ministry was one of the first to be "wired", I sent out a note to the entire ministry noting that I had received their feedback about my performance and that I was extremely grateful to everyone who had taken their time to fill it out. I then summarized some of the key lessons I had learned, and what I planned to do going forward.

My intent was to close the loop; to let those I "led" know

that I heard, and to keep them informed of what my plans were in terms of my improving and eliminating certain things. All of this was with the hope of developing a more trusting culture of learning—and, of course, I called direct attention to the 50/50 split regarding my approachability. "Naturally, while I am surprised by this, I need to understand more about what is at play in terms of my behaviour," I said, before asking folks for further feedback, while also reminding them that, "I hold monthly *Brownbag Lunch with Charles* events that you can sign up for to discuss any issues facing the ministry and our stakeholders. I will ask the next lunch group to assist my understanding of this issue."

And I did. People from all over the ministry could sign up, with applications handled on a first come, first served basis to a maximum of 18 seats at my board table. These were very popular gatherings that only had one condition: no personnel issues could be raised since I didn't want to create a setting in which people might complain about a colleague.

So, I asked the group, "While I feel I am very approachable, obviously many do not. So, what's up? What do you think?"

The first response was not surprising. "Oh, Deputy, you are the most approachable deputy minister I have ever had." Okay, nice, but not helpful at all. Note that she addressed me as "Deputy"—which I despised, but which was a natural aspect of the top-down culture of government (and other settings!).

"Thanks so much," I countered, "but I really need to

understand why 50% feel the opposite. Can someone help me with this, please?"

A pause ensued before someone stepped forward. "Charles, I can easily relate to those who do not think of you as accessible and approachable. We all know how busy you are—not just with the ministry, but with the other things you have taken on government-wide for the Premier. Whenever I've seen you, you've been running in the foyer, going from one place to another... Hardly the image of someone we could approach."

With this encouragement, others weighed in on both sides—again, with an even split. Those who found me to be accessible explained why and how they could and had "approached" me; they noted things like, "Well, everyone knows that you are in your office at 7AM or earlier, so stopping by is no problem", or, "You are incredible at responding quickly to emails; do you ever sleep?" Meanwhile, others noted, "I don't work in Toronto, so how could I stop by, and why would I think a deputy would have time to respond to an email?" What was revealed were distinct differences concerning the perceptions, histories, and differently held beliefs pertaining to one's role and, more specifically, the role of a deputy minister.

Working around this issue served as an invaluable lesson in what to do with controversial feedback—which was, in my case, sending out a note to all that described the results of the brownbag lunch discussion, while also acknowledging my deep respect and thanks for those who had helped me with their perceptions of inaccessibility—perceptions that I had learned were well-founded and based on what they "saw" and believed to be true about my role. Importantly, I noted the ways they could approach me by doing such things as contacting my assistant for a phone call, quickly visiting when they were in town, or simply dropping me an email. Just taking the time and effort to understand and respect the different views presented made a huge difference to the further feedback I received. I also made it clear that it was inappropriate to discuss human resource issues, and that working through appropriate procedures was key. I did not want to reinforce "end runs" around their managers. The notable exception was the occasional issue relating to a case of discrimination or workplace abuse for which I would quickly guide them to the appropriate and safe process.

The results of this process, implemented in plain sight, was a huge boost in terms of the acknowledgement of the importance of trust in the Ministry. At one point, given the complexity and size of the Ministry, and given that it was a ministry that served very vulnerable people, there was a feeling that we needed to ensure that we took care of ourselves as colleagues. Hence, a task force on wellbeing was established, with around 20 colleagues representing the roles, genders, and places of work within the Ministry—all being spread across Ontario. During my time as a member on the task force, our Director of Legal Services was the chair—who, at the very first meeting, asked that everyone introduce themselves and note the one thing that caused each stress.

About halfway around the table, someone said, "What causes me stress? That's easy: when I get an email from Charles at 1AM or 5AM! That sends the signal that just because *he* doesn't need to sleep, *we* should be working harder."

I tried to interrupt with a defensive, "But I don't expect that," but the Chair ruled me out of order.

"It's not your turn, Charles," she said with a firm smile.

When it *was* my turn, I tried to explain—but, again, the Chair suggested I listen more carefully to the message others shared as well. Since then, within a high-trust setting, this deputy minister was given very direct, helpful and public feedback concerning how to improve his behaviour.

It was a highly embarrassing experience—until the next day, when I noted in my journal how incredible—how *unusual*—it was for a deputy minister to get such valuable input in that way. What a gift of trust that they would take me on. It was clear to me that *behaviour* was what counted most. Hence, ever since that moment, if ever there is a need for me to send an out-of-hours email to those I formally "lead", I ensure it is put it in the draft folder and sent out at 9AM—a habit I have actively and consciously developed in an effort to reduce the stress of others.

Seeking feedback is great, but it is only half of a formula that works when it comes to our development. While I am an optimist and capable of giving fulsome "benefits of the doubt", I do not believe that the constant requests we receive from the service industry "to complete this short survey about how we did" are sincere efforts to improve customer service.

Has anyone you know ever received a call or note back about a suggestion you have made with details about what they plan to do with an idea you offered in a survey? Certainly not me. Superficial pretense regarding being open to feedback can foment distrust.

In looking in the rear-view mirror regarding the lessons I have learned along the way, it is also key to understand the context in which I pen these lessons. A day without wondering where to find true, moral, and effective leadership in both public and private places is rare for me. Over the past few years, we have witnessed examples of disturbingly immoral anti-leadership in the U.S., enabled by people who claim to be concerned about their "children's children" while at once supporting decisions that present long-term devastation to the health and wellbeing of their families and their constituents.

In the backyard of my Canada, I also see the same kind of political self-serving tribalism when watching enablers of bad behavior drinking political Kool-Aid—supporting one's "leader" at the expense of a better society. With that said, the chapter that deals with the lessons learned during our COVID-19 "world" underscores how a crisis can provide a change to one's real or perceived leadership—including Ontario's current premier. It is also a time to admire great leadership from the likes of Germany's Angela Merkel and New Zealand's Jacinda Ardern, both of whom bring a level of authenticity and empathy to an all-too-uncommon zenith.

The engine of improvement—doing better tomorrow than

we did yesterday (whether in family, community, or work)—is a constant process of finding effective ways to increase our self-knowledge. Getting help from others in a position to contribute to this process in a way that provides a good deal of objectivity is key, an essential ingredient of the reflective practice of a leader-learner. Additionally, knowing how to both receive and give honest, timely, and constructive feedback should be seen as a gift to the people with whom you live and work. And what about those moments when we feel that someone "simply isn't open to feedback", who seems "so defensive"? That's the time to reflect on how we offer our feedback in the first place. How is our tone? Did we create a positive context for the feedback, noting a few things that have gone well and dressing the feedback in the form of a question (for example, "Have you given consideration to...?") as opposed to a harsh declarative?

I mentioned earlier the story of reaching out to three educators who each had had an extraordinary impact on my life. I mentioned Miss Pond, my Third Grade teacher, but not Professor J. W. Atkinson, from whom I took an undergraduate course at the University of Michigan. Atkinson was a world-renowned psychologist who worked in the field of motivation, and who, as part of a ream of final-project offerings, provided an opportunity to complete a critique of his latest book manuscript. I took up the challenge and wrote what was a rather critical report that challenged a few ideas, pondered the clarity of a few others, and evaluated the general structure of the book draft. Writing a critical review of my prof's book was pretty scary, to say the least—and yet Dr. Atkinson conveyed such a natural, secure, and trusting sensibility, I felt he *deserved* my honest feedback. I will admit I worried about what I had done—and, naturally, when I received my report back, it was also riddled with feedback about *my* feedback, most of which was in agreement. Thank goodness. He also described what he planned to do as a result. Wow, I realized at the time, he really *did* want input.

In this same report, Dr. Atkinson also provided feedback that changed my own life: at the time, I was at the University of Michigan completing an academic/sports scholarship in the hope I would become a professional baseball player while also developing a Plan B regarding the type of job I might seek to pursue if baseball didn't work out. On the back of my "book report", Dr. Atkinson wrote, A++++. *Charles, your response to this challenge was incredible. My fervent hope is that you will consider applying to graduate school to pursue a PhD in our department.* As can be well imagined, this was extraordinary feedback—a reinforcing power that completely altered my Plan B. I applied to the PhD. program just as my baseball dream was dashed after a very short pro-experience the summer after I graduated and by the Fall, I was enrolled as a doctoral student in one of the globe's best psychology departments—once again emphasizing the reciprocal power of giving and receiving feedback.

I also want to note the importance of ensuring the *intentional recruiting of mentors who can provide guidance and feedback in specific areas of desired leadership growth.* For example, when I was first at the Ontario Institute for Studies and Education at the University of Toronto, I established a program in higher education that began to work with Ontario's colleges. I quickly learned that these colleges, established by former Premier William G. Davis when he was the Minister of Education (May 21, 1965), were instruments of social and economic justice—a match made in heaven for me. I began to imagine what it might be like to become a president of one of the colleges. I decided to activate my preferred mode of professional development: shadowing someone from whom I could glean an understanding of the role and its challenges. I approached Doug Light, the president of Toronto's George Brown College—one of the most highly regarded among his peers. He agreed that, after each day, we would sit down, and he would ask what I learned from him and how he might improve. Again: Wow. *Another* embedded reciprocal feedback loop.

I learned much from Doug: shadowing someone is a mode of feedback—watching, listening, observing how others respond, and aligning what you learn about what you do and learn more about what you don't do or don't know. As a result of the feedback I received from shadowing the late Doug Light, I developed enough confidence and courage to wait for the right match. I refer to my wonderful time as President of Sir Sandford Fleming throughout these pages.

Another commitment I made to myself as a leader was to learn more about the issues of First Nations, Metis, and Inuit peoples in Canada. My FNMI journey started many years ago.

In the early 90s, Ontario's Premier Bob Rae—now Canada's Ambassador to the United Nations—became the first Canadian leader to formally recognize the inherent right of the self-government of First Nations peoples in a signed statement of political intent with Ontario's chiefs—a move receiving global attention and serving as a testimony to Rae's vision. The bad news was that, without notice, his ministers and deputy ministers were not pre-warned concerning the historic press conference and its content. Why was that important? Well, for me, I was Deputy Minister of Social Services at the time, which included responsibility for child welfare. Nothing has reinforced the outrageous and recurrent issues related to the health and well-being of Indigenous peoples than Canada's residential schools that took children from their homes to "properly educate" them. Not being pre-warned, I was unprepared to deal with the immediate rise in expectations from First Nations leaders that assumed, understandably, that the responsibility for all of their children caught in the "mainstream" welfare system would be taken over by Indigenous services. Soon.

Within an hour of the Premier's announcement, I heard from Kenn Richard of Native Child and Family Services of Toronto, asking when the transfer of responsibilities could take place. Unfortunately, considering the complexities and government challenges of moving in an intentional and straight line, it took several years for the transfer to happen. I found Kenn to be forceful in his dealings with me while still seeming to recognize my genuine commitment to learning things I didn't know or understand. Thus began an over 30-year journey of trying to understand, empathize, and act when it comes to social and economic justice for Canada's Indigenous peoples.

I have deliberately and intentionally sought out mentors who guide me, correct me, and create a ready platform of feedback to assist my ongoing efforts to learn what I don't know, to understand better what I think I know, and to advise when and how I might support others whose leadership matters when it comes to Indigenous issues. I continue to learn from a "feedback cohort": Cindy Blackstock, an unrelenting crusader for the rights of First Nations' children; Kohontakwas Diane Longboat, a ceremonial leader, traditional teacher and healer; and Jeffrey Ansloos, a young professor in Indigenous mental health and wellbeing in my department at the University of Toronto. All three present examples of the critical importance of securing issue-specific mentors who can provide feedback to ensure a leader's growth. The key lesson is to *find mentors who can guide us in our intentionally chosen areas of personal and professional development.*

Finally, I noted in Chapter One that I have not accomplished a single thing of worth by myself. Nothing. There's not a tinge of false humility to see here; after all, how could I even get away with claiming "I'm the man" when the most likely readers of this book will be those amazing people with whom I have travelled? This actually presents the very core of the next chapter; the critical lesson of ensuring you share leadership with those who can do things either you can't or do not wish to do when it comes to performing your leadership role.

Chapter Two Takeaways

- **The power of seeking and receiving trusted feedback:**
  Key to growing as a leader is gaining self-knowledge by intentionally receiving feedback from others and doing so in a trustful manner that leads to honest and specific areas for development.
- **The value of having issue-specific mentors:**
  Choosing mentors who can provide guidance and feedback in developing knowledge and skill in particular areas of leadership need pays huge dividends to a leader's ability to accomplish worthy goals.

EXERCISE #2:

Please reflect on your approach to seeking, receiving, and giving feedback. How, in specific terms, do you seek feedback about your performance as a leader? In developing an idea or project, how to you seek feedback? How would you rate yourself in terms of giving effective feedback to others? Are you a conflict avoider? Are there helpful ideas you have gleaned from this chapter that you think you will apply? Which ones are they, and what do you plan to do?

In addition to making a few notes in response to these questions, put in place a simple process to gather feedback about something you are working on from people who are in a position to assist. What can you do to ensure you get the straight goods? Once accomplished, how did it go?

Your Notes

Chapter Three
Complement Thyself

NOPE, THE TITLE OF this chapter doesn't have a typo.

We all need to find a humble way to *compliment* ourselves, taking a quiet moment to bow in front of the mirror with an occasional "well done". *This* lesson at hand concerns the simple fact that I have never met a successful leader whose accomplishments were the result of flying totally solo in both good weather and bad. I have met some who *think* their success is entirely due to themselves. However, narcissism aside, those in any position of leadership will immeasurably increase their effectiveness if they work on complementing their skillset, knowledge, and overall approach to what's necessary, both generally and in specific situations. Simply put, *surround yourself with great people who complement who you are, or die on the vine of the "great leadership" pretenders.*

For my part, I have learned—over the course of many years and across many diverse contexts—what things I tend to be good at, and what I would rather not do because of either disinterest or a lack of skill or knowledge. Through useful feedback and the opportunity to learn from my mistakes, I know that I like to lead more than I like to manage. If "leadership" is doing the right things, and "management" is doing things right, as I have already noted, the winning combination naturally is a team that ensures the rights things are done well.

I have learned how much I love to connect the dots of diverse ideas—something I seem to have inherited from my father, Sam; his people skills made him popular with his workers and patrons in his Chicago restaurants, where he knew the names of any customer who visited for a second time. Saying this, Dad's ability to manage a pop stand—never mind a restaurant—was severely lacking. He was great at restaurant design and a wonderful seller of ideas, but he couldn't balance a cheque book—and, sadly, he didn't know it. He was a wonderfully loving father, despite the fact he never really retired. His last 25 or so years provided him with the satisfaction of successfully acting as the "front man" for a timeshare resort in Florida. The key to this later success was simple: it wasn't his resort, and the resort had a superb financial manager who made it all work. Instead, my father generated great ideas that others implemented, and he was superb with the guests.

For me, I *can* do the detail work: I *do* balance my cheque book and much more, but I would much rather work with others in developing shared visions and new ideas and plans—even the detailed plans—to implement ideas. In other words, I can do the "management" stuff. However, when it comes to the detailed and difficult task of carrying out a plan, day in and day out management, I need and want others to complement what I enjoy doing.

When I first became a college president, I discovered that

the college was in miserable financial shape, despite the fact I'd thought I'd done a great job of informing myself of the college's welfare before accepting the position. The VP finance and admin was a wonderful guy, but it seemed that every time I asked him a question concerning a financial problem or an approach to budgeting, regardless of whether that question was simple or complicated, he'd tell me, "I'll talk to my comptroller." With that, he would return a few days later with an excellent and well-composed answer to my questions. After some time, however, I suggested he bring his comptroller to our meetings to save time—which was how I discovered my new gem of a VP finance and admin. With a new and better-matched job for the incumbent, the comptroller took on the VP role and became an incredible complement to our senior team—and, in time, Rod Rork was well-known in the college system in Ontario as the "cream of the crop" administrative VP.

Later on, I had the good fortune to work at the Atkinson Charitable Foundation for 15 years. We had a small team of six people, and, collectively, we were known to "hit well above our weight", as the saying goes. We were able to have a significant impact on the implementation of some key public policy issues during our time working together, including a full day learning for four- and five-year-old children and the Ontario Child Tax Benefit—something that was eventually adopted by Prime Minister Justin Trudeau's federal government for all of Canada.

Small staff, high impact, with what is now called

"strength-based leadership".

The secret is simple: we were high on complementary skills and knowledge, and we knew, in explicit terms, one another's assets. We worked "flat", with little hierarchy. We also informally evaluated each staff meeting, providing one another with constructive feedback, including calling attention (in a playful way) to our idiosyncratic quirks. Our most introverted member would always hold back—that is, until one of us would beckon her with "Okay, now tell us why we are wrong in this discussion." Our performance reviews were always reciprocal: as Executive Director, I would provide draft reviews to discuss with each colleague before finalizing them, each providing me with a performance review in the same manner. We created a high-trust environment in which I would both give and receive constructive feedback. Naturally, I also had a 360 review that provided additional "safety" if any or all required it. Hence, we can see here that our previous lesson—"feedback is the breakfast of champions"—was very much at play here.

However, the true key to our success was the way in which the individual strengths of a small number of colleagues complemented one another in such a way that we were able to create a whole so much larger and more diverse than our solo talents. It is also clear that keeping our team small, "forced" us to form important relationships with external partners, whose talents and knowledge added to our efforts in certain areas of interest and need.

When I started at the Foundation as its first full-time

"professional", I followed in the footsteps of the incredible Mrs. Ruth Atkinson Hindmarsh who had run the foundation for decades and who had recently passed away at the age of 101. Mrs. Hindmarsh was the daughter of the remarkable Joseph E. Atkinson, modern day owner/publisher of the *Toronto Star*, and a significant social and economic justice crusader. From 1899 up until his death in 1948, JEA became Canada's most important force for things like universal healthcare, workers' rights, and social justice in all forms. As an aside, his *Toronto Star* newspaper was recently sold for pocket change to individuals whose track record is the absolute antithesis of what Mr. Atkinson stood for. A sign of the times regarding the challenges of the newspaper industry, perhaps? Indeed, I wonder if JEA would have folded his hand and shut the paper down once he became aware of the notion of selling to those buyers. On the other hand, he was a workers' rights champion, and protecting the employees of the paper would have been a counterweight. Time will tell if the new owners honour his legacy as they pledged. I doubt it. You can buy a paper, but you shouldn't pretend to buy the values you don't believe in.

So, as the first full-time head of the Atkinson Charitable Foundation, I was given carte blanche to hire staff, as well the remarkable opportunity to become a servant leader to support Mr. Atkinson's legacy. A values match made in heaven.

I often think that the only skill worth bragging about is my talent for hiring great people who complement what I bring to the table. My first hire? Christine Avery Nunez, a superbly talented manager and organizational genius with great emotional intelligence. Then, Christine and I hired Liz Chan, another talented colleague. In turn, the three of us continued the hiring process with two things in mind: the fact that I never wanted to have a large team. As I noted, having a small amount of staff ensured that intentional need to form collaborative work with others outside of the foundation, while also providing both flexibility and an ongoing commitment to ensuring complementary talents and knowledge. Secondly, I wanted to avoid the death knoll of "group think", bringing on people with the same style and skillset. Essentially, while we always ensured our hiring centred around the core values of equity and fairness, respect for others, openness to learning new things, and a passion for disrupting the status quo, we ensured diverse skills and knowledge.

As part of this process, Pedro Barata was brought on-board—who, much like Christine and Liz, was a great complement and supplement to our approach to things. Pedro and I discussed in meetings how I would often lead too much from "the front" and how I was often too quick to come in early while he was more prone to "leading from behind", coming in later than he should, both within and outside of the Foundation. As a result, any meetings we shared were opportunities for each to intentionally become a little more like the other: me trying to hold back, and Pedro trying to lead a little closer to the "front".

Years later, when it comes to the need to lead from out

front a bit more, I think Pedro has done far better in doing so when necessary than I have in trying to hold back. He has become an extraordinary social and economic justice crusader, holding many key opportunities to lead for positive change. Meanwhile, I'm still working on my end of the bargain—something that remains one of my lifelong struggles, even though I am self-aware about my seemingly DNA-driven propensity to contribute to a conversation early and often. However, just this self-knowledge has permitted me to make a conscious effort and form a game plan in pursuit of moderating my approach—and, indeed, sharing these aims with others allows them—encourages them—to let me know how I'm doing. You know *they* know, and it can moderate your behavior accordingly. Our Atkinson team also generally knew what we collectively didn't know, which allowed us to complement ourselves with an extended and diverse cohort of colleagues outside of the foundation to guide us; to sound-board our ideas; to do work we didn't have the knowledge or skills to do.

While our skill and knowledge diversity at Atkinson was key, it was the selecting of those core values that was critical, bringing together people who were natural "servant leaders"—colleagues willing to assist one another when one's workload/approach to an issue needs a timely helping hand. Indeed, *while it is critical to have complementarity and diversity of skills and knowledge, high-functioning teams must be bound by the same core beliefs.*

The story about hiring great people to form a high-functioning team, as well as my claim that this is likely my best (or perhaps only) skill worth having a horn to toot, ultimately raises another key lesson learned: I truly enjoy the process of hiring people and coaching others about how best to go about it—and yet think about the costs of hiring the wrong people; think about the investment in hiring the best for what's needed. To state the lesson up-front (with a few stories to follow): *it's always best to select for what you need in a new hire, rather than to train for it.* Too simplistic? Yes, on its own it is. The key is *knowing what you can train for on the job and what you cannot.*

I am asked, on occasion, to assist an organization's board in hiring a new leader. At one point, I also enjoyed a wonderful stint with an excellent search firm to support the hiring of a school board director.

I recall a few occasions when college boards of trustees asked if I would help them before they hired a search consultant. As part of the process, I conduct an initial profile workshop that simply concludes with a list of desirable characteristics making up the "ideal" candidate—a common first step. After a healthy discussion, a draft list of experiences and traits that may guide their search is created. I also encourage them to ensure that a thorough bottom–up approach within the organization to engage all members of the organization in this profiling stage takes place. Then, I ask a key question: "Which of these things can you train for and which require that you hire for?" Simple enough? Sure. But the problem is that, in the past number of decades, things like "fundraiser" and "government relations" have risen to the top of these search profiles far too often. So, why is this a problem? Well, because these things can be either taught and/or complemented by others. In the case of wanting to find someone who is a "fundraiser", the hiring organization will likely have a professional on-board. In the case of "government relations", I have provided both primers concerning how government works, along with key introductions to key people for those less experienced with a particular government. So, what is the key underlying quality required to be successful as a fundraiser or government relations leader? Quite simply, emotional intelligence—that is, the ability to relate to others, to listen deeply to their situation and their needs, and to form long-lasting relationships. This is central to doing these things well. *Emotional intelligence is key to all aspects of leadership.*

These functions require a leader to relate to those within their organizations and listen deeply to the exciting things that can form stories, which can later be told to those external to the organization regarding why their support may be a good match. If you want to *train* for emotional intelligence, it is best to start when the candidate is 18 months old to ensure a continuum of a supportive environment regarding the social and emotional development that builds on their natural DNA. Seriously, emotional intelligence is one of those qualities that takes hold with a touch of DNA and a nurturing early-years environment. Yes, there are many courses that seek to train for it, but they are "tricks of the trade" and help on the margins. Huge and costly mis-hires have occurred, in part, because those hiring failed to learn the difference between what *can* and *cannot* be easily part of on-the-job learning; rather, you have to select for emotional intelligence— something that is central to any successful leader, as we will explore later on.

But what do you do when you have put into play the best of what great hiring is all about, and still make a mistake? How is that possible? Well, here's a story about a lesson I learned in this regard.

When I was President of Sir Sandford Fleming College in Eastern Ontario, we were hiring a new Director of Communications—something that was, for me, an extremely important position, given the emphasis I place on internal and reciprocal relationship-building and external storytelling. We established a search committee consisting of 13 people to ensure diverse participation across the college—a superbly talented and fun group, at that. Given the job was located in the beautiful Kawartha Lakes district of Ontario—combined with the college's reputation—we received over 500 applications, ranging from retired and well-known television and print journalists, to the newly graduated. It was quite the mix.

We finally got down to seven, then five, then two finalists for whom the committee had high praise and hopes. Each of the finalists was asked to perform tasks that simulated the job expectations. We even asked my secretary, who spent quiet and private time with each candidate in the outer office area before the interview, to provide her own assessment. Why? Simple: I have found that candidates oftentimes behave differently when outside the performance arena and when alone, waiting with an "assistant". Are they polite and friendly, or standoffish? Do they engage with the assistant? More often than not, there are no differences; but what about those occasions when a waiting candidate is downright rude or aloof? It is always interesting to learn—and, naturally, just hearing of the gut instinct of another team member who is *not* officially part of the "table" is incredibly useful. I personally did the reference checks myself—which, I admit, I think I do very well—and, in both cases, the reviews were sterling. The debate around the table was lively and intense, and wound up with an unbreakable eight-to-five preference for one over the other. All agreed we couldn't lose with either candidate, but one was most definitely preferred. I was one of the five in the minority, yet I didn't exercise my "position power"; the ideas and views offered by the others were sound. In the final analysis, all agreed to proceed enthusiastically— and, thus, we hired "D", a freelance communications person with 10 amazing clients on retainer who had nothing but glowing reports about her work.

All good? Nope. Within two days on the job, I started getting complaints that D was "abrupt" and "harried". On the third day, more of the same. So, that night, I asked her to dinner.

"So, D," I approached, "after three days, how's it going?"

"Terrible," she said.

Yikes, something *was* amiss. I ordered another beer. "So, what's the problem?"

She told me that, like many freelancers, she had wondered what it would be like to work with a single organization; after all, becoming a member of a team offered some predictability and security. This was not an unusual "the grass is always greener on the other side" response, even for a highly successful freelancer.

"In the last few days, it seems like every single one of the sixty program coordinators want me to develop a fresh marketing plan for their program, and to do it by tomorrow. I can't sleep I'm that stressed," she was saying.

Hiding the fact my *own* stress level had just reached a peak, I responded, "Hey, no problem. We simply need to develop a protocol and do some systems work that will assist in establishing clear and reasonable priorities. My apologies, we really should have put this in place, but we need your expertise to assist with this." I tried to make my tone as confident and hopeful as possible.

"Nope, it won't work," she insisted. "The entire notion of having all of these 'clients' with different expectations and elusive timelines is so different from having ten clients with projects that have a clear beginning, middle and end. I love the process and the money is good."

I took a deep breath and a slug of beer. I tried once more to suggest that perhaps she might wish to give it two months. No good.

"Are you going to fire me?" she asked.

Finally, I gave in. "No, don't be silly. Why don't you try to see how many of your former clients you can secure, and you can let me know when would be best to leave?" Sure, I was hoping a few weeks' or months' delay would help. She was very grateful and seemed relieved, but, once dinner was over and I returned home, I didn't sleep a wink.

The next day, D came to see me at around 1PM. The smile and easygoing energy were in stark contrast to those of the night before.

"Okay, I have called all ten of my previous clients; nine are delighted with my return." She was quite literally glowing. "So, can I leave tomorrow?"

My response: "Nope. I want you to stay until 1PM on Monday, please." I explained to her that I planned to recall the search committee for two reasons, one of which was to have a going away party.

Startled, she said, "Going away party? Today is my fourth day on the job!"

I told her she and I were going to have a *fishbowl* conversation to briefly explain the one thing we hadn't fully understood about her previous context and her new one at the college. I have used the fishbowl technique a number of times; it is an opportunity to actually have a genuine conversation about a critical issue while others observe.

So, on Monday, the one week anniversary of our new communications person, in the middle of the room, D and I repeated the discussion that had taken place, explaining the lesson learned: *clearly analyzing context matters big-time when trying to make decisions and solve problems.* We would explain that we had both totally missed the nuanced differences between a freelancer and a permanent colleague within a single institution. I told D we would then have a quick lunch and cut a cake in her honour, and then she could leave with our blessing. She thought this was both creative and bizarre.

On that Monday, with a bit of heads-up to the committee, we re-enacted the concerns D had outlined in full view, after which, the committee rose to their feet to applaud and thank her for her "service". A lot of laughter, with some tears mixed in, ensued, and, with that, D left. I then convened a formal meeting with the search committee, and we unanimously agreed to approach G, the other candidate, to see if she was still interested and available. It turned out she was, and very quickly she became a key and complementary cog in a very high-functioning team. She performed brilliantly at the college for more than 30 successful years—and yes, of course, I told her the entire story about what preceded her hiring. The lesson to be drawn from this experience is that sometimes you need to work extra hard and even smarter than usual to ensure you have a highly complementary strength-based leadership team. And even when you do, *hiring mistakes can still happen. It's what you do as a result that truly matters.*

The combination of the kind of "know thyself" knowledge of one charged with the responsibility to lead a team, alongside high levels of well-understood and well-utilized complementary skillsets on a senior team, will blow the lid off of productivity and satisfaction levels for an entire organization. If the head of an organization is a pure manager, gets things done on time, and can organize resources to match up with plans, no problem, if they know who they are and what is necessary in a *shared* or *strength-based* leadership model. When the head is a natural manager who complements her/himself with a VP who is a natural leader, creative in their ideas, who can inspire to contribute to a clearly articulated vision, no problem. Allow me to demonstrate.

Years ago, I was consulting with a medium-sized organization's CEO who was entirely committed to ensuring effective, inspiring, and timely communications with his employees; however, while he was a pure manager and knew how to get things done, he was the antithesis of a vision-informed, people-person leader. He was not an inspiring communicator. I observed one meeting during which 200 managers gathered to be informed of the latest "scan" from this CEO concerning both the threats and opportunities facing the organization. Thus, this shy, painfully boring public speaker walked slowly to the podium as though he was about to lay hands on a crop of poison ivy, and began, "It's good to see all of you today. I look forward to our day together, to our workshopping of some new ideas. And to keeping you from falling asleep, I will now hand this over to Jocylyn [name changed to protect the innocent], who will kickstart the day."

Jocylyn then brought the house down with wit, creativity, and inspiration, her "boss" looking on with pride all the while.

He was totally comfortable in his own skin, knowing his talents and complementing them with the skillsets of others to form a successful shared leadership that got all of the right things done well.

Remember the story about how I complemented my leadership as a president of a college? I promoted Rod Rork as VP Administration, and he was superb. Years later, when I left the college to take up a position as Chair of the Ontario Council of Regents (an overseer body for all of the colleges), Rod was appointed acting president by the Board while they conducted a full search for my successor. In my view, while Rod *appeared* to be a first-class manager, I don't think the Board thought he *looked* like a leader. Wrong! He would have made a superb president, and would have ensured, like the president in the story above, that the right kind of complementary skillset required, was included. As I mentioned earlier, Rod went on to be the very best VP in the Ontario College system. The Board then hired Brian Desbiens, who became one of the finest educational leaders in Canada. Go, figure!

What about the flipside? Have you ever worked with or for someone who clearly had no clue about their own skill/knowledge package and had little understanding about forming a complementary team? Painful stuff.

One of the best examples of low self-knowledge and disastrous results can be found by having a close look at Montreal's leadership in 1967 and 1976. The same mayor was in charge both times. Mayor Jean Drapeau's Expo '67 was one of the most creative and successful world fairs ever—and yet, only nine years later, the '76 Olympics, under his charge, was an environmentally destroying, grossly overspending disaster: the Olympic Stadium to the east of downtown Montreal— likely the worst "major" sports setting in North America— remains a testament to the poor planning and implementation of the '76 Olympics. What was the difference? Lucien Saulnier. Saulnier was Drapeau's political partner and a person of detail—a superb manager. He could take the big, dreamy ideas of Drapeau and determine what was feasible and what wasn't; he knew how to develop and carry out an implementation plan, and, together, they did some magical things during Drapeau's tenure, proving that, while *leadership is about doing the right things, management is about doing them right.* Saulnier was totally involved in Expo '67, but he was not involved in the '76 Olympics in any way. Drapeau, like too many pure dreamer-leaders, had no clue how to go about replacing Saulnier's skillset. He didn't know he needed to. And it was this lack of self-knowledge that has cost taxpayers a debt that has taken decades to resolve.

In my view, a similar sense of overly respecting one's own talents and failing to ensure complementary skills and knowledge might have occurred when Ontario Premier David Peterson lost government to Bob Rae in 1990. When the very affable, talented, and popular Peterson lost his Saulnier-like Principal Secretary, Hershell Ezrin, to the private sector, I do not think that Hershell's enormous skillset and contributions were adequately understood. Did David place too much weight on his own considerable talents and not enough on what Hershell brought to the table when he was replaced? I can't be sure, but it is something certainly worth pondering.

Rob Prichard, former President of the University of Toronto, was someone I admired for his approach to strength-based leadership, ensuring that all efforts to recruit the right people were put in place. I once received a call at midnight from Rob asking if I knew a particular candidate for a dean's job. It so happened that I did, and Rob grilled me about him. I then said, "Isn't it odd for a president to be doing reference checks?" Generally, university presidents simply approve decanal committee recommendations, but not Prichard: he wanted to sore-thumb every single recommendation, and, in this case, thought the committee was recommending the wrong person. Hence, he was asking me about the one not offered up. In the end, he had to weigh the democratic ethos of the university culture, and reluctantly approved the committee's recommendation against his own judgment. The chosen one lasted about a year. The committee erred, but Prichard had an instinct for complementary talent that was nothing short of impressive. However, he also understood the need to avoid stomping all over a duly constituted search committee. This goes to illustrate the tough balancing acts needed in sound leadership. (As a footnote, I must admit I also like Rob for his expansive generosity and positive energy—and for arranging for a chance to meet with Mikhail Gorbachev!)

For me, this notion of complementarity is a lesson that is

central to some or most of the public visibility my journey has garnered. My living obituary notes a number of honours, and I can say once again, without even a shred of false humility, there isn't a single example of recognition that would have been possible without countless other people and their own individual and united efforts. Case in point: Just before Christmas 2014, I received a call from the office of Canada's Governor General, who advised that I had been selected for the Order of Canada. I was stunned, and immediately asked if there had been some sort of mistake. Once it became public, family, friends and colleagues wanted to throw a big party to celebrate. Absolutely not. First, notwithstanding my "out front" personality, I am generally shy about this kind of stuff; I had attended extravagant Order parties and found them to be over-the-top. Yes, this extrovert who enjoys the microphone has some issues with honorific things! Contrary to the rules, I rarely wear the Order's pin, and I use no initials before or after my signature line. Eventually, I did agree to a very small gathering, but only with those who were *directly* part of why I was singled out for the Order—those who *knew* they were part of this honour. Still a little shy about it, it was clearly a gathering that celebrated *our* accomplishments. As that old African proverb notes: *If you want to go fast, go alone; if you want to go far, go together.* It's with an ever-increasing dose of self-knowledge that I have been intentional about who I need to travel with—and so far, so good.

To summarize: *high-performing teams have intentionally-created high levels of complementary skills and knowledge, mutual understanding, and respect for these varying assets,* and playful banter about the things each is not particularly interested in or good at. Members share explicitly understood values about how they will work together, and the leader sets the tone with her/his own talents, informed by a humility that ensures "all hands on-deck"—each pair of hands taking on things that showcase their own respective leadership and management stardom. Effective leadership means that the different ways of knowing and being are explicitly understood and built upon; leaders who use effective Myers-Briggs processes, for example, build this stronger intra- and inter-personal understanding about things like introversion and extroversion, as well as various other personal default traits that impact the way in which we approach things—individually and in collaboration—which can be extremely helpful as a catalyst for team-building.

This leads into the next chapter as I explore more of the lessons learned when it comes to the strategic choices leaders make, as well as the options available for actioning directions that improve others' wellbeing.

Chapter Three Takeaways

- **Ensure your leadership team has high levels of complementary skills:**
  An intentional approach to building a strength-based team with highly complementary skills of its members will yield high impact outcomes.
- **While the skills and knowledge of a team should be diverse, all members should share the same core values:**
  While a high-performing team should have diverse skills and knowledge by design, they must also have common values, such as integrity, transparency, and a commitment to a shared "world view" to allow for cohesive and high morale in working together.

EXERCISE #3:

Thinking of a team you are working with right now (or with whom you have worked in the past), write down their names and note their strengths and what they bring to the team. Is there some skill or knowledge base missing? How can that gap be dealt with/managed? Do all members know, in explicit terms, each other's various strengths? Is there a "dysfunctional" member of the team vis-a-vis core values, style of work, or other issues? How should this be dealt with?

Your Notes

Chapter Four
Being Right is Not a Strategy

A FEW YEARS AGO, Michael Fullan and I were discussing leadership and change-making strategies. It was not unusual for us to discuss these things, and, given that Michael is globally known for his transformational leadership ideas and actions, I am always learning from him through informal conversations—or from the pages of his 48 books. Between the time that I first started to think about this book and now, Michael has written at least five. In discussing a real leadership case in point, Michael noted that *being right is not a strategy*. Whether it was a throwaway line or not, this has become a powerful framing of many of the lessons I've learned about leadership.

First, let us use this one-liner as a lens to unpack what we see around us when it comes to various attempts at leadership. When I examine the rhetoric embedded in the public discourse of politics today, whether in the real domain of the electoral kind, or within various public and private places, too much of it suffers from the narrowest protection of the ideas and actions of the political party of choice, or the dominating leadership within an organization. The energy and passion that people of all partisan shades display in proving they are "right"—in turn, being void of empathy for any alternative views—is startling and dysfunctional. Indeed, we can see all around us—both locally and globally—

destructive tribalism at play. One of the best lessons I've come across in terms of win-win discourse, with the best outcomes in mind, is to *seek to understand before seeking to be understood.* I don't care whether you credit Steven Covey as one of his seven habits[6] or Saint Francis of Assisi in the 1200s; the ways in which the responsible and intelligent people try to change the world, while still remaining convinced of their own reasoning while remaining oblivious or simply uninterested in others' views or contexts, never ceases to amaze and concern me.

Self-righteous ownership of "the truth" has defined this kind of tribalism that we see today when progressives like me can't seem to understand why people "fall for" right-wing populism. When the late Rob Ford was elected Mayor of Toronto, a good deal of my progressive friends hooted and hollered about the "idiot uneducated rednecks" who voted for him. The same reaction ensued after Trump was elected in 2016. The same arising after Ontario Premier Doug Ford's (Rob's brother) election. While I hold no patience for those who continued to support Trump in the face of remarkably dysfunctional and dangerous behaviour (which actually hurts the very people who continue as "believers"), I do empathize with the many who thought in 2016, however wrongfully, that they had found a champion for change.

Clearly, I am not talking about those who hold racist, homophobic, and other extreme identity biases, but in the

---

[6] Covey, S., *7 Habits of Highly Effective People,* 1989, Free Press.

U.S. (as well as Toronto, considering the late former Mayor Rob Ford and older brother, Doug, now Premier of Ontario), it is far too easy to dismiss people who are genuinely hurting. Witness the Iranian taxi driver with a PhD in civil engineering who told me why Doug Ford was his political saviour; and witness the African-Canadian MBA who told me why she was voting for Rob Ford back in the day "because the glass ceiling in my company is far too low". Those who represent political entities who lose power need to seek to understand those who didn't support them as the first step. How smart are those politicos who imply that all those who didn't vote for them are stupid and do not know right from wrong? This suggests they are wrong about anything and everything. So, clearly, *being right is not a strategy*; rather, we need to move away from self-perpetuating tribalism that sabotages better solutions to otherwise intractable problems.

Additionally, the anger and frustration that arise from the burden of being right inhibits reason. I think of the many who stake claim to the notion that *anger is a bad advisor*. When opponents showcase that anger, on both sides of political lines or both sides of an emotionally charged issue, the results are often non-solutions to complex and critically important problems. It is my firm belief that *you cannot be angry and smart at the same time*. Those whose choices—political or otherwise—are based on anger have difficulty with basic things, such as evidence. Anger is in firm opposition to reason, and, in my view, it is only through respectful attempts at getting to the root of anger that genuine and respectful problem-solving can begin. Another old chestnut is attributed to Tolstoy, who noted that, *everyone thinks of changing the world, but no one thinks of changing himself.*

How true. "You change; I'm alright, Jack." Not the least bit helpful.

With Tolstoy in mind, I recall an experience when I was Deputy Minister of Education. We were sponsoring a series of seminars in several high schools to support Black students facing not-so-helpful school environments when it came to their aspirations and needs. The program was called Change Your Futures, and, at the time, the Ontario government was dealing with recessionary pressures to cut anything and everything that was considered "marginal". This program was recommended for closure, and I was told it was actually working well and the costs were not high. Hence, it seemed to me that the costs of *not* providing this support would be much higher if, indeed, the program was perceived to be valuable. But then again, we were at the nickels-and-dimes stage when indiscriminate decisions about what to cut were typical.

So, I decided to see for myself. I went to the highly regarded Jarvis Collegiate Institute in Toronto and was met by the usual delegation of school board higher-ups, which I had expressly asked *not* to happen. Top–down stuff; the Deputy is in town, let's have a parade! Anyway, I was led into the weekly two-hour Change Your Future seminar facilitated by a delightful, young, and seemingly competent individual. She explained to the students that an exception to the "no visitors allowed" keep-it-safe rule was being made to host me. She then handed it over to me.

"My name is Charles, and I work in the Ontario government. I just want to get your views on how valuable this program is," I started.

What followed was what felt like an hour of silence crammed into about 90 seconds. Okay, look at your watch now, count 90 seconds, and you will be able to imagine the impact of this deafening silence. Finally, I said, "Okay, I guess this isn't a comfortable situation. I know this is a place of safety for you. Why would you want to deal with a White stranger who comes into your safe space? I guess I should explain one more thing: my job is to decide if the money that supports this program should continue to be provided or be cut. *That's* why I'm here. I'll wait to see if anyone wants to help me decide; otherwise, I will leave so you can continue your discussions. Thanks very much."

Within 30 seconds, one of the students had the courage to start. "Most of the teachers here are White and don't seem to understand our issues at all. They make no effort to get to know us. They think we are all the same."

Another: "One of my teachers treats me like a poor Black kid and makes assumptions just 'cuz I'm Black. Maybe my dad—who is a heart surgeon—should buy him a car for Christmas."

The lid came off. At its heart, the seminar was designed to both provide an airing of issues, but more importantly, to develop active strategies to change the school environment in constructive and meaningful ways. I was blown away and thanked everyone. As I reached the door, one student yelled out, "So, you gonna keep this going, big man?"

"Yep," I replied. "Maybe try to find more money to expand it all."

Leaving the room, the Principal was waiting to escort me to my car. I was silent, still reflecting on what I had heard—and a bit pissed off, actually, that staff had recommended closure. I reached my car, got in, and rolled the window down. At that moment, the Principal said, "Deputy, it's so great that you came to visit today. I'm sure it meant a lot to the kids. They certainly need help learning to adapt to the school's culture."

Oh my God. Two things hit me simultaneously in that moment: one, the awareness that my blood had instantly begun to boil; and two, the understanding that this guy perceived me to be a person of enormous power. How can I deliver a message so I don't destroy him because of his perceived notion regarding my position of power?

To assist my calm breathing, I slowly got out of the car, looked up to this tall guy, and said, "Mr. Principal, this was a truly important visit for me, and I thank you for allowing me to come into the school. I can only say that my lesson learned today is that *schools* need to do the 'adapting', not the kids. Thanks again."

I gave what must have been my most insincere smile ever, got back into my car, drove off, rolled up the window, and screamed. I don't like having to put on a phony face. (And, to go off on a slight tangent, I will admit I have trouble trusting people who are unable to smile naturally. When it comes to public figures, it seems that Doug Ford, Premier of Ontario, former Canadian Liberal Federal leader Michael Ignatieff, former Canadian Conservative Prime Minister Stephen Harper, and Tom Mulcair, former Canadian Federal NDP leader, are all unable to smile a natural smile, which suggests some discomfort with the skin they are in. That's my take on it, anyway. Okay, no more tangents—for a while, at least.)

When I was doing my work as the Early Learning Advisor for the former Ontario Premier Dalton McGuinty, I had a similar "these kids need to adapt" response to a White school principal in Fort Frances in Northwestern Ontario. I was discussing the needs of Indigenous children, just having met with both Indigenous kids and their parents, and, when I hinted at what we might do to *Indigenize* the school, he looked at me as though he had encountered a close experience with a third kind.

When I referred earlier to holding myself accountable for behaviours associated with my core values via a daily reflective journal practice, one of my original commitments was to be an example—that is, to model what's best. Mahatma Gandhi, of course, said it best: *Be the change you wish to see in the world.* A few years back, Dean Glen Jones at OISE conducted a remarkably inclusive strategic planning process; indeed, the process *was* the product, yielding some major commitments to improve public education locally, nationally, and globally—a kind of moral responsibility given to OISE's world-class reputation. We titled this plan *Leading from Within* to emphasize, for example, that, if we want to be a force for ensuring a major change regarding the recurring deleterious effects of the residential schools on Indigenous peoples, we must begin within; we must be intentional about dealing with our own history and the recurrent "colonizing" approaches to education. How can we be authentically helpful and knowledgeable in supporting transformational changes with schools' and universities' ways of dealing with Indigenization? In other words, what can we achieve if we do not embark on a long-term transformation within? Again, this is that *Inside Out* notion at play. Indeed, within any organization—and within each of us charged with various leadership responsibilities—we need to gain a much deeper understanding of the truth before genuine progress through reconciliation can take place. A bit later, I will describe a leadership development process we started at OISE to go deeper within in order to improve our leadership *outside*.

Having been a part of and led a variety of teams and organizations, I have turned one of my key lessons into a mantra that constantly rings through my mind and influences my behaviour—well, most of the time, at least. It's really simple to say, but hard for many leaders to practice:

What is right is more important than who is right.

A good deal of wasteful effort occurs when someone holding a position of power has an almost pathological need to be right. The narcissist in chief who has occupied the White House is Exhibit A of such a figure. What enormous pressure some people place on themselves. What a waste of resources. How damaging to have such a deep sense of insecurity that it drives a need to be "right"—about everything!

As committed leaders who want to make things better, our default terrain naturally includes our experiences and the views and biases that arise therefrom. When I was Chair of the Ontario Colleges' Council of Regents—at the time, the governing body for Ontario's community colleges way back in the 80's—we embarked on a project of renewal entitled Vision 2000. A remarkably inclusive process, the project was led by a very diverse committee of more than 30 leaders from both public and private sectors, spanning education, labour, businesses large and small, and other community-based leaders. Such project tables of diversity usually begin with the approbation "Leave your biases in the cloakroom", What a ridiculous notion! We might as well tell folks to stop breathing. Recognizing this, we did the opposite: we encouraged members to share their biases and the origin of them, to build empathy and understanding, to enable the group to reach for higher outcomes, rather than low common-denominator compromises. Better to have what some would call *hidden agendas* clearly emerge in front of the curtain, out of the shadows. When certain issues created conflict around the table between two or more disparate views, instead of having an extensive debate in which the combatants try to secure the minds and hearts of others at the table, one of the other members would act as a mediator and take the antagonists to a quiet place to work on generating effective resolutions. They would then return when success had been achieved. This was a process that sometimes spanned 20 minutes, other times, days! We built an effective and simple conflict-resolution method—all of this being in service of the "table determining what was right", rather than purely a contest of "winning arguments".

When I was a deputy minister in the Ontario government, over time, I reported to a total of nine ministers across all three politically unique governments. All but one of my ministers were totally joyful and really fun to work with, most being driven by a good amalgam of about 70% substance and 30% politics. Thankfully, I never worked with someone who was mostly (or totally) concerned with partisan politics. That said, however, working with someone who is totally committed, at all times, to substantive goals would be fun... while it lasted. *Getting things done always requires some measure of political acumen, knowing the who, when, what and when of influencing decisions.*

Indeed, political know how is essential for a politician to survive within Cabinet—and publicly—when it comes to gaining and sustaining support for the most essential goals. My most difficult experience was working with one minister who needed to be "right" when it came to moving forward with options to consider in dealing with one issue or another. With the help and trust of the Minister's key political staff, we would have lengthy meetings trying to extract direction from the Minister and learn how to come back with advice that generally began with, "Minister, as you directed, we have taken your suggestions, and propose that..." We learned not to directly advise the Minister, but rather to suggest, argue just a touch, and listen. We worked hard to connect our advice to words, images, snippets of ideas that came from the Minister, and *then* do the weaving, giving the Minister full credit for great leadership. Sound patronizing? Okay, guilty; but we were working with one who rarely accepted others' ideas as worthy. Hey, look around, examine your own experience. All too common?

When leaders have a strong need to be right, a conviction that is driven by whatever insecurities, well... they aren't very able leaders. There is an amazing strength that derives from ensuring that, regardless of the origin, the best ideas should not be the privy of the most powerful in the organization. "What is right should prevail", a marker of great leadership when input is widely recruited—that is, when anyone in an organization can be a star thinker, worthy of receiving credit.

Another example of the potential power of committing to *what* is right rather than *who* is right:

When I was the Deputy Minister of Ontario's Premier's Council on Health, Wellbeing, and Social Justice, I was asked by the then-NDP Minister of Health (now Senator) Frances Lankin, if I would assist her and two other ministers with a problem. All three had parts of a cross-ministry approach to long-term care in Ontario. The problem? The previous Liberal government had conducted an extensive year-long consultation on the issue and produced a report with their findings and recommendations. The ministers had to decide how their newly elected government should proceed, and I was asked to be a neutral facilitator. After several hours of back and forth, it seemed the ministers could not agree: from my vantage point, the unstated issue for a few of them seemed to be, "How can I get some political visibility on this file?" A very powerful force within ego-driven political cultures, to say the least.

At the end of two hours, everyone agreed to meet again, with me as facilitator—but just before we adjourned, Minister Lankin said, "Charles, you've been listening to this. From your neutral perspective, what do *you* think we should do?"

"Well, it's not my place. Each of you has fine deputies who can offer advice," I demurred.

"No, we all want to hear your perspective," said another minister.

I took a deep breath, quickly followed by another. "Well, given that the previous government produced a report not yet released, but which is nonetheless informed by a very extensive consultation; given that the public would like some non-partisan gestures now and again; and given you have a few of your own unanswered questions, I would suggest you release the Liberal report with a letter acknowledging the previous Liberal government's good work, but with the addition of a note with further questions for which you would like input over a period of a few months."

One of the ministers then said, "Interesting option. When should we meet next?"

In-between meetings, two of the ministers said "Absolutely not"; they wanted to conduct a totally new consultation. As I pen this, the COVID-19 pandemic has exposed government after government in Ontario for failing to protect vulnerable long-term care clients. A little more non-partisan focus on evidence and solutions over the years may have just saved countless lives.

Another example:

The current Ford government in Ontario also went crazy-partisan to serve its political ego. In this case, it played political football with its predecessor government's so-called "sex ed curriculum". They portrayed the previous Liberal Kathleen Wynne government's well-researched, modernized curriculum as a deleterious "social experiment with Ontario's children". Total nonsense but Ford used it as a hot button pledge to social conservative voters and as a means to reward one of his leadership opponents—an ardent extremist who helped him win the leadership contest. For over a year, his government spent well over $1 million (CAD) to "research" the issue that included a phony consultation. The conclusion? Ford brazenly released his "new" sex ed curriculum, which, by and large, was the same as that created by Wynne's government—the one Ford used as red meat for his base. In other words, what was old was declared new, and the Premier ran to the front of a parade he had criticized. Holy hypocrisy. The silver lining of this debacle was that Ford's wasteful and ignorant approach led to thousands of students engaging in protest: walking out of classes across the province, likely galvanizing a very powerful voting-block in waiting.

Time to flip it over for some positive versions of how to get things done properly: it's been my experience that one of the very best approaches to developing a new way of doing something, solving a problem, or developing and implementing a new policy is to *catch people and organizations doing things right.* How about the curiosity of Canadian mathematician/playwright John Mighton, whose own math anxiety led him to invent Jump Math[7] to build the self-confidence of kids in dealing with their own math-based fears? Mainstream thinking in government education ministries was slow to recognize the importance of John's ideas. His latest book, *All Things Being Equal: Why math is key to a better world*[8], is a remarkable manifesto regarding how math should be taught and how greater understanding of the power of math can be central to reducing social inequality. Now it's time for mainstream education to catch up to Mighton's work.

What about the person at 3M, who developed—quite by accident—a glue that didn't work; a glue so weak it was repurposed for what subsequently became Post-It Notes. There are millions of examples of how one-off acts of creative problem-solving are captured and developed for widespread impact. Catching something that seems to work on a small

[7] Jump Math, available at https://jumpmath.org.
[8] Mighton, J., *All Things Being Equal: Why math is key to a better world,* Knopf Canada, 2020.

scale and figuring out how to *turn the uncommon into a common solution for something is a remarkably powerful change strategy.*

When I was asked by former Ontario Premier Dalton McGuinty to develop a plan to implement full-day learning for four- and five-year-old children in 2007, our team embarked on an Ontario- and global-wide search for ideas. Naturally, we were pleased with the valuable ideas offered in over 85 roundtables with diverse community partners all over Ontario, as well as the thousands of submissions we received. Many of these ideas were uniquely creative and wielded a direct impact on what is now commonplace across Ontario and beyond. Indeed, many other valuable ideas were already embedded into the creative work being done with pre-school children in Ontario and well beyond.

In Ontario, the future was already being invented by some Catholic and French boards, who'd had full-day Kindergarten in place for 10 years—likely due to the need to have a competitive advantage in dealing with enrollment challenges for their schools. The future was being invented in Reggio Emilia, Italy, with their understanding of curiosity and play-driven learning. The future was also being invented in Scandinavia, whereby parental leave with policy space for fathers to share the leave, was creating a broader and supportive context for quality pre-schooling to have an even higher impact. In our own Canadian backyard, Quebec was already doing the same with modernized parental and family support policies.

However, the story of why there are 250,000 four- and five-year-old children in Ontario today who have access to universal full-day learning (AKA, Full-Day Kindergarten) began with non-governmental leadership. Given that governments (and other organizations) are generally risk-averse in trying new and bold things, at times it is best to lower the risk by proving things *outside* of government purview. The idea is to show, in plain sight, something good; something well-researched and well-communicated to the public that lowers the risk for government. Regarding governments' natural aversion to risk, the key for a change-maker is generally concerned with *understanding where risk exists as a potential obstacle* to moving forward on something important, focusing on how to reduce the risk for folks "in the way" of progress, or *supporting those who can afford to take a strategic risk.*

We understood this, and our approach was also based on *the power of the demo.* The Board of the Atkinson Charitable Foundation in Toronto, where I worked for 15 wonderful years, had determined that it would do all that was possible to establish high-quality early learning and care in Canada. The timeframe? When it was done. So, in 2001, and with the support of others—including Olivia Chow, who at the time was a Toronto city councillor, committed to supporting the wellbeing of children—the Atkinson Foundation sponsored a process that led to Toronto First Duty, a network of five demonstration projects. These projects were designed to experiment with integrated staff teams of teachers and early childhood educators. Part of the experiment included a curriculum that fostered play-based learning that builds on the child's individual differences, including natural interests and knowledge that are already embedded in the young learner.

The First Duty notion was simple: we had to demonstrate what would happen if we could show that the results of the approach had a positive effect on child development, along with increasing genuine and effective partnerships with parents—essential for a child's developmental progress. Another central element concerned the up-front involvement of key researchers, such as my OISE colleagues Professors Carl Corter and Jan Pelletier. Jan and Carl, along with their graduate students, were involved from the very beginning. They asked educators and parents alike what they would like to learn as part of their research, and, naturally, this up front involvement created both expectations and excitement about the project and eventual findings. Our team included Jane Bertrand, one of the world's experts on early childhood curriculum and pedagogy, and Kerry McCuaig, a superb practitioner of what I refer to as evidence-based story telling. Later, I will devote a chapter to this lesson.

The bottom line? The ongoing formative improvement in the demonstration projects, as well as the ability to provide evidence of impact and to communicate this widely, was central to eventually reducing the risk for government. This, in turn, led to them running to the front of the parade to praise Toronto First Duty for doing *good things* and taking its ideas to the rest of Ontario. Bruce School, one of the sites, was saved from closure, when people such as the incomparable late Fraser Mustard, used his bully pulpit to proclaim that it needed to become a laboratory for innovation. This, along with the Atkinson money and City of Toronto resources made available by Olivia Chow, provided what was necessary to keep Bruce School open—and it paid off. Soon, Bruce was the site visit of choice for the media and visitors from around Canada and beyond to see what the future might look like for pre-schoolers; they were "catching Bruce doing things right". Ministers and deputies from other provinces came; the former Premier of South Australia, Jay Weatherill, attended, and described to me afterward at a conference in Adelaide, that Toronto First Duty played a key role in how his State developed an integrating children and youth services system.

But there was one other ingredient to this successful result: Premier McGuinty implemented full-day Kindergarten at a time when he had a $18(CAD) billion deficit! Sure, he was one of those rare politicians who valued evidence; he actually read widely and deeply about education and other fields that drew his attention. With that said, there is one lesson learned that was key to McGuinty's decision to move ahead and eventually appoint an "early learning advisor" (me) to develop the plan.

The lesson? A long one. For me, *lobbying is the giving and getting of good information through trusted relationships on an ongoing basis so that the best decisions are made for the good of the many.* Sure, that's a mouthful, but read it again—

but this time slowly, please:

Great leadership is marked by the ability to form, over time, trusting relationships—and, when it comes to what is considered more pejorative than noble, lobbying should *not* be viewed as short-term, behind-the-scenes pressure driven by quid pro quo, narrow, political self-interests. Sure, that's the common definition and practice, which is why lobbyists need to register doing business with governments with the aim of ensuring at least a little more transparency to understanding the potential for conflicts of interest and that narrow self-interest.

In my view, influencing for the greater and sustainable good flows from my definition of lobbying. There are three important aspects of my version: first, the goal must be driven by moral purpose—something that is clearly for the greater good; second, as noted in this chapter, the obtaining of information, or listening to other side, is crucial, as I have already noted and will discuss further a bit later (after all, lobbyists/advocates frequently lead with *their* proposals rather than getting a deeper understanding of the context of those they wish to influence as a first step); and, third, working through trusted relationships.

As an example, several key people had "lobbied" McGuinty in relation to the powerful evidence underpinning quality early learning when it comes to social and economic progress. We knew that he had already made huge strides regarding Ontario's educational success: at the time, Ontario had become the highest performing jurisdiction in the

English-speaking world on international test scores and was third overall (behind Finland and Singapore). We also knew that this progress was beginning to flatten out a bit: Fraser Mustard had tried, albeit unsuccessfully, to get the Premier's attention. His straight-ahead and gruff manner may have made it difficult for Dalton to listen to the content; being "right" and behaving forcefully in this regard can make it difficult for others to absorb, including those who are either unsure or hostile to an idea.

Later on, the Hon. Margaret McCain, Jane Bertrand, and myself all spent an hour with the Premier, making what *I* thought was a very successful pitch. A few months went by, and we received no response. Then, in a meeting with Jane, Kerry McCuaig, and Christine Avery Nunez (another of my remarkably talented colleagues), held in the Atkinson boardroom, as we were commiserating that we were getting nowhere fast with the Premier, Kerry said, "Charles, aren't you and Michael Fullan close friends?"

Michael was McGuinty's key advisor on their education initiatives and was highly trusted by the Premier and others, such as Gerry Butts, his Principal Secretary. (As all Canadians know, Gerry eventually held the same job with Prime Minister Trudeau, but that's grist for another book.) Kerry's drift? If Michael and I have a trusting relationship, he would totally understand the evidence that 28% of kids in First Grade were seriously behind their peers, with many never catching up. Hence, in order to continue progressing with these kids' success, high-quality and equalizing early learning would be a difference-maker in getting Ontario's international progress moving again. Michael was trusted completely by Dalton. Ergo, we needed to use a different and trusted conduit to convey the evidence to McGuinty.

As I noted, the need to approach and work through the trusting relationships at hand is essential. Kerry's point was clear: "Okay, let's try to get Michael to tell the story to the Premier."

The following Sunday morning, I had breakfast with Michael, and, by the time his eggs arrived, he totally got it. I asked if we would carry our "brief" to the premier.

"Absolutely," Michael said. "This is very powerful stuff."

Later that week, I was working on my porch at home late on a Friday afternoon when I received a call from the Premier. "Chuck, that early learning evidence is really important. We have to do something bold. Can we get together?"

It might be easy to muster up some frustration that visits from the likes of Fraser Mustard and Margie McCain didn't cut it. Hey, the lesson is the thing. *Work through trusting relationships* and get over yourself, Charles! Just because we think we're right doesn't mean we can change the world by pounding on the table of reason. By having Michael Fullan speak to the Premier on behalf of *our evidence*, we were applying a key lesson: *supporting someone who can afford to take the risk.* I would be risky for us to continue badgering McGuinty, but zero risk for Michael, who had the Premier's full confidence. The notion that the government would simply receive compelling evidence and move quickly on its implications is just so rare. Government rarely hangs out in the neighborhood of bold serendipity.

A footnote to Michael's influence with the Premier. The person responsible for introducing Michael Fullan to Mr. McGuinty was actually former U.K. Prime Minister, Tony Blair. Michael had been doing great work in the U.K. at the time, and when McGuinty was in opposition in Ontario, he visited Blair and asked him about the key ingredient to his education success at the time. Blair responded, "Well you should know. Michael Fullan's from your province." That's how our future premier found out about who Fullan was.

Key to all of this is the need for leaders to *overcome being "hard of listening"*. Whether we refer to it as empathy or "putting ourselves in other people's shoes", we must se*ek to understand before even beginning to attempt to communicate our own ideas* with the ultimate goal of getting to *yes* on something larger than our own initial views. If one wants to build a bridge from one side of a river to the other, it might be best to complete a soil analysis on the other side first.

When confronted with something so different from our experience, all too often, our default response is to dismiss or diminish the idea. Listening more deeply to the meaning behind a new and *foreign* idea is absolutely critical if we are to become truly innovative leaders.

When I was a deputy minister in the Ontario government, we had regular meetings with the DM's Council to discuss issues of common concern. From time to time, we would invite special guests to put forward an idea for improving public service. On one occasion, representatives from our cohort of Indigenous public servants came to offer a suggestion. The lead colleague noted that, if the government was sincere about growing the number of Indigenous public servants, it would have to develop some special initiatives. He began to explain that, of the 60 (of 120,000 public servants in Ontario at the time) members of their group, 40 lived on reserve. He explained, in very clear terms, that, "We need to go back to our communities for a week every two months, and, because we live in very remote communities, we need financial support to handle the costs of flying to Northern outreaches." They weren't asking for increased holidays; they were simply asking for understanding. He further noted that, "We are land-based people who need to get back to our own land. If we do not stay connected with our people, they will begin to turn on us as those who have left them behind, working for good money for governments that do not care about Indigenous issues." Although my journal reflects the word "native", the story is indelibly etched in my memory as it is on the page of my reminiscences—as is the ignorant non-response from the government of the day, including the majority of the deputy ministers, who ignored this sage and easy-to-implement idea.

During my 15 years at the Atkinson Charitable Foundation, I grew accustomed to the prospective applicants for our resources coming in with wonderfully glossy proposals. Only once can I remember a prospective applicant for Mr. Atkinson's money—an anti-poverty group—asking me, "Can you tell us about three projects that your board has funded in the past five years that really excited them?" Simple but powerful. What better way to determine the culture and values of another person or an organization! Ask questions, and then listen—deeply. I have been so moved by various Indigenous elders who have taught me the power of respecting our ancestors and the learnings derived by simply asking a new acquaintance, "Tell me about your grandparents, or great-grandparents, if you knew them."

More recently, I participated in a "settlers retreat", facilitated by a powerful Indigenous facilitator and an Indigenous healer and elder. The gathering consisted of 19 other people with whom I work closely as part of our efforts at OISE at the University of Toronto to go deeper with our understandings as part of a long-term commitment to reconciliation. This was part of what I described earlier as our need to lead from within. The opening question for the circle was, "Describe an ancestor whom you value deeply and why." What was revealed was so powerful, so filled with meaning. The respect I already had for the majority of my workmates was already pretty high; but the deepening of my understanding for who each was, and the origins of their personal and professional "gifts" stays with me even now. In my own case, just being asked to choose my own ancestor of choice was a process of self-discovery: my natural go-to would be my grandpa Dave. As I noted earlier, my grandparents lived upstairs and, in this sense, I grew up with two sets of doting parents, but I formed an especially deep bond with my father's father. However, my choice that day was the love of *his* life, Gramma Rose, with whom my grandpa had been smitten since they were 14. Why Gramma Rose? Well, she was the quiet, stereotypic "woman behind the man" of that era. My grandpa was a charismatic guy who lit up the room, and it wasn't until Grampa Dave passed away that my Gramma Rose stepped into the spotlight. Or did the spotlight pick out what had been in the long shadow of my grandfather all along? What was revealed to everyone—including her son, my father—was a strong, bright, articulate woman. Rather than shriveling up, she spent another 15 years displaying an independence of mind and behaviour that was stunning and truly inspiring.

Lessons learned? Tons pertaining to sexist male domination, irrespective of how charming the "package". For this context, however, we need to be proactive in determining what others can bring to our lives and our work. We need to work harder on this; I know I certainly do. It is so easy for me to believe I am right about something and to ignore what others can bring to the table. While my feedback systems have yielded views that speak to my strong empathy and relationship skills, I do admit that words like "opinionated" surface from time to time. Okay, often.

I discovered decades ago how group meetings discriminate against those who are more introverted—those who derive energy from within, taking in what others who lead from out front—those like myself—are saying. Effective group leaders understand this and ensure those leading from behind are intentionally brought into to the discussion. I will often ask a large group to first brainstorm, as individuals or in small groups, as a way of creating more comfortable opportunities for the "laid-back" colleagues to offer up their equally important ideas. One of the most remarkable leaders I ever knew was the late John Evans, former President of the University of Toronto, former Chair of the Rockefeller Foundation, and so much more. This Rhodes Scholar was brilliant—and he was also an introvert. *Really?* One of his remarkable skills was on display in group meetings: whether he was chairing the meeting or not, John always held back, taking it all in, and, when things were all over the map, he was the one who was the great synthesizer—the one who separated the irrelevant from the relevant. With a tone of humility, coupled with a laser ability to focus, he brought everything together. Aided by his natural introversion, he listened deeply to others before he chose a time to be understood. He was usually the smartest person in the room—he just didn't behave like it.

My late brother Roger told me a few stories about his dealings with Barack Obama during which time the former president was an Illinois state senator and my brother was a liberal Democrat activist and accomplished Chicago lawyer. He noted that, notwithstanding my brother's brilliance, Mr. Obama was another who was usually the smartest person in the room (when his wife Michelle was absent!) but didn't behave like it. Obama's natural talents as a conciliator/mediator are a matter of record. The converse is also true when the smartest around the table wants all to know. I once observed a Canadian municipal-level leader who was charming, brilliant, and had the majority of the qualities of great leadership—and yet he was hard of listening. He was usually the smartest person in the room—and behaved like it. The mediocre political results revealed the consequences of the urge to be right—and this is why *what is right is infinitely more important than who is right.*

Flowing from this, I would like to add how critically important it is to understand that *being smart doesn't always mean you are right.* Others dealing with overly smart leaders need to understand this—especially if the person holding the position of power is the smartest person in the room and behaves like it, as I've said.

I once reported to a brilliant leader—a forceful and dominating speaker and thinker, who was terribly "hard of listening", but who more often than not connected the dots and saw what was necessary to move things along. He was also blunt with others, but in a very cherubic way. The net effect of all of this was that the folks around him were too afraid to take him on and offer valuable ideas that may have been of benefit to him and the organization. For me, however, I loved working with him: he didn't intimidate me, and I wasn't afraid to speak up and argue about a point of principle or direction—and he loved that. I learned a great deal from him; I discovered that he thrived on the give-and-take of ideas. The problem lay in the fact that taking him on wasn't easy for many. When I left the organization for another job, I asked him for an exit interview, and, when I arrived for the chat, I asked him if I should go first or whether he would prefer to.

"What do you mean? Isn't this about me giving you feedback about you and your next assignment?" he replied.

"Yes, and it's also a chance for me to give you feedback about *your* performance now that I'm leaving. It's usually a good, safe way for employees to assist the organization they are leaving when they have a hand on the doorknob."

He blushed, and I proceeded to provide him first with a list of several things he did well; then, with a commitment to improving his self-knowledge through the gift of feedback, I described how his behavior had a stultifying effect on others within the organization. How much did my feedback help in the long run? Not much. Later on, when he was in another position, he asked if I would work with his new team because "they aren't listening to me". I told him that I would meet with them one at a time and try to teach them how to "take you on and explain that you thrive on direct conversations". I told him that his job would be to tell his team in very clear terms, "I know I can appear domineering, but here's how to take me on... I truly need your involvement; your ideas."

Still, later on, in another position he was in, someone who was about to work with him as a peer asked me the secret of working with this brilliant and very confident colleague. I replied simply, "Just because he's smart doesn't mean he's always right. Don't be intimidated; share your ideas. You may just have to raise your voice a bit."

I continue to fight against my own propensity to be right. A number of decades back, I started to routinely and deliberately meet with people I perceived to hold views totally contrary to mine, politically or otherwise. Listening to some totally contrary views can be a painful but valuable experience: no pain, no gain. I would often meet with someone who would have a common commitment to reducing poverty as the end game, for example, but their approach to getting there was different. Trickle-down economics to "lift all boats" bullshit is not my preferred pathway. That said, listening to the assumptions behind others' alternative "world views" is useful in two ways: either there is something useful that helps to adopt a new strategy, and/or there is the opportunity to learn about how to better tailor a message that counteracts a ridiculous but widely held view about the "right" way forward. More about strategic communications later.

A few years ago, while visiting my sister-in-law and her partner in their lovely place in the Mexican Baja, they were telling me to stay away from the most "right-wing" nutcase in the village—an Alaskan, and an ardent fan of former U.S. vice presidential candidate Sarah Palin and Donald Trump. Ignoring the advice to stay clear of him, coffee with him became a regular morning ritual, during which I learned his story—a narrative of personal struggle, disappointment with governments of various sorts that hurt his business, and learned of his emerging self-made success. There were authentic touchstones to his "I'm alright, Jack, pick yourself up" attitude. I also learned that he was a short story mystery writer, and I began reading and responding to his excellent efforts. *Seek to understand; it is of critical importance to determine what's right for the many, rather than the few.*

By the end of our time together, he was much more open to my alternative ways of seeing the possibilities. We didn't argue with each other: we listened, told stories, withheld judgment, and made a touch of progress about how the world might be better. While it didn't make my sister-in-law too thrilled to witness ("Charles, hanging out with this right-wing nutcase!"), it sure made me happy—not to mention a bit smarter and a smidgeon less judgmental.

Central to this chapter's message—*that being right is not a strategy*—is how people and organizations determine what is best through genuine reciprocity. This means building on others' ideas, eschewing tribal and defensive responses and the need to be right while always focusing on the endgame. Listening and understanding even the most "hostile" anger-informed opinions can benefit one's perspective and courses of action. Hey, I'm not saying we lie down and let others have their say *and* their way; I'm simply saying that change strategies must be informed through this process of understanding.

Well-known psychologist Kurt Lewin's famous quote: *If you want to understand something, just try to change it.* Well, that's true: if you come into an organization from the outside—as I have on several occasions—and you want to learn about the culture, you have two choices: start making changes and checkout the fallout—those negative resistance and positive responses which lead you to learn about the culture the hard way; or, spend the first number of months as a social anthropologist, listening to the stories, old and new, that provide a sense of the context. Some of these stories are rich with clarity of values and beliefs; some are mythological or apocryphal. Regardless, all are useful when it comes to understanding how to better listen to ideas about versions of the right things to do and communicate your options for moving the organization forward. As I noted, if we want to build a bridge across a river, we should start by completing that soil analysis on the other side first. *Work on understanding more clearly the receiving end of your intent.*

Co-constructing ideas with others through genuine collaborative approaches, working through hard-earned, trusting relationships, and creating something larger than the sum of the ideas that many diverse colleagues offer, takes us well beyond the strong urge to be right as our default approach to life and work. Of all of the lessons noted in this chapter, the most liberating one for me, which almost rises to the level of a mantra—a lesson that frees me from the strong urge to be right—is, *What is right is more important than who is right.* I wonder if this lesson is too long for a T-shirt?

The key to leadership and successful change guided by moral purpose, is the ability to communicate effectively, as well as to ensure that ideas for a better future are informed by evidence, rather than the superficial bumper-sticker misinformation and its dangerous sibling, disinformation, that has become far too normalized. When "effectiveness" audits are performed on organizations, both large and small and both public and private, "the need to improve communications" is often top of the hit list. Ensuring effective communications within and outside of our organizations is essential to effective leadership. This has been so central to my own leadership development over the years that I have devoted the next two chapters to interdependent variations on the communications theme.

Chapter Four Takeaways

- **What is right is more important than who is right:**
  Effective leadership is all about eschewing power and listening to others' ideas in order to ensure the best decisions are made with the best information available. Catching people and organizations doing things right is an incredibly useful strategy for developing a change strategy and is about Covey's notion that leaders must seek to understand before seeking to be understood.
- **Empathy is the most essential quality of effective leaders:**
  Understanding the essential qualities and different and diverse lived experience of others informs the ability to lead through strong and trusted relationships.

EXERCISE #4:

This is a simple but powerful exercise, though it might be a challenging one…

Think of someone in your life—personal or professional—whose views and values are significantly different from yours. Someone you like, but ultimately someone with whom you often disagree. Create a moment—it might be coffee, lunch, or even just a Zoom call—where the sole purpose is a conversation requiring that you listen deeply to who they "are".

Do you know about their great grandparents or their most inspiring ancestor? Do you know about their childhood? Considering a view they hold that is different from yours, can you totally withhold judgment and probe the influences responsible for that view?

Your Notes

Chapter Five
The Power of Evidence-Based Storytelling

EFFECTIVE COMMUNICATIONS AND THE ability to positively "change the world" through the provision of timely and authentic information is sadly lacking. In this age of social media, it seems easier to spread misinformation and disinformation that takes hold of the viewer/listener than it does to generate ideas driven by evidence. Perhaps this is due to the fact-less bumper sticker simplicity that trumps the more difficult nuancing required to convey real evidence and its relationship to a new policy or program idea. Whatever the reason, effective, trustful communications are all too uncommon—and, unfortunately, attempts at providing disinformation designed to deceive are far too common and far too effective.

This is the longest chapter because, in my view, our failure to communicate well—that tribal instinct to wrap ourselves around the tree of the status quo, or to protect or seek power for its own sake—is central to so much of what is causing the hurtful chaos that currently dominates our worlds. Honest, fact-based dialogue deserves attention.

When I was a rookie deputy minister, the Secretary of Cabinet called an emergency 7AM meeting of five deputies, the purpose of which was to determine the options for the government in dealing with a major problem that hit the front pages of the newspapers, as well as item number one on local and national newscasts. I will not deal with the details in an effort to protect the quasi-innocent, but suffice to say that the fact five of us were required to figure out how best to determine the best way for the government of the day to communicate the problems and the "fixes", shows it was a biggie cutting across several departments. After about an hour of conversation, the Secretary said, "Charles, you are uncharacteristically quiet. What do *you* think?"

I replied, "Well, I'm kind of new to my role."

He continued to press me to reveal my thoughts, to which I reluctantly replied, "Why don't we suggest to the Premier and ministers that they just tell the truth? Explain how things went wrong and how they plan to fix it and learn from it."

The response from the meeting? The Secretary of Cabinet, the head of Ontario's public service said, "Why don't we take a ten-minute break."

Yikes. The lack of response to my rookie input was deafening. My initial hesitation about offering up the notion of telling the truth to the public had obviously been warranted. I felt stupid and diminished. Then, facing a wall of urinals during the break, one of my colleagues said quietly, "Good for you, Charles. That had to be said."

"Will you back me up?" I asked, my insecurities on full display.

"Hard to say, but you will learn more along the way about the risk-averse nature of government culture."

Well. Yet another lesson learned.

Yes, governments are very risk averse when it comes to how things are communicated. I get it. I don't like it, but I get it. But that doesn't mean we shouldn't try to change it. Governments live within a "gotcha" culture; but I have also learned along the way that risk aversion can, in itself, be very risky. Too much risk aversion leads to holes that continue to get wider and deeper as more and more inaccurate information, designed to camouflage rather than illuminate, is offered up. It is amazing that Richard Nixon's 1970's Watergate lesson—"It's the cover-up, stupid"—hasn't since penetrated the behavior of so many leaders in both the public and private spheres.

Naturally, the definition of risk is also contextual and situational. When Ontario's Doug Ford decided to scrap the well-designed and necessary upgrade to sex education for Ontario students, he did so because he didn't want to lose the support of his social conservative core. The horrific side of the coin is that this move backward—to the older curriculum—put so many kids at real risk; life-challenging risks flowing from endemic bullying, among other things, that denigrated informed personal choices or identities and behavior toward others. By not wishing to risk alienating part of his base, the result was an embarrassing display of double-talk and confusion, which became much riskier politically in the longer run when the government eventually had to backtrack.

Once in a while, deputy ministers are called before the Public Accounts Committee—an all-party committee that cross-examines deputies on the results of the Provincial Auditor's reports. Unlike many of my peers, I found this process to be really very valuable. As mentioned earlier, *feedback is the breakfast of champions*. Naturally, the questioning can be very rough, considering the all-party nature of the gathering; after all, even though deputies are not politicians and are supposed to be non-partisan, we are working for the government of the day. Far too often, the response to difficult findings in an auditor's report is, "Yes, we knew about that and are doing the following things to fix it." Fine, if genuine—but when you are managing a budget of $12 billion (CAD) with 12,000 employees and flowing money to 7,200 transfer payment agencies—as was the case when I was the Deputy Minister of Social Services—there will always be problems that require attention. During one visit to this committee, as always, I viewed it as an opportunity to discover an outside auditor's perception concerning issues that would likely exist in dealing with the inherent complexities of this large organization. My responses included, "No, we had no idea, but thanks to the Auditor's report, our plans are now underway to figure out what we can do."

On occasion, I would use politically charged moments to attempt to raise the level of discourse and dispel myths perpetuated by ignorance or partisan nonsense from committee members. When I was Deputy Minister of Education, a member from "side opposite" asked me about "bad student behavior in the classroom". He went on to say that "back in the day, teachers had the wherewithal to deal immediately with unruly kids". I played dumb for a while, asking him to explain. Eventually, my dumb persona in full view, he finally stated, "Well, when I was a teacher way back, we could use the strap or the stick."

As expected, I was able to get this guy on the record for believing in corporal punishment. "Oh, thank you, sir," I replied innocently. "Well, you are correct; Ontario's Education Act still has that capability entrenched within, and it is backed up by Section 43 of the Criminal Code of Canada. If I may, as an educator and psychologist, we have learned from the evidence that suggests that modeling physical abuse to deal with unruly behavior, while possessing a short-term fix, has more deleterious effects on the student him- or herself, as well as those witnessing the event. But thank you for your helpful clarification."

When I was in social services, the NDP government of the day was completing some innovative welfare reform work. Minister Marion Boyd was to make a major announcement in the legislature one afternoon. We had all worked hard on her remarks, and Marion had a very strong understanding of what to say and how to say it. Approximately 20 minutes before she was to stand up and deliver her remarks, my communications director called me in a panic, stating that the Minister's script, which was to be delivered to all members of the Legislature, had been altered by the communications boss in the Premier's office. Michael Kurts, a wonderfully talented public servant, read over the phone what had been scripted as the new introduction: "Mr. Speaker, ours will be the first government in history that has taken on the task of welfare reform seriously..." Yikes.

I wasn't happy and told Mike, "That's bullshit, take it out." Mike felt caught in the middle, the power of the Premier's office hanging over him. Using what was a rare use of position power language and hierarchy for me, I said, "Mike, you report to me, not the Premier's guy. If he doesn't like it, he can deal with me." And with that, I quickly turned on my TV to watch Marion's remarks.

"Mr. Speaker, I stand up today to report on our latest efforts to improve our approach to the welfare in Ontario. Building on reforms such as the former Liberal government's Transitions Report, we are going to..."

Brava, Minister, just the way we had agreed—a non-partisan and positive approach. After Marion sat down, Charles Beer, the Liberal critic, rose, and, with an anger rarely seen from this otherwise superb and friendly politician, lambasted Marion for what had been on the awful version that had, unfortunately, already been distributed to the desks of all members in the Legislature. It wasn't held back in time: whether intentionally or not, the grossly partisan version was available, and Charlie decided to read this grossly partisan introduction, as authored by the Premier's communications person, into the record as the "real" beliefs of the government.

A few postscripts:

First, Marion had a chat with the Premier concerning over-the-top interference from his office. Premier Bob Rae was in complete agreement with Marion and apologized for his over-zealous communications guy.

Second, I made two calls—one to Beer, providing him with an off-the-record version of what happened, and assuring him that both Marion and the bureaucrats who served her were fully aware and respectful of what the Liberals had done. He had already suspected this from what Marion had stated, but scoring political points won out, even from someone as even-handed as Charles Beer.

And I called the late John Sweeney—the then-retired former Minister of Social Services under Liberal Premier David Peterson, who had led their remarkable work on welfare reform, and stated the following:

"John, I'm not sure if you were watching Question Period today and caught the Marion and Charles Beer back-and-forth, but—"

"Charles," he interrupted, "I am retired and choose to live a healthy life, avoiding the narrowmindedness that arises in government."

I gave him a full briefing and sent him Marion's official statement. Case closed—except for a few headlines.

Thus, my government experience with communications is that the risk aversion and pressure to make things look better than they are, leads to the staking of claims for accomplishments that all-too-often suffer from hyperbole, over-minimization of problems, or hiding mistakes—all of which lead to further problems later down the road.

In my first several months as President of Sir Sandford

Fleming College in Eastern Ontario, my on-boarding time was spent as suggested earlier: as an amateur social anthropologist listening in on the stories, successes, and challenges offered up through "listening meetings" with individuals and groups. Over the course of the first 60 days, I met with approximately 450 faculty, staff, and administrators, all asking questions like, "What do you expect of me?" and "Can you tell me something that excites you about your work and/or the college?" I also communicated to each and all the principles/values that would drive everything I did—like one of my key leadership lessons: *participation breeds creativity and commitment.* I spoke about my values like "equity" and "authenticity". One day, while visiting our School of Natural Resources in Lindsay, Ontario—a Canadian leader for its comprehensive and leading-edge offerings—I met Chris Yu, our cartography professor, during which I posed my questions.

"Well," he said, "our mapmaking students just won the Paris competitions for the fourth year in a row."

"Wow, that's terrific. Who came in second?" I asked.

"National Geographic, for the fourth year in a row," Chris said, rather nonchalantly.

I was stunned. I asked who knew about this, and he shrugged. While I came into a college with remarkable integrity and commitment to quality education due to the wonderful leadership of founding President David Sutherland, it was not part of the culture to broadcast many successes; if anything, David seemed almost shy about anything that appeared to contribute to a "bragging ethos".

Given the importance of highly visible storytelling to gain students, financial support, and the like, I thought differently. When I was in Toronto a few weeks later, I dropped by *The Globe and Mail*, completely unannounced, to see Shirley Sharzer, the paper's Deputy Editor.

"Shirley, although I've only been at Fleming for a few months, I've got a story worthy of *The Globe*."

"Really?" the affable but skeptical journalist posed.

"Yep! Our cartography students just won the Paris mapmaking competitions for the fourth year in a row..."

"So what?" she replied.

Waiting five seconds to deliver the punchline, I offered, "National Geographic has been the bridesmaid for four straight years."

"Why didn't you say so? When can we talk to the professor and students?"

Three weeks later, a two-page spread in *The Globe*'s weekend edition appeared. Easy win! Evidence, combined with a relationship with a journalist, and the story all but wrote itself.

Several months later, then-Governor General Ed Schreyer visited the college and asked immediately to visit the cartography program: he had read the *Globe* piece, and mapmaking was his hobby. He spent two hours with Chris Yu and his students, throwing his entire touring schedule awry for that day and the next. Thus, Canada's Governor General became an ambassador for a leading-edge program at the college. The wonderful consequences of stories well-told.

While there is a good deal of both hyperbole and outright fake and fact-less communications that seem to have invaded the public space, the best available and well-substantiated evidence should underpin any and all attempts at communicating an idea that intends to impact on improving practice, policy, or research efforts. This is key to my notion of evidence-based storytelling. So, what about the storytelling part? When former Premier McGuinty was leader of his party and trying to gain power, I was invited to a Saturday morning gathering that included all Liberal riding association leaders and more. While I remain to this day an independent non-partisan, my core values are clearly social democratic—with a small "s" and "d". That's why it's easy for me to admire many—not necessarily all—of the things associated with Canadian politicians of different political stripes. So, I have been fortunate to advise and learn from the likes of Ontario's former Progressive Conservative Premier William Davis, NDP Premiers Bob Rae and Roy Romanow, Liberal Premier's McGuinty and Kathleen Wynne, and Federal Liberal Ministers Monique Begin and Ken Dryden. Toronto Mayors, David Crombie, Barbara Hall, David Miller and John Tory have also afforded opportunities to learn about the rough and tumble of the most local of the political endeavor.

So, that Saturday morning, as I stood before Mr. McGuinty and his Liberal colleagues with a few notes literally on the back of an envelope, I began with a true story about my daughter Tai's Second Grade teacher, Jane Mundell. I spoke of her remarkable talents and the struggles she'd had to deal with in the context of a system far from as supportive as it needed to be. I channeled her emotions; I had been an occasional parent volunteer in her classroom, and I'd seen firsthand the challenges this dedicated educator needed to manage. Her struggles became mine; her story held deep meaning for me. Using this emotional story as a springboard, I then spoke about five things the government should be doing to ensure more equitable outcomes for all students, including the need for re-establishing the anti-racism strategy we developed under the Rae government, scrapped by his successor, Premier Mike Harris. To conclude, I went back to the initial story: "If you don't want to do these things for the people of Ontario, if you don't want to do these things so your party can gain government, then, for God's sake, do them for Jane Mundell, who does amazing things, but could do so much more with your support and understanding."

As I write these words again, my eyes well up in much the same way they did when I delivered them that morning: a somewhat tearful and a trembling delivery. A standing ovation ensued. Yes, I can hear the skeptical reader saying, sure, that old political saw, "If you can fake sincerity, Minister, you can really wow them." Sure, *beginning and ending with authentic emotion, while sandwiching substantive ideas in-between, is a formula to capture attention in an attempt to inspire,* but I would never—*could* never—use a narrative that isn't totally authentic. I have to genuinely feel something in order to be effective in communicating evidence-based ideas. Naturally, the stories must fit the audience, but the evidence and ideas don't change. The lesson here is obvious: *leaders must channel their own emotions in order to open up hearts and minds for new ideas to find resonance.*

Dalton was assigned to thank me, and afterward, he and Greg Sorbara asked if I would join them in Dalton's hotel suite. McGuinty asked me, "Chuck, how did you do that? You brought the crowd to their feet; it was amazing. When I am introduced as a leader, everybody stands, but I know it's out of proforma respect for my position."

I explained my formula, and asked him, "Did *you* stand up, and if so, why?"

He confirmed he was motivated by the plight of Madame Mundell.

A number of months later, there was a fundraiser for their party. Greg Sorbara was being honoured as part of the usual money-generating process, and he invited me to attend. I should add that he paid for my dinner (while I do make personal donations to the political process, it is only to support one or two who represent my core values in a consistent and effective way). Generally, this would translate into support for an NDP or Liberal candidate, and, on occasion, a truly *progressive* Progressive Conservative. The main speaker at this Liberal fundraiser was leader McGuinty. Greg introduced him, which I didn't think was a good idea. Why? Well, Sorbara is a master from the podium; funny and comfortable, with a gregarious nature that just lifts everyone up. By contrast, the somewhat shy and introverted leader had to follow this; more often than not, back then, McGuinty, would begin with, "Have you heard the one about..." and go on to tell a pat joke to warm both himself and the audience... A dreadful old formula, in my mind. But not this night... On this night, he began without notes.

"I want to begin by thanking Premier Harris." This was met with laughter, the audience making the assumption it was leading to another pat joke. "I'm serious, friends. The Premier recently took me on the government plane to New York to inspect the 9/11 Ground Zero site and meet local heroes." Dalton went on to describe how Mr. Harris went back to where he was sitting on the government plane ride home and asked how he was doing. "I thanked the Premier for what was a very meaningful experience. I didn't tell him what I was thinking, about what it was like to meet the New York cop and the emergency nurse who were at the Twin Towers aftermath when it counted. In them, I saw the face of government. I couldn't wait to get home to Terri [his wife]. It was through that experience that I wanted to share with her the obvious: that the two of us can't make a road to get our kids to and from school; we alone can't make clear air for them to breathe." He paused. "It was then, on that plane ride back from Ground Zero, that I realized down to my very core why I wanted to form government—a government that matters."

With about 300 people listening to every word, you could have heard the proverbial pin drop. Dalton was clearly touched, clearly moved by the experience he was sharing. I, too, was moved by this authentic story.

A standing ovation ensued. Wow, what a moment; an experience-driven tale—and completely inspiring.

McGuinty learned the lesson that the authentic offering of a narrative that was both real and uplifting, with a clear and emotional message concerning the importance of government, is a highly valuable tool. The ovation was in response to what he said, not the role he held—but he was still learning. Amazingly, unfortunately, he picked up the speech that had been written for the occasion, and for 20 minutes, delivered a dry, boring recitation about why the Liberal party of Ontario deserved support. He wasn't confident enough to know he had already closed the deal with the audience with his ten-minute story. To his credit, however, Dalton eventually became far more comfortable at the podium.

When I was still with the Atkinson Charitable Foundation, and we were trying to increase the public acceptance of the importance of the early years' investment, we did several things to improve our strategic approach to communications. Kerry McCuaig, our key communications partner, suggested we do some market research to test out the early years' language. For a small amount of money, we learned that "childcare" at the time was widely received by the Canadian public as "babysitting"—a sentiment that feeds directly into the conservative or libertarian notion that childcare-spending is nothing more than taxpayer-paid baby-minding. We also discovered that "early learning" resonated quite well with the public: parents were able to relate to the notion that their kids' learning could get a big boost during the pre-school phase. In turn, we learned that we could spend $5 million (CAD) a year for 10 years, explaining that high-quality childcare was a developmentally rich experience that boosted the social, emotional, and cognitive abilities of young children. Alternatively, we could simply adopt "early learning" as the proxy. We did the latter, and, out of respect for the many pioneer proponents of high-quality childcare, we extended it to "early learning and care". To my knowledge, this modest research led to the global adoption of the "early learning" branding. *Finding language that both connects with people and counteracts negative assumptions* was the lesson learned at the time.

Stated differently, we applied the important principle of *enlightened self-interest*. When we spend the time deeply listening to the assumptions behind counterviews to moving ahead, it is more likely we can appeal to something larger that unlikely "supporters" might be able to understand and support.

For example, when communicating about why it is important to get behind poverty reduction and anti-racism strategies, far too many people simply don't see the connection to their otherwise-comfortable it's-not-my-problem existence; but when we use evidence to predict where poverty and the serial assaulting of one's identity may lead when it comes to the desperation of too many who are disadvantaged through no fault of their own, we can move some from narrow short-term self-interest to a more "enlightened" perception about the consequences of going down the wrong pathway.

Extreme desperation and unfair loss of opportunity foments nothing-else-to-lose behavior in the form of crime—and even suicide. When longitudinal research shows that investment in high-quality early education saves up to $7 (USD) or more for every dollar spent, the savings are due to reduction in upstream social service, health and justice system costs. Ergo, it is in our enlightened self-interest to support the early-year investments. A more dramatic question for those who consider anti-racism and poverty reduction as left-wing nonsense is, "Do you want to live in communities surrounded by gates, the materials of which having yet to be invented by metallurgical engineers?" Naturally, it's simply unjust to oppress others because of race, religion, and LGBTQ identities—*just because it is wrong*. But for many, applying the *principle of enlightened self-interest is important to get folks to open up to seeing why the oppression of others will have personal consequences for them.*

And what about other concepts that would propel both individuals and organizations to think less narrowly and more robustly about certain decisions? For example, the quarter-over-quarter short-term mentality associated with many corporate organizations often conveys the notion that investing properly in the professional development of its employees or contributing to the environmental needs of its communities, involves annualized costs, rather than investments that pay for themselves over time. A triple bottom line approach to ensuring a commitment to social good and ecological sustainability, along with the important fiscal focus, should be informed by the enlightened self-interest of any organization—large or small. Unfortunately, this is all too rare.

Finding the appropriate methods and language that changes the minds and hearts of others takes us back to the important lesson concerning the critical practice of empathy, including seeking to understand as a critically important first-step ingredient in effective leadership. Indeed, unless we do all we can to understand the assumptions and broader contexts of others about any particular idea or issue, our ability to lead toward change through effective communications will be less effective or totally ineffective.

When I talk about the importance of evidence-based storytelling, the secret of success lies beyond the critical need for genuine experience and evidence told with narratives that move and inspire the listener: also key to the approach is the storyteller. While audiences are diverse, you cannot—and *should* not—change the "evidence", telling one group what they want to hear while telling another a different version. Perhaps that worked in pre-social media times. Clearly, the evidence should never change, but the narrative can be tailored; most importantly, how the audience perceives the authenticity of the message depends on *who* is telling the story.

Reflect on my earlier reference to how Michael Fullan's relationship with Premier McGuinty was key, and how we recruited Michael and his strong relationship with the premier to tell the evidence-based story about the impact of high-quality early learning. Again, I reiterate, *who tells the story is critically important.*

Central to our approach to more effectively communicating the value of early learning, then was the recruitment of a diverse array of storytellers, informed by the need to have different people able to "tell the story" of early learning to a variety of audiences. We asked the Senior Vice President of Canada's largest bank—the Royal—if he would work with the Hon. Margaret McCain to examine and report on the childcare issues in the city of Toronto. Hence, the Atkinson Charitable Foundation sponsored a short, focused "commission" designed to recruit the Royal Bank's Charles Coffey as a potential storyteller. By the way, we appropriated the word "commission" to elevate its perceived importance, and it worked—and I mean big time. While Charlie was already an unusually progressive banker, working with Margie McCain—former Lieutenant Governor of New Brunswick—and future partner with Fraser Mustard as authors of their Early Years reports—gave the banker a deeper understanding of the economic benefits of the early years story. Since then, Charles Coffey has become one of the best communicators when it comes to the business community's understanding of the economic return on the early years' investment.

As part of telling the early years story more broadly, Charlie and I co-authored an op-ed—*The Banker and the Professor*—in which we explained why two "strange bedfellows" would share the belief about the critical importance of the early years' investment. The "banker" understood that the early years of education were foundational to developing the human capital required for an "all hands on deck economy". The "professor" discussed the human development consequences of getting the early years right, which, in turn, is a contribution to saving money downstream through this upstream winner.

Charlie also penned a piece with Buzz Hargrove, the former head of the Canadian Auto Workers. This time, the banker—a proxy for private sector big biz—was doing a duet with big union. When we were finally ready to release our "best future" report to Premier McGuinty on June 15, 2009—the blueprint for early learning in Ontario—we had ensured that other spokespeople were ready to support the plan. In addition to Charlie, the Toronto Board of Trade, the Ontario Chamber of Commerce, and former Progressive Conservative Premier William G. Davis were among the many other "cheerleaders" offering public support. These storytellers, along with bank economists and academic economists like the University of Toronto's Gordon Cleveland and Pierre Fortin at the University of Quebec, have been key to counteracting the decades-old notion that things like childcare was a "soft church basement kind" of offering, as well as a low-rung funding option when compared with education. Connecting early learning to the education continuum was key, which is why we were so adamant that childcare and early learning needed to become part of the Ministry of Education.

Yes, who tells the story is indeed central.

Another case in point:

For about six years, I have been doing work in Australia, where some very important work has been taking place in the early years space. As an advisor to the largest non-profit childcare provider in Oz, I was having lunch with some members of the organization's board. At the time, it was felt that the very conservative Tony Abbott Aussie government needed to more fully understand the importance of the early years' investment. The Finance Minister of the day was an ultra-libertarian, "trickle-down" guy, who believed in the unfettered market economy as the source of all progress.

The board's chair asked me how we might change his mind when it came to the economic impact of quality early learning, to which I said, "Suppose I could get someone to speak to the Finance Minister who, like him, is a market-oriented individual; who is a very wealthy and accomplished businessman; who is a former finance minister; who tamed a multi-billion-dollar deficit, and was the co-creator of the G-20, without which Australia would not have a seat at any key international table—but someone who also believes that early learning is the best investment a government can make?"

"That would be a miracle," the Chair exclaimed. "Does such a person exist? My goodness, this is someone who might get through to the Finance Minister."

"Yep," I responded with confidence, "Canada's twenty-first prime minister, Paul Martin."

So, I offered to try. Upon my return to Canada, I called

Mr. Martin and explained the situation. My timing couldn't have been worse: he had literally just returned from Australia the day before, having attended a meeting of the Global Oceans Commission. His response: "Great idea, Charles, but these long trips are killing me. Never again."

Tired and jet-lagged... Never say never, I thought. "I'll ask you again in a few months' time, Prime Minister."

He laughed. "You can try, but don't count on it."

A few months later, I called him, but this time with a default card in mind which I decided to play. "Prime Minister, suppose I come to Montreal and film an interview with you that could be used in Australia for television, conferences, meetings of parliamentarians in Canberra, and other communication outlets," I countered.

"What a great idea, Charles! I'd love to."

The result was a tight ten-minute video, in which our former Prime Minister talks clearly and forcefully about the early years' evidence and its rightful place as the "best investment a government can make". Short of getting Mr. Martin to a face-to-face meeting with Australia's Finance Minister, it was a second-best option for sure. The video found its way to Aussie television, conferences, and workshops. Striving to secure well-regarded storytellers is part of the magic of effective evidence-based communications. So simple, yet so rarely practiced.

So, we have had some good success, ensuring that the value of *evidence-based storytelling rests with sound information, communicated by authentic messengers.*

One of the most enlightening examples of this for me involved the need to improve advocacy for those living in poverty. One of the most inspiring people I have ever met, Pat Capponi, recently passed away. A self-described psychiatric survivor and author, her powerful and effective advocacy was based on her own lived experience: she, along with several others, became the go-to people for the media and others who wanted to ensure some authenticity to their own storytelling in regard to poverty and mental health issues. Pat understood two things: the fact that the public at large needed to hear from more than a few "regular" voices; and that public and private organizations needed to do more for those with issues of low income and mental health within their own "backyards". Hence, with the help of several colleagues, I was privileged to work close-up in supporting Pat as she created *Voices From the Street*, an amazing effort to both recruit and train more and more mental health survivors as new and confident advocates. This resulted in more voices who could speak about the necessary changes for both the media and those within their own work settings. Their authentic lived experiences vividly brought to life the human costs arising from non-leaders who simply weren't paying attention.

One of the current catchphrases—especially in the research-rich context of the academy—is "knowledge mobilization". This concept is simple, yet poorly understood in practice. Naturally, its meaning is concerned with taking ideas that arise from applied and basic research efforts and "mobilizing" them into difference-making actions—all with the aim of influencing changes to practice, policy, or further research. National granting agencies, which seek to fund work that will have a high impact, require grant applicants to complete a section on "knowledge mobilization". With the odd exception, way too many of my university colleagues think that writing and disseminating reports and writing journal articles and making conference presentations, fits the bill. Truth be told, their approach to knowledge mobilization is often boring and ineffective; but that's okay, considering the granting agencies' folks don't seem to understand truly strategic communications either. One of my most enjoyable activities at this point is assisting my incredible scholar-colleagues in these efforts at being more strategic about ensuring higher impact for their results, in particular, impact on public policy.

High-impact communications begins with simple questions like, "If my research ideas are well-founded and provide valid evidence for change, how will they be adopted and by whom in order to yield sustainable impact?" Posing such a question leads to decisions being made concerning who needs to know about the research from the onset, not as an afterthought at the end. Who needs to be consulted in the first place about the research questions to raise their interest in the results? Remember how important it was to embed research scholars in the Toronto First Duty demonstration project from the beginning, asking educators and parents alike about what questions they may wish to be answered by the research. Even though the Provincial government was not a funder, we made sure that key bureaucrats—as well as a few politicians—were aware of this early learning work, anticipating that, if we could raise the public's comfort about the early years' investment, the risk would be reduced for the government. And, as it happened, our approach worked.

As I noted earlier, if you can figure out how to reduce the risk for government, eventually the government might run to the front of the parade and take credit for such a good idea—and, in this case, it did. Thus, effective knowledge mobilization should ensure that all key audiences for change are involved in some capacity at the start.

In this regard, I want to emphasize the need to further develop the relationships among and between the following sector leaders for sustainable high-quality impact going forward—always with the hope that good ideas will ultimately be understood and acted upon.

So, there then emerges the need to consider how we can encourage collaborative efforts among and between:

- The Practitioners, i.e. those who implement new ideas to improve delivery of services in various fields (or within an organization),
- The Researchers, i.e. academics and other researchers (including institutional researchers) whom we rely on to provide important evidence to guide practice improvement and decisions that entrench sustainable changes in policy, and
- The Policymakers (and organizational leaders), i.e. those who need to be informed about both practice

and evidence in order to make the right decisions about sustainable policy changes to make it all happen, both now and in the future.

I have worked in the cultures of the three legs of my "impact" model, depicted below.

Leadership Partnering for High Impact Change

Charles Pascal, 2014

There are a number of inherent challenges in each of these cultures:

Those who work in our universities are generally

rewarded for research deemed excellent through peer review, rather than by what practitioners or government policymakers think about their research. Those who work in the public service often work in anti-intellectual environments, whereby the amount of money spent on research to inform policy can be slim—or actually none! Several governments in the not-so-recent past have declared, by their short-sighted actions, their jurisdictions as "evidence-free zones". Former Canadian Prime Minister Harper totally diminished Stats Can—at once considered the finest national statistical organization of its kind in the world. For example, he killed off the long-form census that provides very valuable data for decision-making and research. The Harper government additionally implemented things like increasing spending for prisons, as well as other outdated "justice" measures, at a time when crime rates were actually going down in Canada. A communication plan to throw red meat to his base? Not to mention Premier Ford in Ontario who continues to ignore or eliminate good information today by killing off the critical activities and organizations designed to shed light on key issues, including think tanks and offices that advocated for children, patients, and the environment. When it comes to dealing with the pandemic, Ford's prior actions regarding such decisions have created a weak foundation for fighting the virus crisis—but more on this later on.

Finally, those who deliver services—the practitioners—are generally inactive users of the latest evidence, because they are simply too busy delivering services.

The good news is that there are examples of researchers who form genuinely reciprocal relationships with practitioners, seeking their advice concerning what questions they would like a research project to answer.

In our work in Ontario, the professors involved in our early learning research engaged parents and practitioners in this way—and, naturally, this kind of partnership raises both the practitioners' and parents' level of interest in paying attention to the research findings. Generally speaking, however, unless an academic is a public policy professor, too many academics live with the implicit mantra, "If policymakers or practitioners pay attention to my work, fine, but not my problem."

Let's be clear: any government or organization can make policies. It's easy work to make a policy. Some governments can make a *good* policy! But far too many are not actually very good when it comes to implementation. Unfortunately, too seldom do governments (and leaders of other public and private organizations) effectively involve practitioners—the ultimate implementers—in their policymaking process, both at the beginning and throughout.

More recently, I have come to witness a few more exceptions whereby policymakers and academics have, indeed, also formed respectful and reciprocal relationships. I have also witnessed some policymakers who have a more sophisticated and respectful approach to implementing policy by involving practitioners appropriately, but even so, this requires further improvement yet. Still too uncommon.

The antithesis of this kind of important collaboration is evidenced by Ontario's current Ford government, which has consistently made decisions without the proper involvement of evidence-makers, practitioners, and other "users" of policy changes. Their record regarding a myriad of decisions in education, the environment, and social services, including autism services, has been disastrous. Decisions have been made totally devoid of proper evidence and input from those who know better. They seem to be doing a remake of *The Gang Who Couldn't Shoot Straight*. Among the too many examples to note, here is a simple proxy for their inability to understand effective implementation procedures: their disastrous introduction of a new Ontario license plate. Aside from the fact their new plate wasn't visible at night, it was fine—and yet, after wasting tons of money, they chose to revert to the old plate. Indeed, this is a proxy for the Ford "Ready, Fire, Fail, Backtrack" cycle on so many files. More will be said when it comes to discussing the COVID-19 crisis later on, as well as some good examples of how a crisis can bring into better focus the benefits of good government.

The key lesson in all of this is that, *when those who work in the three cultures of evidence, policy and practice come together and collaborate, the world can change for the better*; thus, the effective development of each of these three professional clusters depends on the reciprocal relationships they have with the other two. Understanding this dynamic should inform the relationships that researchers need to form as part of their work, as well as the key to the evidence-based storytelling that should form the core of mobilizing knowledge.

The lesson for evidence-makers? Recruit partnerships with potential users of research results—policymakers and practitioners—along with potential storytellers, as part of a research projects' "steering" or advisory group. Keep people informed along the way, and supplement the usual and strategically mundane reports, journal articles, and conference presentations with newspaper editorial board meetings, working with electronic chase producers to saturate radio and television current affairs programming. Work with those who can secure mini-documentaries; create meetings with key government players—political and non-political; ensure leading practitioners in the appropriate fields are approached to discuss ideas concerning implementation. Notably, all of this is made easier when key and diverse storytellers who are invested in the work and able to help secure the meetings and activities described above, are recruited at the beginning.

To summarize, communications among and between the "actors" in these sectors, as well as communications to the various publics, must rest with a *combination of quality evidence, diverse narratives that connect emotionally with different publics, and diverse storytellers who add authenticity for different audiences.* Effective strategic communications can move mountains by reducing governments' natural risk aversion by raising the public's level of literacy surrounding the benefits of a particular change in policy or practice.

Listening more deeply and effectively with those you wish to influence or engage with is a must. As noted in the previous chapter, *being right is not a strategy*.

Given the importance of communicating with varied "publics", the subsequent chapter explores the lessons I have learned when it comes to dealing with diverse media platforms.

Chapter Five Takeaways

- **The power of evidence-based storytelling:**
  Communications that embed evidence into stories that capture the social and emotional ethos of each "audience" and "told" by storytellers respected by each audience, will yield a high-impact result.
- **The power of policy- and evidence-makers and practitioner collaboration:**
  Genuine collaboration among and between those in each of these separate "cultures" is key to ensuring sustainable ideas for change that are well-implemented.

EXERCISE #5:

Can you think of a case you were involved in, or which you observed, when those in a leadership position charged with changing or improving upon a policy, properly developed or sought sound evidence and involved practitioners effectively in the process? Or a case that could have been improved with better and clearer evidence and/or better storytelling and/or a more effective storyteller? Please reflect and make a few notes accordingly.

Your Notes

Chapter Six
Ditch the Media Blame Game

BUILDING ON THE PREVIOUS chapter and its exploration of evidence-based storytelling, more needs to be said when it comes to working with the media as part of the process of leading change. I, for one, am a bit tired of those who blame the media—as well as other platforms—for communication woes that were avoidable if we, as self-proclaimed victims, sought to understand a little more about the various contexts in which journalists work. Don't get me wrong: as in any field, there are journalists who are hardly in the business of shedding light on anything but themselves; those practitioners of "gotcha" journalism or the lazy ones who don't take the time to dig for, or verify, a fact.

It is, of course, through diverse media outlets that our stories can reach more people, thereby reaching more voters as we seek to influence policy changes that entrench great ideas for a better tomorrow. I am also concerned with intra-organizational platforms of communications. While we are living in an ever-changing and ever-expanding social media world, traditional platforms continue to require our attention. This chapter will deal with both the traditional and emerging communication challenges and opportunities. The importance of getting one's message out holds for those who lead small and large public and private organizations, not just political entities.

I have learned the hard way that the goal in dealing with traditional media is "fairness"—nothing more, nothing less. The notion of "using" the media for over-the-top coverage of one's most compelling story about change, suffers from a combination of passion and naiveté.

For me, the lessons learned are many, and begin with the need to understand and respect the limitations placed on traditional journalism. Radio, television, and print outlets have been trying to do more with less over the course of the past few decades. The smart outlets have re-engineered what they do with less revenue. Indeed, it is rare to see a TV news/current affairs crew show up with an interviewer, cameraperson, and soundperson unless you are part of a documentary; rather, it's much more likely an interviewer and sound/cameraperson or a journalist with a hand-held camera with built-in sound will be at hand. Newspapers with smaller print and a smaller overall format are now commonplace. And the result for print columnists and reporters? Less and less space to elaborate on interesting stories. For me, I need a magnifying glass to read a newspaper.

I have been fortunate to have my wife, Tassie, in my life for more than 45 years for many reasons. For the purposes of this chapter, given her remarkable career in television journalism, she has been a valuable coach regarding the need to understand a journalist's context. Tassie, in her own right, was a change-making leader, helped turn CBC's Marketplace from a stale consumer show into an investigative powerhouse that continues to pull back the curtain on the malfeasance of governments, corporations, and businesses alike. She has taught me some of the basics, such as the difference between a hard news story's more immediate deadline versus a softer piece that might have a one- or two-week deadline. When I discuss my lessons learned regarding the media, I will distinguish between reactive situations, in which a journalist approaches the "expert" or an organizational leader, and proactive contexts that involves someone with a change-making idea seeking to get their story out into the public domain.

Over the years, I have been on the receiving end of many requests from media outlets for quick turnaround quotes and/or interviews. A few years ago, I was asked to step in and take on an interim job at OISE, during which time I also acted as the main media contact as a broker for many of my colleagues, whose expertise best fit the journalist's request. When approached, the first thing to do is, of course, determine what the story is. Seasoned journalists will usually be very clear about the story, allowing an expert to either agree or disagree on whether their knowledge may be a good match. Furthermore, knowing the deadline is absolutely key. Why? If you are totally at ease when it comes to dealing with the question, then no worries; simply provide a succinct and clear quote or two. More often than not, however, "I'm right in the middle of something... Can I call you back in five minutes?" is a good reply; it provides a brief period to organize what you want to say in order to ensure the biggest impact regarding the issue. I have witnessed so many misunderstood quotes, simply because overconfident or inexperienced colleagues failed to take a moment to pause to think about the story and who was asking the questions.

For example, if I already have an honest and respectful reciprocal relationship with a reporter, then no problem; I can have a relaxed and trusting conversation about the story before either going on the record or brokering to someone else more qualified. On the contrary, if I *don't* know the reporter or chase producer (for TV and radio), I need to be a little more focused; I may need a pause. On the other hand, if the request comes from an outlet that is either philosophically intent on playing "gotcha" to suit their editorial biases, I will, of course, be more cautious.

A few years ago, when Ontario's health curriculum was being modernized (think sex ed), a loud and vocal social conservative minority raised hell, claiming a lack of consultation. The same issue and response reared its ugly head again as an Ontario election issue in 2018. As that great American philosopher and baseball legend Yogi Berra once said, it was déjà vu all over again.

Back in 2015, I brokered an interview between *a Toronto Sun* reporter who requested an expert on the sex ed curriculum and one of my OISE colleagues. First, I should point out that *The Sun* is an ultra-conservative tabloid. While my colleague was, and continues to be, a stellar communicator when it comes to her expertise, she was not well-schooled in dealing with the media at the time— particularly when it came to an outlet hostile to anything remotely progressive or evidence-based. *The Sun* had already conflated the sex ed curriculum with a former deputy minister, under whose direction the curriculum was developed. This deputy had been convicted of trafficking in child pornography and was on Premier Kathleen Wynne's transition team when she became Premier. *The Sun*'s not-so-subtle and horrific message was *Premier Kathleen Wynne is a lesbian. Her former deputy minister was on the job when the new curriculum was being developed and was convicted of offenses relating to child pornography; ergo, the new curriculum is unsafe for our children.* The fact this tabloid would conflate the sexual orientation of the Premier, coupled with the awful issues arising regarding her former deputy in order to attack a modernized and helpful new sex ed curriculum, remains to be one of the most vivid examples of sleazy non-journalism I can ever recall.

Ironically, for the majority of Ontarians, they understood that the new curriculum was designed to assist young people in dealing with things like cyber-porn and identity biases against LGBTQ kids and much more. My advice to my colleague: only answer questions that deal with the way in which the curriculum was developed; the involvement of health experts, teachers, and parents; debunking the silly and stupid things that people are saying about what is actually in the curriculum. I also told her, however, that she would likely be asked to answer questions about the former deputy minister and the "awful" but totally inaccurate non-consultative process, as well as other politically charged questions dealing with Premier Wynne's "bad" approach to the issue. I told her to broker those questions back to me. As per our discussion earlier about knowing the context, *seeking to understand the context before doing an interview, is key.*

Print reporters—unless doing a major feature—are usually operating on a tight deadline, and knowing when to pause and focus, when to broker to someone else, or when to decline when something is not a good match for you, is imperative. The most important element, however, is to respect those tight deadlines under which journalists operate. I think I have done fairly well over the years when it comes to being responsive and timely, and brokering to other expert colleagues if it assisted a better match when my own knowledge and experience didn't match up.

It is also important to recognize the difference between beat or general reporters and columnists: although reporters come in many shades of quality regarding how thorough they are, how much evidence informs their work, and ensuring the usual "on the one hand and on the other" coverage of a story, columnists are opinion writers—not necessarily compelled to apply balance. However, the great columnists—the four or five Canadian columnists I still find worth reading—while still having a "point of view", whether conservative, progressive, or hard to pinpoint—they do their homework. They dig and call a few people to verify a fact, so the arguments they bring to bear to support their point of view are worth attending to. And then there are the lazy ones; those who spout off silly and unsubstantiated ideas. I do not bother reading them, but it seems that many do. These faux journalists are energized by their followers whose anger about something gets scratched. Remember that lesson: *you can't be angry and smart at the same time*.

I definitely respect that the different outlets, whether print or electronic, do have different editorial points of view/biases—that's a plus, really a must, in a pluralistic society; however, key to all of this is to ensure we read or listen to more outlets who do *not* line up with our own deeply held views. Remember: *being right is not a strategy; we need to understand well-put views that differ from ours*. Reading more than one paper is key to understanding at least 70% of any story. Too many of us delude ourselves into thinking that a single outlet will provide all we need to know which is nothing short of nonsense. When we *are* asked to deal with any and all outlets, we need to understand these varying points of view when making decisions about what to say and how to best position our messages. Unfortunately, newspapers are folding or being swallowed up by larger entities that are reducing the diversity of world views—a major blow to the need for pluralism in a democratic society.

When I tell the early years policy story, I need to decide if I push the economic return on investment evidence or the child development side of the coin, or both. Or, in the case of the economic return argument, should I broker in Craig Alexander, former chief economist with TD Bank, Pierre Fortin from the University of Quebec, or Charlie Coffey, former Executive VP at the Royal Bank; or the Hon. Margaret

McCain, former lieutenant governor of New Brunswick, or Steve Barnett from Rutgers University in the U.S. as more legitimate experts or storytellers for the establishment "economic" audience? Should I complement the economic storytelling with the outstanding early years human development expertise of Canada's Jane Bertrand and Kerry McCuaig, the UK's Iram Siraj, or Italy's Roberto Farne, for example?

It is important to note, however, that, even when you know your stuff, even when you know the editorial bias of a media outlet, it can be near impossible to change a single mind of a reader, listener, or TV viewer. When I was in government as Deputy Minister of Education, we had a major consultation regarding the need for all publicly funded institutions, including universities, to ensure they had up-to-date workplace harassment and discrimination policies in place. Indeed, while universities are inherently "free speech" organizations driven by centuries-old traditions of academic freedom, they are also workplaces where power relations can lead to harassment or abuse in various forms. Our consultations went really well, with all the Ontario universities subsequently signing off on a basic template regarding what constituted "acceptable" and unacceptable" behavior, and procedures for handling the latter.

Basically, the Bob Rae government at the time wanted to ensure that public institutions were adhering to the basic policies of the Human Rights Commission of Ontario. Part of our successful consultation was based on the fact that we asked each university to ensure they underwent wide and deep consultations within their institution, along with a final Senate approval. Great? No! It didn't matter who was officially consulted, nor did it matter that the process was totally transparent: the moment the government announced that we had facilitated the development of workplace harassment and discrimination policies in the academy, two professors—one each from two different universities—went on a public rampage about the politically correct "nanny state" that Premier Rae was running. These professors were clear when it came to their position: they believed they had the right to say anything in their lectures or seminars, regardless of how insulting such views would be to their students, or however uncomfortable or unsafe it made them feel. Unfortunately, this view aligned well with certain media outlets and certain journalists, who believed the same views held true for their "freedom of the press" ethos. Thus, they couldn't wait to provide a platform for these professors. Because Premier Rae and my minister felt that, given my bone fides as a professor familiar with the history regarding academic freedom, I would be best to handle the public communications on this file.

Thanks very much for the opportunity, Premier. Yikes. Pretty unheard of for a bureaucrat to be offered up for public defense of a government initiative! Nonetheless, those were my marching orders. Thus, I completed a number of interviews and held my own in print, carefully providing examples of how racist or homophobic remarks seriously affect students, in turn forcing a few notable columnists to agree and nuance the difference between freedom of the press and falsely yelling "fire" in a movie theatre. Other columnists defended even worse comments by a professor and the results with populist garbage like: "Students need to learn it's a tough world out there." Nice sound bite for their readership. Much tougher for me, though, were a few phone-in shows on right-wing radio slots: with the station's home-grown crowd phoning in and asking, "Why are girls so sensitive?" (making reference to university-aged women), and "So what if a Muslim is offended? They can go back home to study!" It was indeed a bit of a challenge keeping my cool, and all while being attacked as a "politically correct flake". Out of about 15 calls in an hour (thank goodness for a few news breaks!), it seems I managed to convince one caller that, in 1994, it wasn't acceptable to attack one's identity to the point of creating extreme discomfort—and, for me, while the experience was a little uncomfortable, I'm glad I did it. Why? Well, first, I did my best to research and understand the context and bias of the media outlet; more specifically, this particular radio station and host. Given that I had time to listen to the same show, format, and approach of the host before I was in the hot seat, I had more perspective going in. And the second lesson? *If you are confident in your message and story, and you can stay calm, it's always good to* firmly and respectfully *fight ignorance with empathy and evidence.* Finally, that phone-in show was research—listening in on a swath of Toronto people with strong views and reasons for those views, is all part of the seeking-to-understand formula; useful for sharpening the messages down the road. For those unsure of dealing with a little (or more) of this kind of hostility, I would advise declining the invitation.

Flash forward to today when we recently witnessed the same issues at play with a particular University of Toronto professor, whose misogynistic and homophobic views have made many students feel unsafe along with many who are harassed by the harmful but effective use of social media by the professor and his many followers. The good news is that many universities are reinventing workplace harassment and discrimination policies and procedures—although implementation continues to require more in-service training to make these processes effective and safe.

So, in dealing in a reactive manner with requests from the media, seek clear understanding concerning the story and deadlines; try to understand the outlet's values and approach, and buy a touch of time, when necessary, in order to prepare accordingly, or alternatively, broker to another colleague. I would also add that, if you are asked to be part of a panel for radio or television, it is perfectly acceptable to ask the chase producer about who else is on the panel, as well as about the format. For me, this has had important benefits: first, I have been able to prevent participating on a panel of all White males, which continues to happen in this day and age. Second, as in the case in a radio interview, the outlet will often want to have a "pro" and "con" voice dealing with an issue (one person followed by a second one)—which is fair enough, although I always ask politely but firmly to go last, depending on who the other voice is. From time to time, what seems like an effort for balance is really a quest for entertainment: let the sparks fly! In these cases, I want to be able to do some myth-busting if I think the other voice is offering up fake facts to make an ideological point. Sure, you may ask why I think my point of view is superior—more than a touch arrogant, perhaps. So be it; I would rather follow someone who says that "provincially sponsored early learning and care is nothing but state-sponsored babysitting" than to allow for that bumper-sticker nonsense to hang, unchecked, in the airspace as the "last word" in a radio or TV segment. I have had too many difficult experiences as a result of being blindsided by both the format and the other selected participants, chosen based on their entertainment value rather than an informed view of an issue. Overall lesson learned? *Responding in a timely, prepared, and respectful way to media requests offers opportunities to impact on positive change.*

Thus far, I have focused on how to be prepared and responsive to media requests—that is, dealing with the reactive side of the coin. Indeed, being proactive in getting messages out about key evidence-informed ideas about improving practice or implementing a high-impact policy, has the potential to provide tremendous opportunities for positive change. As I noted earlier, the objective of what I refer to as "evidence-based storytelling" is to raise the "literacy" of the electorate or an organization's stakeholders in regard to why a particular idea is worthy of attention. The beauty of being proactive in telling the story is that you are in charge: you are in control of how the story is told, to whom, by whom, and in what media "space".

There are a myriad of vehicles that include the usual. For print or online newspaper websites, writing an op-ed can be a useful tool in framing your story; in my case, I have published too many op-eds to count, and have done so in various print and web outlets. Once published, these 600- to 850-word laser-focused mini essays can naturally be recirculated through social media for increased exposure. I have also learned that, oftentimes, it's best to seek an op-ed co-author with a bigger profile and/or authenticity regarding the piece's editorial intent. I have often been successful gaining higher impact with a piece as the junior author to a well-known "expert". I will admit that, in order to advance the public dialogue about a certain issue, I will recruit, and act as a ghostwriter for, someone with unquestionable reputation and knowledge on the subject. Longer form blogs or podcasts can also take ideas deeper, including actions concerning the implementation of a new idea or policy, and can be posted and sent to a wide variety of journalists, editors, and producers who work in newspapers, magazines, radio, and television as "backgrounders", ultimately leading to others picking up a story for coverage. In addition, these various communications can be sent and/or discussed directly with politicians, bureaucrats, and various other public and private leaders.

Something else worth mentioning: the majority of

governments have pretty sophisticated clipping services at hand that provide both bureaucrats and politicians with timely access to ideas and concerns "in the news".

But, as we discussed earlier, knowledge mobilization is not about sending around long obtuse reports; rather, mobilizing good ideas is about asking, *Who can make the decision(s) to implement an idea that will make things better, then working backward to determine what and who will influence them?*

For better and for worse, political leadership, regardless of stripe, uses polling and focus groups to determine which way the wind is blowing, the results of such methods often yielding what the public wants, rather than what it needs. The process is all too often focused on how best to sell a predetermined idea and how best to package it. With this in mind, it is more critical than ever that those who elect governments have a higher and deeper understanding of the efficacy of various policy directions and how they were developed. *Effective leadership means doing everything possible in order to raise the understanding of those who ultimately influence the decision-makers*—something that is increasingly difficult in our social media frenzied world, in which superficial bumper-sticker slogans—repeated ad nauseam—can be difficult to overcome, as we have seen with the skillful and destructive Trumpian practice of proffering fake facts as news and attacking evidence as fake. This fact fabrication virus doesn't respect borders, having invaded, for example, the DNA of Ontario's Ford government. More will be said about dealing within this social media context later on.

Dealing directly with major influencers is very important but knowing how is too rare. I continue to be amazed that progressive think tanks—most of them now defunct— continue to send, at one time, four or five reports on key issues to the editorial boards of major Canadian newspapers, rather than making an appointment to meet directly with the most appropriate editorial board, beat reporter, or columnist. Influencing a policy change based on some good evidence can and should be presented and discussed directly to and with a minister, deputy or other senior public servants directly. Yes, I know it sounds harder than it is, but not if we work through various networks. Our degrees of separation in Canada are small: remember, it was through Michael Fullan's relationship with Premier McGuinty that we were able to tap into getting the Premier's attention concerning the impact of full-day learning for four- and five-year-old kids. And it was Prime Minister Tony Blair who first mentioned Michael to McGuinty.

When I was at the Atkinson Foundation, we were approached by an anti-poverty group for some money to launch a public campaign with the aim of getting the government to make a small change to a social service regulation; they wanted a huge chunk of change to raise voter awareness and seemed startled when I asked if they had met with the Minister or Deputy, or one of their assistants. Nope—they hadn't thought that it would be possible or effective. Hence, through our networks, we brokered a breakfast meeting with the Deputy Minister. The group presented a clear case regarding this minor change to the regulation, and, in due course, the change was made. All for the cost of breakfast.

It's important to emphasize the importance of influencing through trusted relationships. When working backward from a key decision-maker, as I have noted, we need to simply ask the question regarding who and what influences her/him. If you want to influence your dean, head of a community organization, president, minister, premier, or mayor, you have to come to know who influences them and how your existing relationships connect with the ultimate object of influence. How can you, slowly, over time, increase your relationships in an honest and mutually rewarding manner? In government, it is often unelected political staffers, as well as talented bureaucrats, who carry a good deal of weight when it comes to influencing major decisions.

I've already mentioned other things we did at the Atkinson Foundation that paid off, including the use of demonstration projects to portray how the future would look if we were to have the universal full-day pre-school learning programming, for example. In one way, the Foundation was a communications organization; a great deal of our work began with the changes that may improve the lives of the many. So, what various policy and programming options should be considered? What kind of information would be helpful in deciding upon the best possibilities? As noted earlier, this resulted in research and evidence, as well as the generation of demonstration projects we sponsored to showcase the future. This work illustrated the possibilities as part of telling the story in various ways to various audiences by relevant story-tellers.

When it comes to supporting some of Canada's most remarkable and effective storytellers for social and economic justice issues, one of the best vehicles we developed at the Atkinson Foundation was our Economic Justice Award. How did it work? With no applications, nominations, or processes, from time to time, the Board would decide who would be best to support when it came to issues the Board felt were critically important in achieving a better future. This was a tap-on-the-shoulder kind of thing for people for whom a boost of support would provide major resources to continue doing their thing and accordingly bring visibility to an issue. So, we tapped people on the shoulder and provided an initial $100,000 (CAD) per year for three years. They could use the money for any purpose that would help them achieve a higher impact. All of those chosen while I was at the Foundation were highly recognized for their knowledge, integrity, experience, and ability to communicate with clarity and passion. Want a few examples? Sure you do.

In 2002, Armine Yalnizyan, one of Canada's most progressive economists, was working on her growing income gap research. She needed support for this work, and we were fortunate to be able to support this remarkable thought-leader. When her first report came out, the clarity of the report, quality of its short form summary, and stunning nature of the evidence regarding the growing gap between rich and poor in Canada, led to total media saturation in Canada. Say what? Our media-tracking showed that every single daily and weekly newspaper, as well as every single television and radio newscast, covered the story about Canada's "growing gap". In addition to this, Armine's uncanny ability to communicate so clearly in the avalanche of interviews that followed—as well as her ongoing work in this area—has altered both the ways in which we discuss income disparity in Canada, and how Stats Can now reports on it. Want a sample of Armine's ability to communicate clearly when it comes to complex economic issues? Well, she remains a ubiquitous go-to person for radio and TV segments. Indeed, Armine continues to be one of the most effective voices regarding ways in which we can develop the economy as an instrument for social betterment.

Another example? Just after former Saskatchewan Premier Roy Romanow tabled his report with Prime Minister Chretien on the Future of Healthcare in Canada, one of my board members raised the following question: "Charles, do you think Mr. Romanow has the financial support required to continue communicating the importance of his commission's findings on retaining and improving our universal healthcare system? If not, we should give him our Economic Justice Award."

I replied that I simply did not know, but that it was not unusual for a government to receive a commission report, thank the commissioner, and send him/her on their way.

"Well, Charles, call him up and offer our support," the board's chair, Betsy Atkinson Murray, said.

"Okay. All in favour?"

Unanimous—and, simple as that, I was dispatched to call Mr. Romanow.

While I had met Mr. Romanow when he was Premier of Saskatchewan and was consulting with him regarding his post-secondary system, I naturally did not have his home phone number. Working through those small degrees of separation and the kind of good working relationships to which I have referred, I phoned two Bobs—Rae and McMurtry. The first Bob, Ontario's former premier and now Canadian Ambassador to the U.N., needs no introduction; meanwhile, Dr. Bob McMurtry had worked on the commission with Romanow, and was a superb health policy and research-oriented M. D. I left messages with each of the Bobs, and Dr. McMurtry was the first to phone with Mr. Romanow's home number. With that, I called him and reintroduced myself (he did recall our meeting in Saskatoon a few years before), noting our mutual friends. I then asked if he would accept the Foundation's support to continue his important work.

Silence. Then, "Charles, do you believe in God?"

Yikes. Deep breath, then, "Well, while I am a values-driven person, I can't say I'm a religious person." I was trying my best to avoid a simple "no".

"Me too," he replied. Instant relief flooded me. I mustered

the courage to ask him why he'd posed such a delicate question. "Well, I just got off the phone with a big-time American speaker's bureau, and they offered me a huge amount of money to put me on the international circuit. I turned them down; the idea of getting rich talking about universal healthcare didn't seem right. Then you called."

He asked about how it would work if he accepted, and he made it clear that some money for travel, further research, and communications support would be helpful. Given that he was not someone who became rich while in politics—and while he was doing some teaching at the University of Saskatchewan—I had to work hard to convince him to take some of the money for a modest stipend.

Again, the rest is history: Roy was able to continue speaking out about the importance of the Commission's work in Canada and beyond, and a few other things arose directly from Roy's association with the Foundation. Given that his commission did not emphasize the critical importance of upstream investments regarding the determinants of health, he supplemented this serious omission with extensive communications—and, importantly, Roy became the Founding Chair of our international steering committee that oversaw the development and implementation of the Canadian Index of Wellbeing (CIW).

A word about the CIW: as part of the Atkinson's commitment to ensuring the provision of effective and publicly available information dealing with the things that generate wellbeing, we set out to bring together Canada's best minds to explore measures of genuine national progress. The notion was that emphasizing the things that measure the determinants of health would support upstream investments that get the short shrift compared to rising costs of healthcare that strain government budgets; in fact, we don't have a healthcare system, we have an "illness system" that tries to solve health problems, not prevent them. By generating and reporting information concerning how Canadians are doing with the things that prevent illness—factors dealing with education, environment, living standards, and community vitality—it is hoped that communities, voters, and government decision-makers will respond accordingly. The GDP is regularly reported as a proxy for how a nation is doing, notwithstanding that it is a narrow measure of consumption and economic production; the treating of serious illness and natural disasters contribute to the GDP. Now, situated at Waterloo University, the CIW has eight measurement domains, with eight indicators for each domain—and, while the CIW is still not quite being reported regularly in the news like the quarterly GDP, it is being used by several municipalities and community health centres to organize their work and track progress.

During the latter stages of development of the CIW, I chatted with the then-Finance Minister Paul Martin about the idea of Stats Can eventually taking on the ongoing development and reporting of the CIW. He liked the idea, and, by the time a possible transfer was feasible, Martin had become prime minister before eventually losing government to Mr. Harper, who then, as I noted earlier, eviscerated Stats Can. Please take the time to visit the CIW website[9], and you will see the remarkable potential to steer decision-makers and those who elect them to the better use of our taxes. Whatever leadership objectives you have, *developing clearly understood and viable measures that track progress in a transparent manner can attract human and financial resources to the work at hand.*

Back to Roy Romanow and the dividends he paid as an Atkinson Economic Justice Fellow: Roy was the one who introduced me to Dr. Danielle Martin—who now, in my view, is the most effective spokesperson for the efficacy of universal healthcare in North America. The manner in which she took on misguided American senators during a Senate hearing a few years ago is a classic, as is the work she did more recently with U.S. Senator Bernie Sanders. It's the stuff of legends. However, well before her important and visible communications work (including her book *Six Big Ideas to Improve Healthcare,* 2017, Penguin/Random House Canada), she needed support to start up a new movement in Canada to guard against attacks on our own single-payer system. Canadian Doctors for Medicare was thus founded in 2006 with help from the Atkinson Foundation as its founding funder. All of this is thanks to Roy's introduction to Danielle—all of this from our support of Roy.

While Roy was doing his research for his Royal

---

[9] CIW, available at https://uwaterloo.ca/canadian-index-wellbeing.

Commission on the Future of Healthcare for Prime Minister Chretien, two highly regarded McMaster research professors approached the Atkinson Foundation for financial support for a timely topic: their study of studies focused on whether for-profit hospital care had an impact on patient mortality compared to non-profit hospitals. Put crassly, I wrote in my diary a simplistic version of their research questions: *Does the profit motive kill when it comes to human services?* Their meta-analysis included millions of patients in thousands of for-profit and not-for-profit hospital settings in the U.S.

When Principle Investigator, Dr. P. J. Devereaux, described the work they wanted to do, I said, "Sure, we will support this on one condition: that you do all you can to ensure that, whatever results are obtained, you will try to secure fast-track publication in key medical journals." Why did we insist on this? First (fingers crossed), our working assumption is that privatizing human services introduces potential challenges regarding cutting corners—and, while these researchers brought impeccable independence to the work, we thought an extra sense of independence would be carried if the results were reviewed independently by journals' independent experts and published accordingly. Again, independent refereed journals as the "storytellers" would create a strong sense of credibility. They agreed, and when the results *did* show that the profit motive yielded poorer mortality outcomes, P. J. had managed to get both the *Journal of the American Medical Association* and the *Canadian Medical Association Journal* to publish the results. The story—

that Canada's not-for-profit approach was superior—was widespread, boasting great coast-to-coast coverage; however, we were far from satisfied with Canadian media saturation given that, for better or worse, we are subject to how we are seen by the U.S. concerning who and what we are. So, before the release of the journals' findings, I called the offices of the two American senators who were fighting for Canadian-style single-payer healthcare at the time: Teddy Kennedy and Hillary Clinton. I spoke with their healthcare policy directors, and asked each if they would like an embargoed copy of the journal articles so that, when they were published, they could disseminate the story through their channels if they so wished. They enthusiastically embraced the opportunity, and, upon publication of the results in 2002, not only did the storyline receive massive Canadian coverage I noted, but, through the senators' media machines, the U.S. coverage included *The New York Times*, *Washington Post*, CNN, and more. The lesson? *Piggyback on those who have the resources to do your bidding to carry effective public messages of the things you care about.*

Okay, I can't help it: here are three more examples of the power of this lesson, as applied through the Atkinson Economic Justice Award. Anyone who cares about affordable housing for low-income people in Canada, anyone who cares about the homeless and their recurrent need for proper shelter and care, will know about the remarkable "street nurse," Cathy Crowe. Again, the Atkinson Board asked me to tap her on the shoulder, and, in this case, my boss, Betsy

Atkinson Murray, asked if she could join me in asking Cathy if she would accept $100,000 for three years to support her crusade for the most vulnerable in our society. Through an instant flow of tears, Cathy nodded a "yes". An out-of-the-blue opportunity to support so many out-of-the-cold initiatives led by Cathy, who is still going strong as *the* most effective advocate for the homeless and affordable housing in Canada. Just ask a run of Toronto mayors who have been forced publicly to answer to Cathy's evidence-informed and public admonitions to do better... much better.

In 2008, we tapped community researcher and advocate Uzma Shakir on the shoulder with the view of supporting her critically important work on immigration and "colour of poverty/the colour of change" project. This dynamic leader was an extremely important force for change for the communities she served. Uzma was also key to the Foundation's ongoing efforts to ensure that our own development as an organization was informed by a greater understanding of race and poverty.

Finally, given the Foundation's commitment to early childhood development and our increasing awareness that we needed to learn more about Indigenous issues and support initiatives that would help us with this learning, we asked Dr. Cindy Blackstock if she would accept our support. Cindy is considered one of the most respected Indigenous leaders in Canada.

At the time (2009), she was in the initial stages of taking on the Federal Government regarding the fiscal injustice regarding support for the social and health needs of the First Nations' children. Her foundational concept of Jordan's Principle is named after a child who died during his two-year wait while the province of Manitoba and the Federal Government squabbled over which jurisdiction should be responsible for dealing with Jordan Anderson's complex needs. This child-first principle means a child-first response to needs is paramount, that jurisdictional arguments should not delay attending to a child's needs. Importantly, the overriding policy goal is to ensure that the support that children receive in First Nation communities should be equivalent to non-Indigenous support off reserve. This fight for fiscal fairness guides everything that Cindy does in her unrelenting, high-visible crusade for social justice. The timing of our Atkinson support provided a much-needed springboard to advance the case to and through the Canadian Human Rights Tribunal process, which ruled in favour of strong and expanded support of the application of Jordan's Principle. Since 2017, the Tribunal has continued to issue further directives to the Federal Government to get on with fiscal fairness for these Indigenous children. To this day, Cindy continues to urge the current Trudeau government to get on with a full response to the Tribunal's directive. Without commenting on our current Federal Government's overall record, I find its hypocrisy regarding Indigenous issues simply shameful. When Mr. Trudeau was first campaigning to become prime minister, upon the tabling of the Truth and Reconciliation Commission's report, he noted, naïvely, that he would "implement all 94 Calls to Action" noted in the TRC's final report. Jordan's spirit is still waiting for that promised fairness.

Think of the ongoing work of these five individuals—Armine, Roy, Cathy, Uzma and Cindy—and the direct impact of their work on the others who follow in their footsteps—and all of this because of the simple lesson noted earlier. Stated differently: *find, learn from, and support the best communicator, the best change-making person, or the best organization that matches up with your issue.* Yes, I hear you: you don't have the resources or network of an organization like the Atkinson Charitable Foundation! But you *can*; through the small number of degrees of separation we enjoy in Canada or your country, determine who fits your end game aspirations for a better future and find ways to support them. It's easier than you think—*much* easier if you want to make a difference. As noted earlier, it wasn't difficult for me to find the phone numbers of two iconic American senators, Ted Kennedy and Hillary Clinton—both of whom, given our common cause of universal healthcare, were more than delighted to use our sponsored work to support their agenda by using their enormous communication "machines" to advance the cause. This is why U.S. Senator Bernie Sanders has used Canadian Dr. Danielle Martin, supported in her original advocacy work by the Atkinson Foundation, as a superb myth-buster against the many self-interested Americans who provide false impressions regarding our Canadian healthcare system.

There are other things we can do in a proactive manner to achieve a greater impact through more effective communications and various channels. Why do I find the Fraser Institute, located in British Columbia, to be such a challenging organization for me? Is it because of their interesting historical reliance on certain funding sources (such as American money from the right-wing Koch brothers, for example)? Or could it be that some have claimed concern about the voracity of their evidence informed by their clearly noted ideological ends? Nope, none of these things. In actual fact, my consternation flows from a grudging admission that their approach to communications is remarkably—and unfortunately—effective. For example, they stretch the use of Ontario testing data to inappropriately rank schools in "reports" that support their view of the world regarding public education. And it attracts attention. Yes, they are very good at grabbing headlines and ensuring their network of their so-called "experts" wind up on radio and television panels and are quoted in newspapers. I always find it interesting that some in the media often refers to them as a "think tank", but reserves "left-wing think tank" for organizations like the Canadian Centre for Policy Alternatives. One of most inventive things Fraser does is their Tax Freedom Day: the day when Canada, as a whole, has allegedly earned enough to pay its total tax bill for the year. Designed to build resentment concerning the very notion of paying taxes, it's very clever, purely ideological, and very effective.

Not to be outdone, Hugh McKenzie—one of Canada's

most thoughtful and progressive economists—produces an annual report noting how quickly the highest Canadian wage-earners earn the annual salary of the average Canadian worker. It usually takes no later than the mid-afternoon of January 1 each year for the richest corporate leaders to earn what an average Canadian worker makes in a year. Both are examples of clever communication devices to convey a clear message about an issue.

Naturally, there are many other ways to be proactive in obtaining evidence-based stories for public discussion and possible impact: opinion pieces, blogs, and more recent modes, such as podcasts, short videos, and Instagram, can all go viral if well-conceived and creatively constructed. I personally love the power of podcasts filling my soul with leadership inspiration. My two recent favourites? Former CBC journalist Connie Walker's *Missing and Murdered* series should disrupt the attitudes of anyone uncertain about the recurrent and extreme forms of racist attacks on Indigenous peoples.

Another inspiring podcast series? More than 300 people have risen to take the helm of prime minister or premier in Canada, and only 12 have been women. Political science instructor Kate Graham's *No Second Chances* podcast series chronicles the endemic challenges that women face in seeking and retaining political leadership. Both of these podcast series should be inserted into the education curricula across Canada.

I also believe in being proactive with beat reporters and

columnists who are working harder and harder with fewer resources and less space on the pages of an ever-shrinking print world. These journalists are also finding their way onto webpages. The grind of being productive, producing article after article, column after column, means they are always looking for ideas. You can wait for them to call, wait for them to "get it" *vis-a-vis* an important issue, or you can politely offer up ideas that need exposure. So, go for it—or ask someone who already has a relationship with a journalist to pitch the idea for you. I am always pleased to coach others with great ideas on how to take their ideas to the various media "markets"—and nothing gives me more pleasure professionally than to assist others who have great ideas by editing their draft op-eds and providing coaching on how and where to get them published.

And what about dealing with social media to get your ideas discussed with a view to impact change? By the time you're reading this book, it is quite likely that what exists in the social media world now as I write this will be replaced by something new. A few years ago, I was chatting with my then-14-year-old granddaughter, Indiana, telling her proudly that I had joined Facebook (shortly after which I quit) and Twitter.

"That is so yesterday, Papa Chuckie," she replied.

With Instagram and Snapchat in full-bloom, I asked her, "What's next?"

Her wise and strategic rejoinder: "It hasn't been invented yet, but it's gonna be cool."

Okay, so I admit: I'm a rookie regarding the use of social

media, but my observations to date are that, with rare exceptions, there are serious issues when it comes to intelligent discourse and messaging out coherent ideas; the fast-paced, real-time, and brevity requirements of Twitter, for example, reinforce the kind of emotion-over-evidence that seems to deepen the divide between alternative-world views, rather than moving to solutions that might actually work. This is all part of the bumper sticker right wing populist approach to communications made infamous recently by various politicians. Opinions, or intentional dis-information offered in 280 words or fewer aimed at the visceral level, do not advance thoughtfulness.

More and more, it appears that people are uncomfortable living in the grey zone, more comfortable with the extreme accusatory, I-am-right-and-you-are-wrong, rhetoric. Unfortunately, it is in the grey zone of complexity where we must stave off the simplistic and strive for something greater than the parts of our prideful, too-easily-formed notions of some form of truth. Remember: *being right is not a strategy*; as Oliver Wendell Holmes so famously noted, "For the simplicity that lies this side of complexity, I would not give a fig; but for the simplicity that lies on the other side of complexity, I would give my life."

One of Michael Fullan's latest books, *Nuance* (Sage, 2018), underscores the notion of eschewing oppositional thinking and the need to go deeper regarding the requirement of understanding the underlying assumptions at play when leading a change process. Building on the systems theory notion of "simplexity", Fullan cautions against knee-jerk tendencies to view the complex as simple, and what appears to be simple as complex.

This has been a struggle for me, as one who is quick to connect the dots for *the solution* way too often. As an aside, in certain situations, I also am also too quick to share my quickly formed ideas with others which can shut down further creative problem-solving. It's part of that constant need to learn to lead from behind a bit more. Learning to live more comfortably in the grey zone is a lesson that requires intentional training and self-control, building on those other notions discussed (e.g., what is right is more important than who is right; seek to understand before seeking to be understood). With the exception of those remarkable viral postings of a picture or video—those proxies of a million words of expression—social media, more often than not, does more to create simplistic and harmful division than move constructive discourse forward. And in an age where there seems to be diminishing opportunities for independent and diverse investigative journalism to thrive, I worry deeply about the loss of the availability of the kind of intellectual capital and patience required to deal with increasingly difficult issues.

Finally, in dealing with the media, whether reactively or proactively, what do you do when the media *does* get it wrong; that is, when they have seriously—unintentionally or intentionally—misrepresented facts? As I have noted, the major burden for clarity rests with those of us who wish to ensure our best ideas carry potential for enabling positive change. That said, either through unprofessionalism, laziness, or being overworked (as media outlets try to do more with less), serious errors of editorial omission and commission do happen.

First, if there is a very minor mistake regarding a quote, for example, let it go; however, in those situations where the very meaning of what was noted on the page is unfair and misleading, don't hesitate to respectfully follow up with the journalist to clarify. Keeping a good relationship with a beat reporter is important, and sometimes good feedback will be helpful for the next time. Writing a short letter to the editor to correct a serious error will likely be published, at least in the eyes of the few who read letters to the editor. And social media can be used to provide additional public correction under your control. And if the journalist is hostile to fair feedback that has been constructively offered, then just avoid her/him going forward.

Additionally, if a print reporter persists in misrepresenting the evidence that informs an issue you care about, you do have further recourse. Here's an example from my own experience.

As you know from these pages, I care deeply about the importance of high-quality pre-school education and its impact on the social, emotional, and cognitive development of young children. A particular Canadian beat reporter continued to misuse specious American research to slam Canadian research that showcased the benefits of early childhood education. His cherry-picking of research that bore zero application to what we were doing in Ontario was absurd. This was not a problem at first: with a good relationship already built, I simply explained why the research comparison lacked scientific voracity; however, his approach continued, and when he told me at one point that he wasn't going to send his four-year-old to Ontario's Full-Day Kindergarten program because "she was better off at home", I got it: the journalist was justifying his own decision on the pages of his newspaper with totally—and I'm certain—unintentional non-research. In my view, this was an innocent example of resolving cognitive dissonance—one that so happened to be very damaging to the public conversation. Thus, I put together a case for the ombudsperson of his paper, providing all of the articles and explaining the misuse of research that resulted in extremely biased reporting. After investigating the matter, I can only say that the reporting changed on a dime. I also made it clear that the reporting was so biased that, if the paper didn't provide effective leadership, I would taken the case to the Ontario Press Council, the ultimate arbiter regarding fairness in the print media. Footnote: to this day, my relationship with this reporter is stronger than ever.

Here's a story from the electronic media world:

Back in the day, when I was Deputy Minister of Social Services in Ontario, there was an item on the Canadian CTV network's current affairs program, W-5. The segment dealt with the horrific challenges of a woman trying to hide from the predatory behavior of her abusive estranged husband; the issue dealt with the need for more safe-haven shelters for abused women, given that the woman featured was hiding in a non-shelter situation. While her face was "masked", her voice was not—and, making matters worse, the location of her makeshift "shelter" was revealed with a single wide-shot included in the piece. Horrified at this location disclosure, my staff called me at home and made me immediately aware of the situation. That evening and throughout the next day, I did everything I could to reach the show's Executive Producer: I left messages indicating the issue, and noted that he had a moral responsibility to contact the woman in question and ensure a safe and immediate alternative place for her. A couple of decades later, I still haven't had the decency of a return call—and, while I still harbour a deep respect for the media and its many talented professionals and the limitations on various outlets, there are times when I deeply resent the very notion that, while I am totally committed to returning calls from them to assist "their" story in a timely manner, that it is not always reciprocated. Even now, I am not sure why. Embedded arrogance? Not overly-organized folks? Regardless of my work flow or role over many years, I continue to find it irritating when people compliment me for returning their call or responding to their email in a timely manner: sure, nice feedback, but these comments serve as a proxy for how uncommon it is for people to respond to others in a timely and decent manner. How often do your legitimate calls or emails go unanswered? How often are you made to feel like a nag for following up a week or two later?

In summary, with this and the previous chapter, I have attempted to emphasize the simple notion that great leadership carries the responsibility to continue improving one's capacity to bring clarity of message through effective communication practice. The overall aim is achieving a broader understanding on the part of more people concerning why we should vigorously pursue more productive pathways to that better future. This is what great leaders aspire to do—and, naturally, a good deal of this is about being clearer about the outcomes we seek. The next few chapters focus on a few lessons learned about *getting there*, being clearer and relevant about the ultimate destination that defines the changes we seek.

Chapter Six Takeaways

- **The importance of effectively responding to media requests:**
  Understanding the limitations placed on journalists, knowing about their deadlines, editorial bias, and ensuring your own clarity about the messages you wish to convey, can greatly assist public dialogue about issues you care about.
- **The big benefit of being proactive in getting your messages out:**
  Learning about, and using, the many communication vehicles to get public exposure for your ideas and plans is key to controlling the quality and impact of your message.
- **Find and support the best communicator, the best change-making person, or the best organization that matches up with your issue:**
  Who in the public sphere is making a difference communicating the importance of the issues you care about? Working through networks that reduce the degrees of separation, determine how you can support them and/or form an "advocacy relationship".

EXERCISE #6:

Taking two of the takeaways from this chapter, describe how you might improve your ability to impact on the changes you seek to make by applying each lesson. Alternatively, you might describe, in detail, how you have already successfully applied the takeaway. Or you might use a case you have observed that illustrates the lesson's value.

Your Notes

Chapter Seven
Improvement is the Enemy of Change

WHEN IT COMES TO changing things for the better, the notion of improvement takes centre stage. Whether we are examining the change processes within government, education, a community, or an organization, it always seems to be about "*improving* child welfare", "*improving* math scores", "*improving* waste management" or "*improving* company morale". Huge efforts, marked by investments in time, money, and human sweat, are offered in pursuit of such improvements—and yet results often fall short... way short. Why? Because *improvement is the enemy of change.*

Using education as an example, the response to bad practice or unmet outcomes far too often surrounds "making improvements" around the edges, holding constant the real things that make a difference while tinkering with the low-hanging fruit that makes no fundamental change for the better. I've had enough of non-improvements that do no more than maintain the status quo but which are nonetheless sold as major advancements that are actually a waste of time and money.

A few examples:

At the post-secondary level in Canada, it's good to see many institutions trying to respond to the Truth and Reconciliation Commission. The TRC, headed by now Senator

Murray Sinclair, was established with the aim of examining the negative effects of Canada's residential schools that sequestered Indigenous children to *make them Canadian*. It contained 94 Calls to Action. The salient response to date from Canada's universities seems to be the implementation of required undergrad courses pertaining to the history of residential schools, as well as the recurrent and horrific consequences that continue to sabotage the aspirations of Indigenous peoples. To some, this appears to be a great improvement to our collective understanding. But it is enough?

Several years ago, I was addressing the graduating class of Ontario's Laurentian University. Before the event, Laurentian's President introduced me to the Dean, who, just the day before, had managed to get Senate approval for one of these mandatory courses dealing with our collective, unfortunate, and recurring behavior regarding Indigenous peoples. Later, standing before the graduates and their families, I caught the attention of an Indigenous family with *traditional* clothes, further self-identifying with an elderly woman holding an eagle feather at the centre of their gathering in the audience. Without hesitation, as someone painfully unable to stick to a written script, my spontaneous response was to congratulate the Dean, who was successful in bringing about that undergraduate course. I then noted, "Mr. Chancellor, Mr. President: if an undergraduate course is a useful way of educating students about the horrible impact of residential schools, why doesn't your university ensure that all staff, faculty, and administrators undergo extensive anti-oppression training to change the colonizing effects of a culture that actually ignores or perpetuates obstacles to genuine reconciliation?"

My off-the-cuff bluntness was met by the thunderous applause of about twenty or so people. Pretty isolated response from the gathering. A bit too *in your face* bold for the masses. Okay, there it was: notwithstanding the tepid response that proved my point, I did notice that eagle feather pointed in my direction. University convocations are generally concluded by the chancellor. In this instance, the chancellor was *TVOntario*'s Steve Paikin, who thanked me for my "typically challenging nature" before turning to the President noting, "I guess we have our work cut out for us."

Good. I really did put Steve—one of Canada's premier journalists—and then-President Dominic Giroux, on the spot. Good for Steve for punctuating the essence of doing better at the university. Saying this, such examples of public and private Canadian organizations that are truly and intentionally committed to a long-term, integrated truth and reconciliation journey, are few and far between. Having a university "truth" course for undergraduates without a strategy to intentionally, over time, change the overall culture of the university, will not sustain any legitimate progress of reconciliation. They will not alter the colonizing research and teaching practices. These superficial, short-term fixes may look good on an organization's annual report or election brochure, but they actually set real change back.

This case in point illustrates how little change will ensue unless truly transformational cultural change takes place. *Real change requires the serious disruption of the status quo; playing around the edges and appropriating simple solutions for complex problems will not yield the required progress.*

Real change *will* disrupt the status quo. Great change agents will be both clear about the endgame, and both tenacious and patient about the long road ahead. This was brought home to me on a deeply emotional level with the recent passing of U.S. Representative John Lewis. Mr. Lewis urged each and all to *get into "good trouble"*. A remarkably simple but powerful admonition to emphasize that, unless we seek genuine change, unless we disrupt the status quo, real change will remain elusive. Like Canada's Tommy Douglas's fight for universal healthcare, John Lewis's clarity of vision over his eight decades of "freedom fighting" for racial equality was crystal clear. He took every opportunity to move things forward. He was beaten and jailed, and yet, with grace and courage, battled on. He was always getting into "good trouble". Great leaders do.

When it comes to genuine and sustainable change, strategies must be informed by a clear understanding of the problems that require attention. If I had to recommend elements for leadership development programs, high on my list would be the *critical importance of systems thinking.* The all-too-common absence of this skillset gives way to what seems like an epidemic of superficial attempts at change. Determining the root causes of a problem is a necessity, and, without this key systems ability, attempts at solving important and complex problems will suffer from treating the symptoms, while the resistant underlying forces continue to persist to entrench obstacles to genuine progress. As part of this challenge, we need to *avoid adopting solutions in search of problems*—solutions thrown at a problem that have been successful in dealing with one situation that are then assumed to solve issues in another context, despite them having seriously different root causes. For me, Peter Senge's *The Fifth Discipline*[10] provided me with a great primer on the critical importance of focusing on the underlying causes of a problem and avoiding skating on the surface of what he called *symptomatic barriers.*

One huge challenge facing societies around the world is the ever-growing prevalence of mental health problems—and Canada is no exception. Public attention to mental health challenges in Canada seems to be at a fever pitch. Approximately 1.2 million Canadian children and youth—or one in five—experience a mental health challenge, with less than 20% receiving the appropriate treatment. A shocking 80% go without proper support. Indeed, from the earliest years to our seniors' population, mental health issues seem truly epidemic. The current pandemic has provided both additional evidence to these challenges and a re-emphasising of the situation by triggering latent mental health issues for far too many.

[10] Senge, P. M., *The Fifth Discipline*, 1990.

A few years ago, I was giving a speech to an audience of about 1,000, and, at the end, I asked all those *who did not know* someone with a serious mental health challenge—those aged 18 months to 80 years—in their immediate circle of friends, family, and next "circle" beyond, to raise their hands. Of those 1,000 present, five hands went up. Five out of 1,000 said they didn't know anyone with a serious mental health challenge—and, who knows, maybe these "lucky" ones actually did know someone whose challenges were not obvious.

In the past number of years, millions of government and philanthropic dollars have been spent on dealing with mental health issues. So, are things abating? Are they getting better? Here and there, yes; but, generally, not much. From our youngest citizens to our oldest, way too many are falling through the gaps and cracks of a non-system. The fragmented efforts currently being dedicated to the problem here and there just aren't sufficient. In short, nothing less than a whole-system approach that begins with early childhood diagnostics and intervention involving wraparound initiatives from totally integrated community resources will do—to begin with.

Here is another case in point. The first obstacle in the way of a long-term vision, such as, for example, aspiring that Canada become the healthiest place in the world, is that we do not have a totally integrated, seamless service system in our communities. Really? Many providers believe that high levels of collaboration among and between service providers equals integration, when it does not. Rather, the systems work required to achieve true integration would start with the need for a community-based process that results in each individual service *doing fewer things better rather than all things less well*. Would this begin with every service related to children and youth placing all of their resources on the table? Scary, but yes. And does this mean services would actually have to stop doing things that others could do better? Yep. Would some services need to shut down so their resources could be used by the newly arising system? Yep. Would the government need to seriously alter its funding approaches across several ministries to reinforce this transformation? Indeed. Absolutely.

For example, if this is all done well, a "no wrong door" result would emerge: no matter what agency a family enters in a new and genuine system, they would immediately enter *all* of the systems' resources. The job of the initial agency of entry would be to diagnose the issues at play, and if their agency matched up with the mental health requirement (or some other issue at play), then proceed. What if what was required would be best served by another agency or "node" in the system? In this case, the agency would broker the client to the other agency with a better match for the client in mind. Easy? Well, not unless the initial agency gets "paid" by the government for the brokering behavior. Why? Increasingly, governments pay agencies with a very narrow piecemeal approach—one client at a time. Unless brokering behavior is rewarded by a tweaked funding mechanism, it won't happen.

Service organizations will hang onto clients, even if the match for success isn't ideal. It won't be informed by an intent to do harm; just a natural, contorted effort to do the best for the client—even if the intervention approach isn't the best match for the issue.

Imagine someone going into a Neo-Freudian clinic with acrophobia—a fear of heights. They may leave one hour or two years later hating their mother. Okay, not so funny—especially for you Jungian therapists who think you could do the trick. But if this initial clinic got paid to broker the client to a service that specializes in phobic issues—one that offers systematic relaxation therapies, for example—better results would ensue. Creating a whole larger than the sum of its parts is a lesson worth pondering, whether we are talking about this kind of major systems change work or developing a strong and effective leadership team with an intentional effort to ensure complementary skills and knowledge.

So, even if a jurisdiction did this very difficult systems change work within each community, if the funding arrangements fail to adjust, it will simply be another case of layering a new program onto fundamentally flawed structures and methods that will not yield sustainable results. Indeed, *effective change will require approaches that intentionally and strategically disrupt the status quo.* We simply need to go deep. *Holding constant the most important levers for a better result and playing around with the symptoms that hang out on the visible edges simply will not yield the changes required.*

Let's take a peek at what happens when we fail to have a

continuum of diagnostics and effective mental health interventions along the way, beyond the foundationally important early years. In Ontario's elementary and secondary schools, a student presenting issues related to serious learning challenges can be assessed via a diagnostic process reviewed by a school and school board committee process. When the process works well, a student receives an Individual Education Plan (IEP)—a clear accommodation plan for the teachers to implement, along with the provision of other supports. This is great when it works in a timely fashion—and herein lies the problem. Back in the days of Ontario's Premier Harris, a major cut to education funding led to the loss of the majority of the school boards' diagnosticians in Ontario—and things have only become worse under Ontario's current regime of serial short-sightedness.

Earlier, I discussed some lessons learned from my daughter Tai's book chronicling her educational journey from age four through high school. Tai was a book author at 17, preceded by a few op-eds at age 14. Sure, I am very proud of her accomplishments, but the story behind her "stories" is that of a Third Grader with serious learning disabilities and who transitioned from someone having problems with school to a confident honour roll student. As a first story in this tale, her teacher, Madame Brigitte, pulled me aside when I was doing the after-school pickup:

"Charles, have you noticed a disconnect between Tai's verbal expressions and what she writes on paper?"

Doffing my clinical hat, I went straight to a father's

defensiveness. "Absolutely not."

"Okay, but perhaps you might have a closer look. No worries," she countered.

Given I was the homework support parent, I tried to leap over my defensiveness and paid closer attention. Sure enough, despite being shielded by an overly optimistic and hopeful perspective about each and all of my children, Madame was right.

When I tell this story, without identifying at first that the student in question is my daughter, I ask my audiences, "How long do you think it took the parent to locate an expert diagnostic psychologist, take the results to the school, and secure a successful back-on-track IEP to accommodate this student?"

Informed by their own experience, people shout their guesses—usually in the one- to three-year range. Three years to get this done? I then reveal I was the parent and the student was Tai. I note that it took me six weeks. How was that possible? Well, quite simply, rolodex and money. First, it took me three hours to locate one of the best diagnosticians around through my network—who also happened to be the former head of diagnostics for Canada's largest school board, Toronto's public board. He put Tai (and Tassie and me) through an extensive testing process in a timely manner; the results were then provided to the IEP process—and, with the leadership of a great school principal and her teachers, it was indeed a major back-on-track experience for Tai. The rest is history: a pathway to successful honours completion of high school. What happens with undiagnosed issues? With Tai, like others, it could likely lead to despair, lack of self-esteem—in essence, the kinds of things that can go wrong for individuals and outcomes for taxpayers who foot the bill for costly "downstream" social, health, and correctional services. What about Tai's experience with colleges and universities? I will get to that shortly.

But first, before you understandably start screaming about White privilege, should rolodex and money be the public policy default? Hell no. It's an embarrassing story to tell. I was able to locate the best diagnostician and pay him the $1,500 required, receiving the majority of that back because of my benefits package. Money and rolodex should be the antithesis of good public policy. What does the average family do when it comes to serious challenges related to learning disabilities, pent-up test anxieties, or autism symptoms that can show up as early as 12–18 months of age? What would we need to change in order to facilitate for all the kind of timely intervention that propelled my daughter down the more productive pathway? Professor Yogi Berra's notion of "When you come to a fork in the road, take it"! Notwithstanding my love of baseball, I prefer Robert Frost:

Two roads diverged in a yellow wood,
And sorry I could not travel both
And be one traveler, long I stood
And looked down one as far as I could
To where it bent in the undergrowth;

Then took the other, as just as fair,
And having perhaps the better claim,
Because it was grassy and wanted wear;
Though as for that the passing there
Had worn them really about the same,

And both that morning equally lay
In leaves no step had trodden black.
Oh, I kept the first for another day!
Yet knowing how way leads on to way,
I doubted if I should ever come back.

I shall be telling this with a sigh
Somewhere ages and ages hence:
Two roads diverged in a wood, and I—
I took the one less traveled by,
And that has made all the difference.[11]

It's that pathway *less traveled* we need to embrace. The creation of genuine and sustainable systems that achieve real

---

[11] Frost, R., *The Road Not Taken and Other Selected Poems*, 2015.

results is really very difficult; it takes time and tenacity. Saying that, however, ignoring it and dealing with shiny "improvements" is no fix, and will continue to yield terrible human cost and wasted public and private resources.

At times, I feel as though I am witnessing—both in real life and real time—one of worst movies ever made, *Groundhog Day*. In the midst of self-isolating due to COVID-19, it is interesting how often I hear people make reference to this "every day is the same" theme. How often do we leap to solve a problem only to witness its reoccurrence? We need to *avoid the ad-hoc monster of keeping underlying causes untouched.*

So, when one of my children came home from middle-school and told me "one of the kids had a gun in his locker and the police were called and we all had to go outside", I asked if she had a note from school. Nope. It took two days for heartsick parents to receive a note from the Principal explaining that the gun was a fake. Sure. I went to see the Principal, who explained that she wasn't allowed to communicate anything until she received an okay from the Board's "central office". Talk about a problem that required an easy systems-change fix. Of course, my privileged rolodex at play, I then spoke to the then-Director of Education, whose "improvement" response left me with the unfortunate notion that there would be further reoccurring breakdowns in communication. I could fill a book listing other examples that ignore the lesson that a *problem worth solving creates opportunities to ensure system change work prevents reoccurrence.* And if a leader has no systems-change acumen (which is a very, very common problem), they should then refer back to the major lesson of "Chapter Three: Complement Thyself." *Know what's needed, know what you don't know, and bring in a damn systems thinker!*

Regarding the early years story, Tai was fortunate to have a teacher whose training and/or instincts provided sound understanding about what her observations about Tai might mean. We do not need teachers to be sophisticated diagnosticians about things like language encoding or decoding issues; however, it *is* critical their training provides much more about what to watch for and what to do if question marks arise about a student. That's all it is: the ability to raise a question. The same is true when it comes to the others involved in the lives of young children: parents, of course, are included in this group, but what about pediatricians? Is the "average" pediatrician effective when it comes to noting irregularities in a child's development? Unequivocally, maybe; it would depend on the doctor. While there is specialty training that some have undergone, too many children still continue to fall through the cracks or are forced to have to wait for far too long for adequate diagnostics and support.

Thus, it is evident that the ensuring that the training of all professionals, as well as increasing parental knowledge, needs to be part of the system's work. One of the reasons we selected teams of certified teachers and early childhood educators to support full-day learning for four- and five-year-old children in Ontario, is because of the school routines and knowledge that the teacher brings to the table, as well as the more advanced knowledge concerning child development contributed by the ECE.

So, if we wanted to transform the Individual Education Plan (IEP) process to ensure that any student—from pre-school age onward—for whom a question mark is raised receives a timely response, what else would be required? Well, the lowest hanging fruit in an otherwise-challenging orchard of what's required relates to the relationships between educators and parents/guardians. For sure, a good deal of effort appears to have been devoted to "involving" parents. "Parent involvement"—or its more active expression of "parent engagement"—seems pretty widespread. And yet how genuine, how deep, is the kind of partnership required to effectively support the needs of the children/students these would-be partners "share"? Indeed, given the remarkably important impact the home environment has on children, as well as the value deriving from these partners sharing information about what each knows concerning their common charges, genuine and respectful collaboration is critical. Yet it remains all too uncommon. Sure, there are parent–teacher nights, but how effective are they really? Who shows up? And more importantly, who doesn't?

I remain fortunate enough to continue to receive invitations to visit schools around Ontario and well beyond, both in Canada and internationally. I can recall an indelible experience from one of these visits to a Toronto school set in a very diverse low-income neighborhood with a very high immigrant population. Based on previous expectations from visiting "similar" school environments, I was amazed at the number of parents—both mothers and fathers—who were present as volunteers. The place was teeming with vitality and diversity, and, at the end of the visit, I asked the Principal, "Given that so many of our *newly arrived* neighbors do not feel welcomed in our schools, what's going on here?"

In a matter-of-fact and humble manner, he noted, "That is true, and *was* true with this school when I arrived. Many immigrant families see the school and its teachers and principals as elusive 'authority figures'. Few had the confidence to show up at parent–teacher events due to this—and language barriers."

"So, what changed?"

"Well, I decided to do two things: naturally, when teacher vacancies arose, I was intentional about ensuring that diversity of culture, race, and language informed our new hires. I got great support from my superintendent, and, six years later, we are now on our way to ensuring our staff is closer to matching our communities."

"What else?" I continued.

"Well, I started attending various events across different communities in our area; things like community kitchens and other cultural celebrations."

"So?"

"Well, dressed in my 'civilian clothes' and withholding any initial mention that I worked in the local school, I would ask a few folks here and there—those who seemed open to a conversation—if they had any kids in the local school, and proceeded to ask if they were having a positive experience and whether they thought there were any improvements that might help. Over time, I would run into the same parents and parents in different communities, and the comfort level eventually seemed good enough to reveal that I worked at the school. I asked if they would ever consider coming to the school to help me improve the experience for their children."

Talk about the road less-traveled!

"At first, about five parents had the confidence to show up. I listened, involving a few linguistically appropriate staff members to assist, and ideas arose that were worthy of implementation. These parents then went on to tell other parents who had observed some of the simple ideas that were now common in the classrooms. And that's how it all began."

Of course, I was curious about examples of specific things that made a difference when it came to increasing immigrant parent participation in the school. The initial group of parents noted that their kids' cultural differences made them feel isolated, even from other racialized kids—not just the White students and White teachers—and, while the majority of the children spoke some (or fluent) English, it might be nice, they suggested, if the teachers asked *all* the children to share words and phrases in their current dominant/heritage language. With White English-speaking kids included, they could explore, with their parents or grandparents, their heritage language, thereby destigmatizing the idea for the immigrant students; a simple idea with a powerful outcome. In basic terms, this principal is a natural systems aficionado. He understood the underlying obstacles that stood in the way of his vision of an authentic community school for *all* families. He understood that community peers would be the best recruiters for increasing enough trust for other people to participate in the school's activities.

This story reinforces the need to train and supply more systems change-makers for the future; in the meantime, we need a massively increased understanding that those "natural" or trained systems thinkers that *do* exist need to be central to any organization's hope for genuine improvement. As I have noted, it also reinforces the need for leaders to know what they don't know. Big problem.

This also raises the reason as to why improvement strategies often suffer from what I call the *hardening of the categories* in which the key, necessary parts for a particular change strategy are the purview of another department in an organization. Want to improve health or educational outcomes for people? Great, but what's your plan to ensure that a systematic anti-poverty and anti-oppression strategy is in full and sustainable bloom? But that's another department or ministry's responsibility, you say? Well, here's the deal: if we care about evidence, then we know that children living in poverty are:

- More likely to be low-birthweight babies and have weight-related diabetes and poor nutrition,
- 2.5 times more likely to have a disability,

- More likely to have learning, behavioural, and emotional problems,
- More likely to be exposed to higher rates of abuse and violence,
- Less likely to be supported by extended health plans,
- Less likely to have access to preschool, cultural, recreational, and after-school programs, and
- Less likely to have the digital supports at home required for a future that will increasingly depend on remote learning.

Unless there are more horizontal and holistic approaches to the challenges at hand, leaders will continue to illustrate the problems by *putting new wine in old bottles*, and, as with this analogy, the results will be vinegar—not even suitable for salad-making. Trust me, I learned that culinary lesson the hard way.

The key is to *avoid pseudo-innovations*—those "improvement" solutions that simply waste time and money—and, worse yet, do not actually improve things. One of my favorite non-starter examples is the proliferation of the "offices of...." solutions to things like equity, anti-racism, or Indigenization. I just found out that another Canadian university hired someone as their Associate VP of "diversity and human rights". Great, depending on what else happens in the organization as a result of this new "office". Will the incumbent be charged with ensuring that all deans and department chairs are given performance objectives that deal explicitly with any issues arising with the rights and needs of

LGBTQ staff and students? Will all the university's leaders—the President, VPs, deans, chairs—receive in-depth training concerning the issues faced by Indigenous and Black staff and students? Will these performance objectives have some accountability? Will the progress of achieving these objectives by university administrators and faculty be tracked? Really? That just isn't happening.

More often than not, the best these "offices of..." can do is to provide publicly available statistics about who is doing what to whom, who is being hired by what procedures, who is not being hired because of seriously flawed recruitment procedures, and how many suicides/attempts are arising with students in the first semester of their first year due to the totally inadequate systems that "assist" with diagnostics, screening, and adequate and timely interventions. And how many of these "offices of..." would be permitted to pull back the curtain regarding these data and publicly post them? Few to none.

Getting back to post-secondary education and its failure to adequately deal with the students they inherit from our schools, let me refer once again to my story about Tai and success regarding timely intervention and support that is too uncommon. The good news is that, when it comes to learners entering our colleges and universities, there should be fewer vulnerable students because of our early years' investments. When the IEP process works well with elementary and secondary students, as it did with Tai, the increased readiness to take on post-secondary education should be improved. On the face of things, Ontario's high school graduation and post-secondary participation rates have been excellent. Under Ontario Premier McGuinty—and with help from Michael Fullan, among other advisors—Ontario's high school grad rates went from 68% to over 86% in five years. Among the OECD countries, Canada leads, possessing the highest level of the population with post-secondary education, helped along with our excellent college systems across the county. However, beneath these glowing statistics, those cracks and gaps are causing serious impediments to health and wellbeing for too many.

So, what's the problem? When Tai chose to go to university, she was an honour student who was accepted at all three of the universities to which she applied because of her successful IEP support in high school. As part of her research, she discovered that all three—like most Canadian colleges and universities—had "access to success" centres designed to provide the same services that had led to Tai's school-based IEP. She chose one of the three—the one that matched her interests at the time—and then the domino effect of doom began.

First, she wanted her IEP to be understood and acted on well before she started classes, and yet nothing was available until the end of August, with the onset of classes looming. She then discovered, just as classes began, that the diagnostics that informed her IEP had to be repeated; an updated version was necessary. Interesting that there was nothing ahead of time that might have generated a more timely and updated report. Okay, no problem; the same psychologist who had supported her back in Third Grade fast-tracked an update, providing Tai and her university of choice with the updated information. Alright. Very nice and helpful that the people in the "access centre" worked with this information, and, in discussion, developed a superb plan for accommodation for Tai. All this was done as classes began—not perfect timing, but it could have been worse. The plans for Tai were then sent to each of her professors—and that's when the roof caved in. Unlike her school experience, where an "all hands on-deck" approach was applied with the leadership of a principal and vice principal who assured effective implementation, each professor at this highly regarded university was "free" to consider *if and how* they would implement Tai's university "IEP".

One professor said at the beginning of a lecture with 200 students, "One of the students here needs a volunteer note-taker. Anyone interested?" There was no regard to quality note-taking, and no regard to the public call-out and how it might affect Tai (she so happened to be fine with it, but others in a similar situation might have been mortified). No hands raised; no note-taker. As time passed toward mid-term exams about six weeks hence, she did her best with notes, although listening to meaning *and* taking notes was a very challenging part of her world.

And then there was another professor, who told Tai, "Hey, I just received this report about your learning needs. I am very pleased to help. I will make my slides available to assist you with your homework—but this thing about 'providing an alternative way to test your learning'... Well, that wouldn't be fair to the other students." Okay, so here we have it: a professor in a fine university who doesn't know that equity does not mean "sameness". The results of all this? As mid-term exams—offered in traditional ways—were looming, Tai's anxiety rose to a fever pitch. She dropped out, and, with her permission and because of the privilege of my rolodex again, I spoke to the President and Provost about their systems' issues, as well as how it was affecting one student: my daughter. Both were very sympathetic and actually followed it up but couldn't do anything in a timely way. I had to suppress my "hang in there and tough it out" attitude in favour of my overriding love for my daughter and my concern for her mental health.

The rest is a success story of resilience. First, Tai wrote a three-page brief to the President and Provost about all of the issues that needed fixing, including professor training, negotiating with the professors' "union" about the need for "access reports" to be binding, and the need to pay quality note-takers already chosen for all large lectures (McGill University in Montreal does this), among a host of other related changes. I was very impressed with her resulting report—something that would likely cost $50,000 (CAD) if the university hired a consulting company to genuinely improve their "access to success" outcomes. Strangely, it is a university's enlightened self-interest to improve all of this since they lose grant money when students drop out. In

Ontario, universities bend over backward to try to keep students in their classes until at least November 1, when enrolment for grant purposes, is counted. The worst form of keeping a lid on mental health issues is when student health services uses an expeditious "medical model" and dispense drugs to calm things down for stressed-out students. Something else that is also strange and disturbing is that the President and Provost who received this totally well-intentioned brief from Tai—a report totally void of rancour, comprising a simple, "I hope this is helpful to you, and I am available to chat" conclusion—have never replied to Tai. I am still amazed that her advice wasn't even acknowledged.

But, as the Bard said, all's well that ends well. Tai used an unanticipated gap year to take a few more courses, work, and complete an enormous amount of research to find a university outside of Ontario (in the U.K.) that provided what was necessary—and, sure enough, she graduated with honours. She did find that Ontario's community colleges were a little better than their universities but had nowhere near what was necessary.

One lesson I learned in all of this was *the importance of genuinely involving those served by a service or innovation in its development and/or formative evaluation.* The consumer as the consultant, when totally genuine, rather than a we-really-want-your-opinion pretense for looking as though they care, can be powerful. *Tapping into lived experience carries with it a kind of natural and inductive notion of systems thinking.* The President and the Provost who received Tai's report needed to understand and action this lesson—and yet they didn't. Yes, while not wishing to name and shame them here, I will send them this excerpt—now eight years later—to contribute to their development. After all, feedback is the breakfast of champions. Guess what? I did send this to them. The then provost is now the president of this university. His response. "Great that things worked out for Tai." No ownership, no apology... no leadership.

Here's another example of the throes that accompany ignoring the real things that can bring about genuine improvements to our efforts at leading change. Many decades ago, psychologist J. B. Carroll conducted some research concerning the concept of aptitude. Generally speaking, when we discuss the concept of *aptitude*, we are referring to whether or not someone has "it"—as in, "you have an aptitude for woodworking or second language-learning, and I don't." You either have the ability to do something, or you struggle with it. However, it was Carroll (among others) who redefined aptitude as "the difference in time it takes different people to achieve the same learning outcome".[12] The significance of this? Well, if you look at how we structure the conclusion of the Canadian school year in June, some students in a math class will get As, while others languish in the C-or-lower range. From the perspective of Carroll's work on aptitude, the net effect of our school year structure is to *hold time constant* while *allowing success to vary* from student to student,

---

[12] Carroll, J. B., A Model of School Learning, Teachers College Record, 1963.

subject to subject. From a systems change perspective, a continuous learning approach that provides each student the time and resources to learn what is required when it comes to their "lower aptitude" subjects would flip it all over, holding success constant and varying time for our more challenging learning outcomes for each student in various subjects.

Naturally, all of us, excepting the "uber learners," are "good" at some subjects and less so in others. This does not mean, however, that I don't acknowledge how daunting the prospect of totally overhauling how we go from our entrenched status quo of learning delivery to a mastery model would be. It would be nice to see a few demonstration projects that test out continuous learning approaches. In the meantime, are there more modest structural changes that may help student achievement for all students in their areas of struggle? After all, the reason why we have a two-month summer break in-between grades is because our current approach is based on the historical need to have our children available during a mostly agrarian economy when working on the farm with all hands available during the summer was a necessity. Of course, that's no longer the case—and yet we still stick to what was.

A two-month hiatus isn't helpful when it comes to consolidating newly and hard-won learning outcomes. This is why Australia, for example, structures its school year into four terms with two-week breaks in-between. This is a terrific structural change that assists with continuous learning challenges. So why is this not the case in Canada? Indeed, while we have an array of interventions and inventions to improve learning for all students, these improvements won't make the big differences we seek regarding student success—that is, unless we disrupt those bigger core obstacles. As noted in our book, *Too Far from Perfect*, Tai noted that "if we care about kids' learning and their success, we would allow the time they need according to how different kids learn different things." One of the possible, even hopeful, benefits arising from the challenges of the pandemic is how we can reimagine everything—including education. Based on the lessons learned from the virus crisis—which we will go into later—it is clear that the demand for a return to the old "normal" is a non-starter.

So, effective transformational leadership requires systems thinking—period. But are there other obstacles that result in those marginal "improvement" efforts that waste time and resources? When considering RIM's (Blackberry's) almost-fatal end to their very existence, it begs a very scary question: why is it that too many successful organizations don't see a looming cliff on the horizon? In the case of RIM—a truly global Canadian success story—I think the problem was success itself: far too often, *success is the enemy of success.*

Say what?

The most sustainably successful organizations are always aggressively paying close attention to the "what-ifs", seeking out possible threats and opportunities, rather than ignoring them. Thinking way outside the box to discover subtle opportunities and determining when to stop doing certain things should be an embedded, continuous habit—and yet, too often, very successful leaders seem to dislocate a shoulder patting themselves on the back.

The inherent threat of success is not to be taken lightly. We see a natural tendency toward overconfidence with early—or even sustained—success. A young tennis player who has early wins often begins spending too much time on commercials and less time on the hard things required to take things up a notch. Think about the many politicians who are sky-high in the polls, and who cash in their popularity on a dime when it comes to decisions and behavior that simply do not match up with their espoused values. This latter example is usually followed up by the classic, "If people have taken offense to my actions, I am sorry." More on this issue in a subsequent chapter.

Overconfidence is not a helpful quality. Success without humility and lacking passion for being even better, can be a poisonous preventer of any serious attempt at effective leadership. Arrogance is a leadership killer.

Once upon a time, the late great scientist and advocate for peace, Dr. Ursula Franklin, provided me with one of the most important lessons ever regarding leadership. *When it comes to thinking about your latest accomplishment, ask yourself "So what?", and then say "So what?" about your* answer. Her message was clear: be critical about research results; don't make more out of something than it is. With a careful and "secure" eye, embrace what needs improvement. To paraphrase what Tai said in our book about great teacher/leaders, we *should be more excited about what we have yet to learn than arrogant about what we already know.*

How does this apply to my work as a professor? Easy: when it comes to the academy, there is very strong value placed on publications in journals. Far too often, more often unintentionally than not, research results are placed in their most positive light. Sure, but overstating what we *think* we know in the sciences—basic and applied—is a natural part of an unnatural and unhelpful process at times. I preach Dr. Franklin's *So What?* mantra to my doctoral students and my younger professorial colleagues.

One of my colleagues—a real superstar—was hesitant to apply for the rank of full professor. She thought she didn't have enough publications. The fact of the matter was that she had plenty, not to mention the fact they were high-impact articles, but she *could* have had many more. Journal editors rejected many of her submissions because she was specific and honest in describing why her results were inconclusive. So what? She was offering details about experimental failure and a critical lesson about leadership; the need to embrace mistakes as nuggets for learning. I like Tolstoy's notion that, "An arrogant person considers himself perfect; the chief harm of arrogance is that it interferes with a person's main task in life—becoming a better person."

Unfortunately, the very notion of embracing things less perfect and learning from the process can be elusive for too many. In higher education, government, and other private and public organizations, there are enormous pressures to overstate things. In our university culture, positive acceptance of our research results can lead to promotion and additional grants; for high-flying scholars who are cash cows for generating grant revenue and philanthropic donations, the rewards are huge for the university. Overstating results becomes natural. And fraudulent findings happen, cases of fudging results—and more often than you might think. Really? In the ivory tower? Yep.

In government, the constant quest for popular support also means that making things *appear* better than they are is an art form of amazingly creative proportions. Naturally, political parties seeking power do the same thing, staking claims that a particular approach or a "major improvement" regarding an otherwise-challenging file will yield wonders, is endemic in political cultures. Complex and huge omnibus bills are now commonly brought to legislatures as Trojan Horses with the intent of obfuscating the real intent of buried daggers of destructive public policy. A governmental game of hide-and-seek. Fabricating or skewing evidence—whatever it takes.

You may be wondering if politics has its truth-tellers? Absolutely—but, ever-increasingly, the public is finding it harder to discern what's real and what's fake. Ontario's current premier has taken things to such an extreme regarding the offering of disinformation nonsense that an increasing number of constituents don't believe a thing he says. He and his Minster of Education, note the intention to take a "failed education system" and make it great, while at once continuing to implement things that are seriously harming what was an already-high-performing system.

Interestingly, one of the other major obstacles to genuine improvement is that those being asked to "get on-board" believe that what is already being proposed is actually not new and has failed in the past. Like extreme success, past failure can be very hard to overcome, and distinguishing between what might actually improve things from "we've seen this before and it didn't work", is the work of highly trusted leaders with exceptional storytelling capacities. In addition, overcoming the lethargy-driven "seen this, done that" attitude in the electorate and followers of leaders in various organizations, isn't easy either. Here, this hard-earned lesson about overcoming the "we've-already-done-that" syndrome, speaks to how you marshal those you need as supporters and partners for change.

Speaking of the current Ontario government, their approach toward the importance of providing autism services to more people in need illustrates many of the challenges associated with how improving the wrong things and failing to think in systems terms can worsen a problem. In all fairness, intractable problems in this domain have been around for several governments, but the current Ontario Ford government's handling of this has been a case study of exactly what *not* to do; though I actually hold the view that the two ministers who have dealt with the challenge of providing autism intervention support for the thousands of children on the waiting list, are well-intentioned.

However, this is a government that claims it is "for the people"—the very same people who it actually never listens to or involves on a broad scale when it comes to determining the nature and possible solutions to problems. It has falsely claimed that "we have held the largest consultation in the history of Ontario" for various arising files and issues.

So, without proper and widespread conversations with families battling various emotionally challenging autism issues, and without properly consulting with service providers and expert researchers, it launched into what *they* thought would be a "winning" announcement—eliminating the waitlist for over 20,000 children. This was without consideration for the endless amount of variations pertaining to what is needed by what children at what ages and under what circumstances. Instead, they rolled out their plan, and the emotionally charged response was deafening, ultimately resulting in a ministerial replacement.

I will not go into all of the problems that arose; rather, I will simply illustrate what I believe to have been their biggest oversight. In my view, the root of the problem was that they wanted to serve more children with the same amount of money without any consideration for innovating with the methods of *delivering* autism services. By ignoring this key variable, as you can well imagine, very little has been achieved but chaos.

Among other things, families currently receiving services were appropriately fearful that their children would receive less so that the government could add services to those on the waiting list; however, unless the methods of service delivery are altered—including who provides the specialized interventions and more accountable assessments for who actually needs what and when—the heartache and anger that has risen from lack of support for far too many, will continue to be present.

When this storm was at its peak, I wrote an op-ed noting that, when I was a professor at McGill University, I ran a clinic at the Montreal Children's Hospital, in which I ran training workshops for parents, guardians, and all who were part of the lives of children with serious challenges—including those with autism spectrum disorders. I believed then—and *proved* then—that the delivery of interventions, such as Applied Behaviour Analysis (ABA), was over-professionalized, and therefore very costly. I asserted that there were great benefits to be reaped if all those involved with a child could be trained in ABA. Ironically, I reported that the current minister's own department was already sponsoring demonstration research projects on "parent-mediated autism models". The Minister and her Deputy Minister, were clearly unaware of the promising results that were being generated in their own back departmental "yard". Further, the previous Liberal minister responsible for the autism file when in government—who is now in opposition—ranted and raved against his under-siege successor, yet still never mentioned the alternative delivery research taking place in his former ministry. Holy head-scratcher.

Michael Fullan often channels Michael Masterson's

"Ready, Fire, Aim" approach, where a good deal of up-front collaboration and strategic analysis kick-starts action— followed by ongoing recalibration based on the experience of the actual doing. This is part of a typical continuous formative evaluation and improvement approach. Some observers inappropriately use Fullan's phrase with a different intent when it comes to the current Ontario government. Perhaps its approach is best defined with a more cumbersome, but apt, phrasing: "Superficial Prep, Let it Rip, Clean it Up, Blame Others, Repeat". The beat of this approach continues.

The Minister who originally led the charge regarding the provision of autism supports was, indeed, replaced. As noted previously, I really think she cared about the unserved children and youth—so much so that her concern was matched by a skin too thin. This led to an angry response and ensuing emotional attacks from rightfully upset parents. As noted earlier, you *can't be angry and smart at the same time.*

Before being replaced, she established an Autism Advisory Panel—something she probably should have considered *before* concocting a policy without a chance. She asked if I would be on the panel, and, upon examining the very limiting terms of reference and its structure, I declined. Perhaps she genuinely wanted my input, or perhaps she wanted to make a point of having a critic on-board to portray "openness". Regardless, the reporting deadline, as well as her other terms, was simply set up to fail regarding genuine input. While the challenges remain, her successor opened up the potential of this panel with some useful tweaks and has since tried to make some good use of the experience and expertise of its members. This minister also reached out to me to see if I would join the panel, and, although I declined once again, I provided private input—including the observations and research offered in this chapter. It seems, however, that not much has penetrated the actions of the government as of yet.

I think this story provides a good transition from this chapter to the next. In this chapter, I have underscored the importance of doing the tough systems work in an effort to *determine the real root causes that entrench an unworkable status quo;* that without this hard and smart work, improvement will continue to be the enemy of change. The Ontario government's approach to autism also underscores what happens when a bold, relevant, and long-term goal that drives change is absent from the process. We should have another walking-on-the-moon goal that in 10 years, all those in need of autism support in Ontario should receive timely and appropriate services in less than one month following an independent diagnostic evaluation.

Earlier, I discussed the remarkable power that would be displayed if we had genuinely integrated child, youth, and family service systems in every community that would provide timely diagnostics and interventions. If you recall my story about asking audiences how long they had to wait for this kind of service support for their children, you'll remember that the responses tended to range between six months and three years—and not only for autism, but for a myriad of other issues facing our children, youth, and families. We recommended the need for truly integrating and integrated services in our *With Our Best Future in Mind* (C.E. Pascal, 2009, Ontario Government) to Ontario's premier. At the time of release, I spoke of the need for a "moon-walk goal". I noted that, "...from the time a question mark regarding a child or youth's progress is raised from a teacher, parent, pediatrician, or another significant other, to the time it should take for free diagnostics and the implementation of a back-on track-plan that generates demonstrable progress, should take no more than eight weeks."

Imagine how a true commitment to this goal, complete with timeframe allowing for all of the transitions, systems and communications work in communities and within government, would drive changes. Think of the human costs avoided; the human potential gained; the millions of dollars saved to our social services, health, and education expenditure—all by ensuring the early and sustained support of those who are disadvantaged through no fault of their own, held back by short-term/superficial thinking and lack of horizontal collaborations.

We need to *overcome short-termism and the hardening of the categories*, whereby government departments and local providers and departments currently avoid pursuing genuinely new ways of ensuring cost-effective synergy. In our 2009 report, we recommended a major shift to how five ministries needed to overcome this hardening of the categories to better support integrated children and youth services. The results to date? Not much. Too much ministerial vested interest. Lots of nagging was required to bring about *some* structural changes. We managed to convince the government to move childcare to the Education Ministry to give Ontario a global lead in developing a developmentally enriched human development continuum—and by tying it to education, high-quality childcare is better understood to be an educationally important early years change-maker. But the more ambitious changes we suggested? Well, not yet.

Saying this, I am a very stubborn advocate, and, as such, devised a simpler way for the government to get its leadership act together when it comes to fostering a government-wide commitment to supporting the healthy and safe development of our children and youth: I proposed what I thought to be the simplest change to how government could do its work to achieve the highest impact for Ontario's children and youth. I will explain shortly. This case presents another example of how best to develop new organizational improvements for achieving goals. Far too often, *major* structural change within an organization is the default approach to achieving improvements to productivity and quality progress—and, sure, this is appropriate at times. However, *moving too quickly to the big, dramatic changes often creates a level of negative disruption* that is costly in terms of resources, morale, and other unintended consequences that ultimately backfire. So, *when deciding on a path for real change, a leader should always choose the route with the least amount of unnecessary disruption and the least anticipated resistance in mind of achieving the best outcome.*

At the time, the government had established a Ministry of Children and Youth—something that was, in my view, another example of an "office of..." that might remove responsibility from all other departments to adopt healthy child and youth policies. In light of this, I recommended that this ministry be downsized, sending most of its work back to the ministries of Social Services and Health.

I hear you: "Charles, you didn't think this would face resistance?" Of course, but wait—let me finish! The newly designed and focused Ministry for Children and Youth would take on one major task—screening every proposal from *every* ministry that would go to the government's Planning and Priorities Committee, prior to Cabinet, for its possible effects (positive, negative, or neutral) on children and youth. Each draft Cabinet submission would have a single page provided by the newly reconfigured Ministry of Children and Youth, which would analyze a proposal's evidence-based impact on the health and wellbeing of Ontario's children and youth. Regardless of whether the Cabinet submissions came from education, social services, health, the environment, natural resources, tourism recreation and the like, the Ministry would provide an independent, fact-based one-pager.

Other more complex mechanisms were available. It was a pleasure to act as the Deputy Minister of the Premier's Council on Health, Wellbeing, and Social Justice, set up by Premier David Peterson, strengthened by Premier Bob Rae, and scrapped by Premier Mike Harris. The Council, as reformed and chaired by Rae, included six Ministers and a coterie of some of Canada's leading minds and practitioners, charged with developing mid-range and longer-term policy frameworks. It generated useful work, including setting the stage for subsequent early childhood education initiatives. Perhaps it might have been a useful body to evaluate current and projected cross-cutting initiatives.

Simpler approaches fall into the "superficial improvement" category—comprising inter-ministerial committees on children and youth that bring together deputies from many ministries. I chaired this committee when I was DM of Social Services, as well as when I moved to education. We had great discussions, agreed on some very promising directions, and then went back to our ministers, whose self-interest in solo stardom makes horizontal cross-departmental collaborations in government and other organizations difficult, to say the least. Just like Canada's Council of the Federation—in which the premiers of all 13 jurisdictions "come together annually so they can go their separate ways" (thanks to Roy Romanow for this very apt line), inter-Ministerial committees are "improvements" that don't add up to much.

Considering more complex/superficial approaches that don't work, I thought my suggestion of having a small ministry act as a screening device was a good one, as well as being relatively easy to implement. Apparently, not. Two different premiers have told me that my solution would be too upsetting to ministers, as well as very tough on the minister who would be a "gatekeeper" with the "burden" of ensuring healthy public policy for children and youth. Yes, a gatekeeper with the best interests of our children as a priority—that's kind of the point. We either care enough to do the unpopular thing and lead, or we don't. My only retort was that the choice of the "gatekeeper" was key.

I said to one premier: "If you choose a minister who is high on emotional intelligence, a genuine collaborator, and popular around the table, why not try a demonstration of the concept to see how it could work?" Nope.

This still makes me a touch miffed by leaders who are far too risk-averse. But, never too late, I guess. I hope. Maybe one will try something that actually works in generating truly horizontal integrating policymaking to overcome the hardening of the categories.

One additional footnote regarding governmental efforts at dealing with extreme issues that hurt people. Ontario used to have effective independent advocates who called public attention to problems with government actions. What about the Children's Advocate and Environment Commissioner? Did these offices do a good job pulling back the curtain and identifying issues requiring attention? Yes—and they were scrapped by current Premier Doug Ford, along with a myriad of other evidence-providing agencies in Ontario. Shameful, ignorant, and short-sighted. COVID-19's most disgraceful revelation deals with the awful conditions and high number of deaths in Ontario's long-term care facilities. As I write this, Mr. Ford bellows out indignation about these numbers from his tele-prompted script, failing to call attention to his previous major cuts to public health in Ontario and major cuts to the inspections of these facilities only a year before the pandemic struck. As I noted earlier, in fairness, many of these challenges beset earlier governments as well.

One final case in point when it comes to the importance of systems change that is informed by horizontal thinking. For the past number of years, the world has been abuzz with discussions about the remarkable power and the remarkable unknowns regarding the impact of artificial intelligence (AI). All we know is that AI is already disrupting the way certain things are unfolding. How deep and wide the disruption will be along the way informs the content of global conversations. My concern from the start is that the leadership for the AI juggernaut is being led by brilliant engineers. Nothing wrong with brilliant engineers and new-age technical geniuses. I once had lunch with one once upon a time. But seriously, my issue is simple: given that the algorithms that drive robotic outcomes are based on historical data—gazillions of data points—this input information needs to be screened for nasty historical constructs: racism, homophobia, sexism, and more. We need to ensure that social scientists are working side by side with the engineers. More recently, seems like more and more attention is being paid to this but too much has been done without this necessary synergy.

In summary, *yielding to short-term fixes with solutions in search of a problem generates hopelessness and resistance to new ideas.* Allowing the time to deal with complexity, showing through demonstration projects some delivery alternatives, and providing some compelling evidence-based storytelling, on the other hand, can build support, as well as the momentum required to move a mountain—or two! However, at times, the mountaintop of effective change is too-often clouded over by superficial "short-termism" and "hardening of the categories" that prevent horizontal collaboration.

The foregoing pages, then, have emphasized the challenges of avoiding wasted efforts at marginal improvements without a hope of meaningful and sustained change. The next chapter focuses on the many issues associated with determining and tracking progress toward clear meaningful goals and objectives. Let's explore the power of a bold, morally driven, and compelling long-term goal as the driver of real change.

Chapter Seven Takeaways

- **Improvement is the enemy of change:**
  Far too often, complex problems are met with tinkering on the edges, dealing the symptoms of the problem while at once avoiding the root causes that sustain the ongoing presence of the problem.
- **The importance of overcoming hardening of the categories:**
  Organizational progress often suffers from the lack of integrating horizontal collaboration that is required to deal with all that is required to solve a problem. When thinking of solutions, choose the least disruptive approach that will yield the impact desired.
- **If you don't have leading edge systems thinking to plan and implement a change, find it and use it:**
  Systems change know how is in short supply and education and training programs that deal with any aspect of leadership and management, should commit to including this skillset. In the meantime, change-makers need to "borrow" this talent when appropriate.

EXERCISE #7:

Think of a change project you were involved in or observed that illustrated how dealing with the underlying obstacles were identified and dealt with. What were these core issues? How were they dealt with? Conversely, describe a project that failed to deal with the real reasons for an entrenched issue for which superficial attempts for "improvement" failed. Do you have access to sound systems thinking capacity? Describe.

Your Notes

Chapter Eight
Choosing and Achieving World-Changing Outcomes

I HAVE SPOKEN ABOUT the lessons learned in regard to leading change—whether personal or organizational efforts—in an effort to move things forward. But to what ends? If we do the systems' work required to deal with the root causes of problems, if we ensure we have leadership teams with high levels of complementarity of skills and knowledge, if our emotional intelligence and our ability to empathize and understand others' views informs our ability to lead through relationship-building, then how will we know we are making progress? As the fly-by-night pilot notes, "Ladies and gentlemen, we are making good time, but we're lost." Or, as the Cheshire Cat in Lewis Carroll's *Alice in Wonderland* points out, "If you don't know where you are going, any road will take you there." Or we can consider that Yogi Berra attempt to channel Robert Frost: "When you come to a fork in the road, take it."

On a personal level, as I have emphasized, we can complete the *Inside Out* reflective practice work and use different feedback approaches for gaining self-knowledge concerning how to align our leadership behaviour with our individually chosen values; but when it comes to accomplishing general goals and more specific objectives *as a result* of our leadership, we must be clear about the outcomes we seek personally and/or organizationally. Far too often, our goals are either too ambiguous, too tame, simply irrelevant, or too short-term in perspective. Want to lead genuine change? It is obvious to say, but I will regardless: there is an *essential need to develop very clear and relevant long-term outcomes with short and medium markers along the way*. Sure, simple, but what do we mean by "relevant"? Will achieving this goal yield demonstrable improvements for the people you lead, or the organization you "run"? Will it provide increased mental health and wellbeing outcomes for people? Is there a moral purpose that drives the outcomes you seek?

You will recall my notion that the *process is the product*; that the ways in which you select your directions and plans to get to a better place are key when it comes to ensuring that all who are necessary for implementing appropriate actions "own" the goals and plans to achieve them.

Storytime! Back during the halcyon days of Ontario's remarkable Premier William G. Davis, the late Dr. Bette Stephenson—notably his very able and tenacious minister of education—was asked the following during Question Period: "Mr. Speaker, I find it extraordinary that our Minister of Education is presiding over a system that has absolutely no goals, no values that drive progress. We are moving fast to nowhere. Minister, when are you going provide these?"

Rising to her feet, the diminutive but forceful minister said, "Mr. Speaker, the honourable member's question is both excellent and timely, for we are in the process of developing exactly the kind of vision-directed values he is asking for."

"When will they be available?" the member responded.

"Perhaps the member didn't hear me, Mr. Speaker; I said they will be released in a *timely* manner—likely next week, or the following week."

Another great stand-up performance by one of my favourite parliamentarians of all time—but let's pull back the curtain.

After Question Period, the Minister rushed back to her office and called in her Deputy, Harry K. Fisher. "Harry, I want you to involve anyone you want and work through the weekend developing Ontario's goals and values for education. I need them for Monday."

Harry was already accustomed to the Minister's bold directives. He took a breath and asked, "How many?"

"You decide; but not too many, and not too few."

Sequestered in a hotel room for three days, Harry, with a few colleagues in tow, developed five values, including the usual ones, like "respect". These were then reviewed by Dr. Stephenson and read into the record the week after the Minister had been asked the question in the House.

Two months later, every school and board office, every college and university, received plaques, almost like tablets from on-high, complete with Ontario's Values for Education, all to hang on the walls of the boardrooms of Ontario's education institutions.

Lesson? It's easy to develop a vision and related goals. Anybody can do that, and it doesn't take a lot of time, but to develop a vision, values, and goals that will carry momentum for change requires a thorough and transparent process of involvement. It is the back-and-forth discussions regarding what various values and mission statements mean in practice by all he members of an organization that ensures the kind of "organizational ownership" that fuels effective implementation. These discussions—productive arguments, even—raise the level of literacy of everyone in an institution regarding what will be expected to carry out the plans that arise.

Years ago, I conducted a strategic planning workshop for post-secondary leaders, including several college and university presidents. I thought it went well—that is, until about six months hence. I was flying to Vancouver. It turned out that I was sharing the flight with one of the participants of that workshop. This university president stopped by to say hello, seating himself in the empty seat across the aisle.

"Good to see you, Charles. I have been meaning to call you to thank you for that workshop. As a result, I am pleased to say that I developed a strategic plan for the university, and I'm very proud of it."

Naturally, my heart sang when he began with praise for the workshop—and then sank when he described his takeaway: "I developed..." There are reasons why I do not like the phrase "strategic planning". Too much of what is attributed to this activity is ineffective; its process is too stagnant in its implementation. The "I" rather than "we" was bad enough, but when he also noted develop*ed*, the suffix was suffocating. All of this spoke volumes about someone leading a large and venerable organization implying how pleased he was with a document that he delivered to his senate and board in a glossy form suitable for fundraising. Any planning document worthy of prideful impact should bear the fingerprints of the many who contributed, as well as the sense that it is an organic document that will be adjusted as new threats or opportunities arise over time; not something that was develop*ed*.

Regardless, this incident was great feedback regarding the changes needing to be made to my thinking in relation to the ways in which my workshops dealing with leadership and change could be improved.

By the way, without alluding explicitly to this incident on the plane, I subsequently sent a note to all of the workshop participants: *Now that six months has passed, I want to find out how effective it was—how effective I was. So, briefly, could you tell me if you led any planning process as a result, how you involved all members of your communities, and if a "living" planning document was developed? I just want to learn how to improve the approach. Thanks so much.*

I heard back from most, a few promising responses; however, most noted how their busy lives had taken over. Thus, I can't stress enough that the "how" and "with whom" elements of our goals-establishment, matter.

What follows are a few more tales that I hope will speak to the challenges of choosing the right goals—and avoiding goals that may lack long-term relevance.

As noted, I remain a huge fan of Ontario's 18th Premier, William G. Davis. I recently attended his 90th birthday party, and the non-partisan cross-section of friends was typical. Naturally, my respect for Mr. Davis derives largely from his remarkable accomplishments as the "Education Premier", when he continued to support the things he accomplished while in the role of Minister of Education. He created Ontario's college system, expanded the university system, and launched our public broadcaster *TVOntario* and OISE. Not bad! And my affection for him? Well, simply put, he is also a nice person, loyal to friends while remaining publicly partisan and privately very non-partisan in seeking the best for the many. He is painfully witty. It is damn hard to dislike Bill Davis—and very easy to like him. I have cherished the friendship I have enjoyed with him. I love the calls I still receive from him about the current state of affairs in Ontario, and am eternally grateful for some of the kind gestures he has sent my way, including an invitation to join him and 38 others to hop aboard the Royal Yacht Britannia to have dinner with the Queen and Prince Phillip on September 30, 1984.

And, speaking of Queen Elizabeth II, Premier Davis and I have had only two policy issues where we have been at odds: the retention of the monarchy in Canada; and the extension of funding for Catholic schools in Ontario in 1985. Regarding the former, I won't go into that here, except for the call I received from Mr. Davis the morning he read my op-ed in the *Toronto Star* about ending Canada's "relationship" with the monarchy. I was taking my daughter to an event while on speakerphone with Mr. Davis, who was playfully but firmly railing at me for my royally "misguided" stance for the entire 45-minute car ride. At the end of his sermon, he asked, "What do you have to say for yourself, young man?"

"I thought you didn't read the *Star*, Premier," was all I could muster. He laughed, and that was it.

Regarding extending funding for Catholic education, the disagreement continues. I continue to believe that the decision to extend separate school funding was short-sighted, and, while constitutional considerations supported Catholic elementary school funding at the time, further entrenching the use of public money to support the education of a single religion remains a public policy mistake. The two most Catholic provinces, Quebec and Newfoundland, have moved to fund a single secular public system, having dealt with the constitutional issues. But not Ontario.

Always curious concerning the pressures that led to Mr. Davis's decision, I had the opportunity to put it to him directly. As President of Sir Sandford Fleming College, I recommended to our board that we give Mr. Davis an honorary diploma (the first of its kind in Ontario's college system at the time), and so, in the spring of 1985, over an informal brunch prior to the convocation, I casually inserted the burning question.

"Premier, I've always been curious about your decision to extend separate school funding. How about a multiple-choice question? One, your very able Attorney General, Roy McMurtry, came to see you and noted, 'Premier, constitutional clouds moving in'; two, you and your young and talented Chief of Staff, John Tory (now Mayor of Toronto), are driving along St. Clair West in Toronto, and you note, 'Lots of Italians in Toronto. They're generally Catholic, yes?'; and three, you and your friend, Cardinal Emmett Carter, are playing golf. On the 18th tee, you are into your backswing, and the Cardinal grabs your club midair and says, 'Now, Bill, now's the time!'" I paused. "Premier, is it one, two, or three—or all of the above?"

I was so pleased with myself. Just the two of us having a quiet and informal chat; surely, I am about to gain some historical intel. I leaned forward with anticipation.

He paused for five interminable seconds. Then, "Charles, could you pass the salt, please?"

And that was it.

Back to later on. In mid-August 2007, I received a call from Mr. Davis. "Charles, as you know, John [Tory] will beat Premier McGuinty in the upcoming election [October 10, 2017], and I will need your help."

Naturally, as a non-partisan yet supporter of McGuinty's campaign pledge regarding early learning for four- and five-year-olds, I said nothing other than, "How can I help?"

I was also a relatively close colleague of John's, so was kind of curious about what WGD was up to. What he proceeded to say ensured I would actually do all I could to support Dalton's re-election and John's defeat. "Well," he said, "when John wins, he is going to appoint me as his commissioner on how to extend funding to *all* faith-based private schools in Ontario. Charles, I want you to join me as a co-commissioner."

My God. Speechless, light-headedness set in, and I almost fainted. Breathing again, I said, "Premier, two wrongs do not make a right. Using public money to support Catholic schools was wrong in the first place; this will not be helpful to the people and will ensure John never gets to the corner office." I was upset that I had to be so blunt with one of my heroes, but I was also so concerned that what John Tory was about to do was fundamentally wrong. "Premier, not only must I say no to your offer, but also that I will do anything I can to lobby against John's plan."

That night, John called me at home—a long listening event for me, during which he played to my core notion of equity, noting that extending funding to all faiths was a matter of fairness. I truly believe that John was sincere about that, but I also believe he was on the wrong side of sound public policy. I subsequently did spend energy in adding to the public debate during that election, crafting an op-ed that was subsequently signed by 50 notable Canadians, including leaders from various faiths. This op-ed became a printed leaflet, used door-to-door by opposing candidates. In seeking names for this, I actually contacted one of Mr. Davis's longest-standing allies and friends, his former Attorney General Roy McMurtry. While Roy was sympathetic, he was also very close and loyal to both WGD and John Tory.

Dr. Bette Stephenson, Minister of Education when Premier Davis extended funding to Catholic schools, told me,

"Charles, I can't sign on to the op-ed out of my loyalty to Mr. Davis, but I warned him that this day would come." Obviously, she had not agreed with the extension.

John Tory's loss, including his personal loss in the riding held by the incumbent Kathleen Wynne, was largely attributed to his stance on funding for faith-based schools. Had he not taken this position, many believe he would have beaten Dalton McGuinty; instead, McGuinty won a huge majority, and Ontario has universal full-day pre-school for 250,000 four- and five-year-old children as a result. Interesting fork in the policy road. Yes, choosing goals that matter regarding that better future won out in this case. As political faith would have it, John Tory is now in his second term as a very popular and effective mayor of Canada's largest city.

Let's continue to explore the good, bad, and the ugly of setting the right goals. When goals that are clear, bold, and informed by a moral purpose to improve the lives of the many, are chosen, it truly disrupts and moves things beyond that entrenched status quo. There is a reason I use the phrase "walking-on-the-moon goal" as the first step in a plan to disrupt the status quo to achieve a worthy outcome. As we know, in 1961, U.S. President John F. Kennedy famously announced that "landing a man on the moon and returning him safely to the Earth" would be accomplished before the decade concluded. Not so long ago, the 50th anniversary of Neil Armstrong's first step on the moon was celebrated—a bold goal, clearly stated. Imagine what was required to achieve this goal: systems overhauled, and new money provided to get the right things done and old things repurposed. Mistakes will have been made: two steps back, three forward. The goal totally disrupted what had been and replaced it with a purposeful—sometimes messy—pathway to achieve an outcome that few could imagine possible. Choosing the right goal and thinking long-term drives change. Did the goal have a moral purpose? That depends on where one sat back in 1961—and how you view the many scientific advances made since.

Naturally, the majority of observers chalked it up to Cold War competition with the Russians, who were clearly out in front in terms of space exploration. Interestingly, Kennedy's decision didn't poll well at the beginning. If one looked at the pursuit of the moon-landing goal through a scientific lens, Kennedy's "new frontier" held remarkable promise—a promise that has paid enormous dividends regarding inventions that have improved the wellbeing of Americans and those around the world. To be sure, JFK's sales pitch to Americans and to Congress was informed by the scientific advancement promise. Eventually, the public "got it", and, notwithstanding the ebb and flow of the process, sustained support was critical to achieving a longer-term goal. Big risk and big reward for that "giant step for mankind" on July 20, 1969.

In our current uber-partisan world, trying to set and achieve a goal that will take a decade or more to achieve naturally requires a clarity of purpose and perceived benefits in order to be wildly popular with the electorate required to sustain government leadership.

Regarding particular issues, for example, I do not believe—bolstered by evidence—that the profit motive has any place in the delivery of human services—a notion that would certainly cause an uproar from certain quarters who choose ideology over evidence! Naturally, many human services have private delivery as part of an overall "system", including "health" care. That said, in my view, there should be no reason to permit for-profit childcare in Ontario or anywhere else, for starters. Are there private providers who aren't cutting corners, not making huge profits, or providing safe environments for kids? Sure, but when we examine the key factors related to the high-quality provision of childcare, such as the qualifications and salaries of the educators and "directors", health and safety issues derived from proper ratios, a supportive environment (alongside the intentional use of curiosity driven play-based pedagogy), a publicly funded non-profit and a well-inspected system is far, far better. And what about unlicensed childcare? I have suggested to several consecutive governments that they should set walking-on-the-moon goals that, in 10 years' time, there would be no unlicensed childcare in Ontario—and in 15 years, for-profit childcare in the Province will be a thing of the past. Why these timelines? Because Ontario is suffering from a serious lack of childcare spaces. The right policies and investments will take time to implement as a new approach evolves that allows—and even potentially rewards—for-profits to evolve into non-profits.

Furthermore, in addition to a supply-side problem, governments of all stripes will be perceived to be anti-small-business by driving out "Mom-and-Pop-Shop" childcare, unless there is time to adapt along with supports and incentives to assist. Part of ensuring the long-term public support necessary to keep any and all governments committed to the goals will be the need for ongoing and unrelenting evidence-based storytelling that explains to parents, as well as the general public, why unlicensed and for-profit childcare is generally not a healthy and safe option.

While I will talk more about the issues arising as a result of the pandemic later on, it is abundantly clear that the goal of a national universal high quality child care program is essential for our social and economic progress. Great. One was developed under Prime Minister Martin, then scrapped by his successor, Stephen Harper. More on this devastating short-sightedness later. But this is the worthiest of an essential goal.

Being clear about the long-term destination is a must. Overcoming expedient short-termism is a must. *Communicating "imagine when" clarity about a better future is key.*

I will always cherish my lunch with Canadian icon, Tommy Douglas, in 1983—one that triggered my journal entry the next day when I wrote about *the beauty of visionary incrementalism.* Tommy was crystal clear about his long-term goal of having universal healthcare and talked about the ups and downs of this long-distance journey. During our long, relaxed chat, he reaffirmed that, while it took over 20 years to achieve universal healthcare in Canada, not enough was being done on the prevention upstream side of things. He also reiterated that his long-term plan was to ensure that all Canadians were covered for prescription drugs (and dental care). Today, Canada remains the only country in the world with a universal healthcare system that does not have a pharmacare component—notwithstanding it is now on political agenda for consideration in one form or another. It is never too late for this critical part of Tommy's vision to arrive on the political radar.

In the meantime, one of my favourite quotes regarding the importance of vision and goal clarity comes from the highly regarded American global issues analyst, William Van Dusan Wishard:

> *Vision is seeing beyond the immediacy of the day. It is understanding the temper of the times, the outlines of the future, and how to move from one to the other.*

> *Vision is seeing where life is headed, and how to make the transition from here to there most effectively.*

> *Vision is seeing what life could be like while dealing with life as it is. Vision is having some sense of the inner impulse of the Age.*

> *It is sensing what is felt, yet unarticulated, in the public*

soul and then giving it voice. Vision is seeing the potential purpose that's hidden in the chaos of the moment, yet which could bring to birth new possibilities for a people.[13]

As Van Dusan Wishard notes, managing the transition from here to there is essential. We need to ensure that the pathway to a robust change-making goal is paved with markers that are designed to indicate progress. Having the right short and medium benchmarks that move things along is critical.

Furthermore, on the topic of clarity of vision, we need to create an intentional notion of where we want to be later on down the road. I am a big believer in the process of envisioning—imagining a time when life can be better, with a quiet dismissal of the current chaos that surrounds us. I love the book *Inner Game of Tennis* by Tim Gallway[14], which is all about creating a quiet, positive mindfulness regarding what success feels like, and the glory and peacefulness of imagining accomplishing a goal.

With that said, a crisis with full-blown chaos can also present an opportunity to think long-term as a way of reinforcing values and imagining better, clearer visions and goals going forward. I will use the Ontario College's strike of 1984 as an example in the subsequent chapter—and, because

---

[13] Van Dusan Wishard, W., 1992, American Future.
[14] Gallway, T., *Inner Game of Tennis*, 1974, Penguin.

the COVID-19 crisis has provided a new and devastating example of what constitutes a crisis, I will use it later on as a demonstration of a redefining opportunity to reimagine that better future for the many.

When we talk about setting relevant goals, we also require the effective tracking of progress toward those goals based on indicators that can be measured and reported. Over the past 20 years, the concept of Key Performance Indicators (KPIs) has become a popular accountability vehicle for governments and other organizations. Easy enough: provide measures of progress and publish them as a guide for decision-making options, including continuous quality improvement and distribution of resources. However, the problem with KPIs is that they are too often chosen for what's available on the shelf, often suffering from a bit too much simplicity: they are easy to measure, and readily available data; graduation rates and the related employment status after attending a given educational institution provide good examples of what is common. There is nothing wrong with simplicity—as long as it delivers what is needed in order to secure a genuine sense of impact. So, the question arises as to whether six months after graduation is long enough to measure the true impact of a college education. Far *too often, the easily measured isn't worth measuring*. We talk a good deal about the importance of creativity as an educational goal, but nonetheless spend precious little time developing outcome measures that come close to measuring things related to creativity, such as divergent thinking—in other words, connecting rarely connected dots. Oftentimes, the default response is, "Well, we know it when we see it, but we really can't measure those intangible things." Total nonsense. Is it easy? No, but it *is* worth the effort. The work that Canadian Annie Kidder's People for Education organization is developing—the *Measuring What Matters* project—is designed to do the hard work in this regard. If we can develop real signposts for the ultimate destination and stops along the way, we'll get there. We *will* have a national pharma program, someday.

Years ago, I was working with a colleague at McGill—an English professor who was a proxy for the default excuse of not taking the time to operationalize his ultimate goal for his Shakespeare students.

"I really want them to truly understand the universality of Shakespeare," he said, "but it's really hard to measure this, of course."

I posed some simple questions. "Do you hand out grades to your students?"

"Don't be silly, of course I do," he replied.

"Okay, then great. The last time you handed out an A or A+, what had those students done that led you to believe that they understood the universality of Shakespeare?" I asked.

"Well, that's an easy one: just a few weeks ago, one of my very best students wrote an essay analyzing key issues regarding our mental health challenges in Canada today using Hamlet and King Lear content to illustrate his conclusions," he proudly noted.

Responding, I said, "Wow. So, fairly straightforward then, you define understanding the universality of Shakespeare as the ability to take any one of his almost 40 plays and apply its themes to an analysis of a current social or economic issue. Correct?"

"Of course," he agreed, stood still, and you could see the wheels turning: "I suppose I could make this clearer to the students, *and* teach and provide feedback about how they express this *ability* in their work."

Well, that was easy.

Sometimes, it's much more difficult to develop these "impact measures", but we simply must pay more attention in this regard in an effort to truly answer Dr. Ursula Franklin's admonition about work as a researcher and leader. Remember the follow-up? So what?

As I've stressed, it is absolutely crucial that leaders continuously seek input from others; that we listen deeply to what diverse people both within our organizations and beyond, have to offer. Former Ontario Premier David Peterson established two "Premier's Councils": one for the economy, and one for health. These advisory groups brought together a remarkable cohort of grassroots leaders and big-idea generating experts. As I noted earlier, the Premier's Council concept was a superb example of how to build in regular input from a diverse group of individuals, with the aim of developing ideas, mid-range and long-term policy goals, objectives, and so much more. The trap here is to ensure that when advisory groups are set in motion to advise leaders, the membership must be regularly refreshed in order to avoid group think. Their work also needs to be done in plain sight. In this way, stakeholders at large can provide further input about the group's ideas arising.

Finally, there is another key lesson to be understood when it comes to choosing goals: simply put, if you have too many, you have none. *In a forced-choice environment, do fewer things better rather than all things less well.* Too many walking-on-the-moon goals sap already limited energy and resources, creating chaos over the focus required to progress in meaningful ways. I love that anonymous quote that sums it all up: *Starve your distractions and feed your focus.*

In 1972, Federal Progressive Conservative Candidate Robert Stanfield was two seats shy from beating Canada's Prime Minister, Pierre Trudeau. This high-integrity albeit lackluster guy became known as "the best prime minister we never had"—that is, until Bob Rae came along, in my opinion. When Rae was premier of Ontario, I had a front row seat as a deputy minister to observe his approach to leadership—the lessons I learned from what was happening and, no doubt, the ones he eventually learned. After about a year and a half in office, he and the Cabinet had a retreat to determine the government's priorities, after which the Secretary of Cabinet handed out manila envelopes with the priorities assigned to each deputy minister at our next council meeting. If you are familiar with the TV show *Mission Impossible*, that was the scene. "Open up your envelopes to discover your mission." I was Deputy Minister of Social Services at the time, and I had three priorities listed:

1. Overhaul Ontario's welfare system to ensure fairness and fiscal responsibility,

2. Develop a modernized childcare system in Ontario that is accessible, affordable, and developmentally supportive of children, and

3. Overhaul the delivery of the ministry's 7,200 transfer payment agencies to reduce redundancy and increase service effectiveness.

That was our ministry's mission: impossible—and one of these, if accomplished well, would have been sufficient for an entire government's overall success. But these three for one minister and his ministry? Overall, the deputies conferred, and the total number of government priorities exceeded 50— which meant it actually had zero priorities. Of course, each minister had fought for "big" success in the political sun, and yet even with this enthusiasm, the lack of discipline to ensure the government's goals were manageable in number was an issue. Bob Rae went to the Federal level, completed the Churchillian dance of changing parties, ran for the Liberal leadership, lost, and eventually became his party's interim leader while waiting for Justin Trudeau's first victory. Rae continued to head-up important inquiries and make a difference, including through his recent appointment as Canada's Ambassador to the U.N. For me, his story illustrates that his training period regarding leadership—his one term as Ontario's premier—and the lessons he learned *equalled* his tenure as a leader. He never had a chance to apply what he learned regarding heading up a government. Far too often, search committees, elections, or leadership campaigns fail to understand the difference between mistakes made and genuine lessons learned as a result. Bob Rae is, indeed, the best Canadian prime minister we never had.

To summarize, we need to *develop clear and relevant goals, gather appropriate and transparent tracking information to plot progress, and make necessary improvements that take us to that better place.* A mouthful, I know.

My recurrent mantra regarding my love of, and commitment to, education is that it's *the* cornerstone of that future that is necessary for safer, healthier, and more prosperous environments and opportunities for the many, rather than the few. For each part of this personal view of the future, we can define and provide information pertaining to our progress regarding things like whether they are "safer" and "more just". Having clarity of purpose and the ultimate "destination", as well as an increased understanding of "how we're doing", ultimately allows us to adapt along the way.

In the domain of education, my clarity of its "purpose" drives my commitment to improving measurements of progress. In recent times, it has been the core of my criticism of Ontario's current government, and, in this regard, I have been accused by some of being partisan. On the contrary, as a non-partisan, I remain driven by evidence regarding what education can provide a society's future—and, as a result, I become pretty cranky when I observe things that sabotage that future. *Having long-term relevant goal clarity provides a useful way to distinguish between things that hold promise to take us forward and those ideas that either unintentionally or deliberately sabotage progress toward that better future for the many.* We need to think twice about whether what governments, or other organizations, put on the table is the real deal, or simply cards dealt from the bottom of a phony deck.

Chapter Eight Takeaways

- **The critical importance of having clear and relevant long-term goals:**
  Leading meaningful change should be driven by clear moral purpose-informed goals in order to ensure that energy and resources are dedicated with intention. In addition to clarity, achieving long-term goals that are relevant to the many, requires uncommon tenacity and the ability to coalesce diverse and widespread support through public and private communications.

- **Participation of the many in setting goals breeds creativity and commitment:**
  Building and sustaining momentum toward long-term goals requires the active inclusion and ongoing involvement of all stakeholders in order to build ownership of both the process and intended outcomes. Leaders must understand how to build and sustain a consensus and a process that can survive their own tenures.

EXERCISE #8:

Can you describe your involvement in developing a long-term goal for a project or an organization? Depending on your context, it could be that "long-term" might be a year or ten, but what were the obstacles that needed to be dealt with? How? Did you have a way of tracking progress and making adjustments along the way? How were others involved in both setting and achieving the goal?

Your Notes

Chapter Nine
The Graceful Power of Apology and the Opportunity of Mistakes

A S I HAVE NOTED, leaders who develop collaborative ways of adopting long-term goals informed by moral purpose and committed to intentional pathways forward will, by definition, disrupt the status quo. No matter how hard we try, eggs will be broken. Not everyone will be happy with change all the time. Obviously. But there will be times when we will make unintentional mistakes that do harm to others and/or our reputation as leaders. Other times, a mistake will arise from an attempt to cut corners that shouldn't be cut from a moral perspective, hasty decisions to get something done. Regardless of circumstance, great leaders own their mistakes. Great leaders apologize. Great leaders learn from their mistakes.

I've spent more than a few pages on the importance of honest, evidence-driven communications as being key in ensuring widespread support for our boldest efforts to improve the futures of the many; but the best of us, when leading change, make mistakes. Intentional or otherwise, such mistakes provide opportunities for reinforcing the best in us or otherwise reveal our deepest insecurities. It is how we handle our human, unforced errors that will either deepen hard-earned trust or erode it on the spot. We do make mistakes, and I continue to be amazed at how difficult it seems for those with leadership responsibilities to offer up genuine apologies in a timely manner. Naturally, this is true within personal relationships. However, when serious errors are covered up by public and private organizations and their leaders, teachable moments are lost, and effective momentum for meaningful change is stopped in its tracks. In this deeply divided world, I think of trust as a precious public good.

As noted earlier, one would have thought that the early 1970s' Watergate scandal would have embedded its key lesson in the DNA of any and all who lead organizations in public and private places: that the truth will come out, and that trying to cover up such truths generally backfire—and do so big-time. The leadership lesson for all of us is painfully obvious and hard to practice when it comes to covering up a mistake. *Tell the truth in a timely manner or pay the price trying to crawl out of an even deeper hole.* For this space, I will focus on those more public unforced errors and the either unintentional or intentional efforts to cover them.

Earlier, I told the story of an early-morning meeting of deputy ministers to discuss the way in which the government of the day should handle a serious scandal that cut across several ministries. The focus was centred on how to tell the story to the public in an effort to minimize the embarrassing fallout. I was a rookie deputy, and, having listened to an hour of song-and-dance regarding communications "positioning", I was asked by the Secretary of Cabinet for my opinion.

"Why don't we advise the Premier and ministers to simply tell the truth about what happened—how and why it happened, and how a reoccurrence will be prevented?"

My reluctant intervention was met with the kind of silence reserved for addressing a large crowd with my fly down—or, worse yet, a piece of broccoli stuck in my teeth at a cocktail party. My comment was deemed naïve in a culture of covering up. I never liked the saying "putting lipstick on a pig", but it's hard to come up with something more accurate. In this case, the option chosen by my more seasoned colleagues fit that old saying.

Well, the public didn't buy it. Investigative journalists did the digging, and there you go: the government's hole became as deep as it can get. The cycle of covering up ends badly most of the time.

The cover-over propensity goes against everything I hold deeply in my core. I just don't get it. For example, there is enough on the public record regarding the Canadian Federal Liberal's handling of the so-called SNC-Lavalin (a major Quebec-based company) "scandal" that rocked the Justin Trudeau government in 2019. Other than to note that the issues related to the perceived or real political interference with the justice system by Trudeau, I will not get into the details of "who did what to whom and when"—with one exception. On the morning of March 7, 2019, Prime Minister Trudeau held a media conference to "set the record straight" regarding the SNC-L issues. He made a very passionate opening statement regarding his version of what happened, noting correctly that no law had been broken. Yada, yada. It was then that a journalist asked, "Do you owe anyone an apology?"

With a confidence bordering on arrogance, Trudeau responded, "The only apology I am making is later today, when I head North to apologize to the Inuit people."

A missed opportunity to calm the waters. Why didn't he simply say, "It's obvious to many—and lately to myself—that I didn't handle the situation well; that regarding my Minister's [the scandal's 'antagonist'] position in Cabinet, I truly offer my apology to her and to others concerning how I handled it." Full stop. Rip off the band-aid.

But no; instead, he spoke of the importance of "moving forward", which was essentially code for, "Well, you don't expect me to keep her in the Justice Ministry just because she asked. Can't have a minister telling a prime minister what to do, can you?"

Well, here's the deal: generally speaking, it is absolutely not cool for a minister to "direct" a PM—but, in my view, it would have been better to have listened to her pleading. Better inside the tent than outside. And yet he didn't step back, breathe, and think of the longer-term consequences that were easy to predict. Okay, tough call, given his caucus's increasing concern about this particular minister. Nonetheless, my opinion is that this was a mistake. Why not issue a genuinely contrite admission and apology? Well, I am told by some seasoned politicians that one should never apologize, that it's a sign of weakness. I call that total bullshit.

So, from that missed opportunity in early March 2019, it all got much worse for Trudeau going forward, although he did win the 2019 election, albeit with a minority government.

Along that electoral path, Trudeau, who loves to appropriate the local dress of visiting places like India, was slow to explain another of his Mr. Dress-Up mistakes: the use of blackface back in the day. Okay, that was a 10-day wonder on the hustings—so what's the big deal, you might wonder? *Leadership* is the big deal—and the trust required to accomplish things can be diminished to such a degree that even an electoral victory can still carry a bad taste. To be clear, that case at hand regarding the perception or reality of political interference is not a one-sided story: there is much to say about how others handled themselves during the SNC-L saga, including two former ministers. However, when something like this arises, I tend to focus on those with the most position power and what they/we might have done differently. Was putting a rookie MP in high-profile and complicated portfolios at the beginning of Trudeau's first mandate an intelligent thing to do? Or, in this case, was it ticking a box full of strategic, short-term, symbolic messages? Why was it so difficult to offer the minister in question a genuine apology? Ego? Short-sightedness? Anger? Remember our earlier lesson: *you can't be angry and smart at the same time.*

While I am picking on Prime Minister Trudeau, I should add another case in point regarding his judgment and issues of diminishing trust. In the context of his otherwise excellent leadership during the pandemic, he announced a program that would provide post-secondary students with an opportunity to earn money during the summer months. This almost one-billion-dollar (CAD) program was awarded to the WE charity without a tendering process. Criticized for failing to ensure due diligence and a competitive bidding process, Trudeau claimed it was the public service that determined that WE was the only vehicle for doing what was necessary in a timely fashion. Well, it turns out that Trudeau's mother, his brother, and his finance minister all had direct ties to the charity. His mother had received $250,000 for speaking at WE events. The conflict of interest was clear and ran deep. The PM first claimed it was the public service that had made the decision, and implied he wasn't involved until we learned that Cabinet approval was necessary, and that he and his Finance Minister did *not* recuse themselves when the vote was taken. When all hell broke loose, Trudeau finally and reluctantly apologized, but only for failing to recuse himself from the final decision. Nothing about his handling of this passes the smell test, including the lack of due diligence regarding many ethical issues regarding the charity itself.

And all of this connects with an earlier case when the PM and his family accepted a free Christmas trip in 2017 to an island owned by the Aga Khan at a time when the he was discussing funding for projects with Trudeau's government. Trudeau's first comment when this was revealed was "Well, the Aga Khan is an old family friend." What does that have to do with violating a most basic conflict of interest tenet?

I strongly believe that genuine and timely apologies regarding mistakes breed forgiveness. I think most people are genuinely forgiving about others' human foibles when genuine contrition is offered. Timing, however, is most critical: when pressure builds and time passes due to political operatives' discomfort with apologizing, the value of better-late-than-never apologies declines: the longer we wait to apologize, the less "credit" accrues concerning the actual strength it takes to own up. Indeed, the fallout is often viewed as external pressure for contrition, rather than a deeply held notion that "I made a mistake and I am sorry". *Inside Out!*

For me, mistakes made both in plain sight, and less obviously, provide incredible opportunities to build trust through heartfelt apologies. On the micro level, those daily leadership reflections concerning my previous day's application of my core values that I have spoken about is an opportunity to check to see if I think I owe someone an apology. Did I cut someone off in conversation? Was I too harsh in a meeting or on Twitter? Yep, I have had to clean up after myself far more than I would have liked—and I still do.

I don't have a huge list of pet peeves. Trucks passing other trucks slowly in passing lanes on major highways is one of them. Those who continue to misuse "imply" and "infer". People with power taking credit for the work of others is also one. But even higher on my short list of pet peeves is the insidious non-apology: "If people have been offended by my actions, I am really sorry."

That was even difficult for me to type out!

Let's consider for a moment all of the associated nonsensical rhetorical defenses, such as, "It was taken out of context" or "I didn't say what I said"—a paraphrase of another of Yogi Berra's quips. An apology delayed is not an apology. A genuine sense of regret and the perception of others that one is taking full ownership of a mistake must be immediate. The passing of time, whereby others are calling us out publicly and others within are urging us to "get out there and apologise", simply doesn't cut it.

What do we do when the big problems arise—those we might even categorize as a "crisis"? The popular notion that the two Chinese characters that spell out "crisis" translate to "danger" and "opportunity" is interesting in this regard. Well, a crisis can be an opportunity to reveal the core values that drive us or a dangerous misstep that inhibits our movement forward. When the going gets tough, who are we really? Did that SNC-L case reveal an opportunity for Trudeau to reinforce his commitment to his mantra of "Let's do politics differently"? Hardly! Did accepting an all-expenses-included Christmas vacation from the Aga Khan help his "sunny ways" brand? Hardly, and yet when this conflict of interest was pointed out, his refrain was, "He's an old family friend", rather than "I wasn't thinking; it was wrong".

Sure, I have been picking on Mr. Trudeau—who, by the way, is an easy target for two reasons. First, he's our prime minister and therefore a big target who has shown very bad judgment as noted; but secondly, on the plus side, I have found that those who are very clear and very public about what they stand for—their core values—the easier it is for others to pounce on them, including me. Would we rather have leaders who are transparent about what principles drive them, or those who play hide-and-seek without a compass? So, kudos to Mr. Trudeau for his clarity regarding his values. I, personally, like what he says he stands for, but it is also this clarity that provides natural gaps between the reality of his behaviour and his self-proclaimed values. Clarity regarding values makes it easier to see the hypocrisy gaps as they arise. Sure, but this book is about the importance of leading from *the Inside Out* based on increased clarity about what's at our core. When and how often you share your values is another thing.

As I mentioned earlier, when I was a newly minted rookie college president, I was crystal-clear and public from the outset about the principles that would guide me, one of which was "participation breeds creativity and commitment". The problem was that, over time, the principle of more democratic involvement of the college community rang hollow due to the front-line leadership differences being displayed by various department chairs.

In my first year as college president, I learned about the need to ensure that behavior and values commitments are well-aligned early and often; but then again, I would rather have a Trudeau who is clearly committed to feminism than one who is not. It is easy to criticize anyone who is clear about their values, so perhaps it needs to be made clearer that core principles and values are always aspirational, that we are committed to closing the gap as we travel along our leadership pathways.

This is the purpose of my reflective journaling: to establish how I can be better aligned tomorrow than I was yesterday. Regarding Trudeau and feminism, in retrospect, perhaps it would have been better for him to avoid saying up-front before his first election that his Cabinet would be at least 50% women. This naturally gave the dinosaurs a chance to claim that some (or many) women were not chosen on the basis of merit. Rather, it would have been better to simply appoint a Cabinet and then let the pundits do the counting. The lesson for me is to be *clear about who we are—while perhaps toning down the frequency with which we "crow" about it. Let our actions speak. Behaviour is what counts.*

Here's that story about how a province-wide strike that affected Ontario's colleges provided me with valuable experience regarding going from *the Inside Out.* In 1984, the union representing all of the educators in Ontario's community colleges went on strike. In my view, it was a thoughtfully taken strike by the union: many of the founding college presidents were top-down command and control leaders from industry, and the main strike issue was that faculty were being treated like lemmings—no input sought from them regarding how to deal with increasing student numbers, for example.

As the prospect of a strike was looming, our senior team at Fleming College spent hours and hours determining what first principles would guide the way in which we would handle a province-wide strike. Why did this take hours and hours? Because we needed to establish our own deep commitment to them, as well as how these core principles would actually play out in plain sight if there was a strike. After a few days of deep reflection, we came up with two principles that would guide how we would handle things locally if a strike were to occur: 1) quality of education; and 2) what relationships we wished to have with our professors 14 months after the strike had come to an end. Regarding the former: you can't claim to be a great educational institution with outstanding educators if you hire scabs to fill in while our educators are on the bricks. This meant we totally shut down all offerings, including continuing education. As well, we did not want neighbors to be crossing the lines led by neighbors. This contributed to the latter principle—our long-term relationship with our faculty. Administrators and support staff did go to work, and we *did* cross the line; but we spent time talking to our colleagues, bringing them coffee and muffins, and empathizing with the province-wide issue of the non-involvement of the faculty in decision-making. All of this worked to reinforce a core value I had put into play at the outset of my tenure: that *participation breeds creativity and commitment*. Behaviour counts, and this crisis proved beyond a shadow of doubt, the indelible commitment to that value.

In other words, this crisis presented a wonderful opportunity to ensure our behavior during the strike reinforced a new and exciting commitment to a collaborative culture that became a hallmark of the college. Yes, I took a good deal of criticism from other presidents; I was dubbed the "Pinko President" by some. It also reinforced my view that local bargaining for everything except financial support from the government would be best. The problem with province-wide bargaining was that those who wanted to lead union negotiations often came from colleges with less-than-effective leadership—meaning the entire system was wagged by low-common-denominator issues at the bargaining table. Local bargaining would generate a more direct accountability for working out college-specific issues, in turn creating constructive tension for change at the local level.

How a crisis is dealt with sends clear messages—good, bad, and ugly—about what leaders stand for; and making mistakes, both big and small, provides opportunities to learn from them and use genuine contrition where appropriate. I will further explore the impact of a crisis regarding leadership in the ensuing chapter on COVID-19.

A footnote regarding the handling of a crisis that can advance or inhibit organizational progress is the notion of the wonderful opportunity of the teachable moment. One huge advantage of being clear about one's core values and associated behaviors is that you don't have to spend a good deal of time figuring out how to respond to tiny mini-crises, or the moments of conflict that arise almost daily for those with leadership responsibilities. The mishandling of something "small" can create bigger challenges when it comes to moving forward and building trust. I have always thought that admitting mistakes, genuinely owning them, acknowledging them, and apologizing for them, shows strength not weakness. Sure, it hurts at times. It's embarrassing to make a silly or big error in judgment; but own it, and most will forgive. I know it's hard, I've made more than my share, but it gets easier over time because of the positive response from a forgiving world.

Regarding my experience as a college president, I have already discussed the notion that being too bold too early in regard to what I "stood for" created problems whenever my colleagues within the organization weren't "feeling" those claims for a "better world". However, after six months on the job, I decided to hold a "let's-pretend-we-all-work-at-the-same-college" barbecue, bringing colleagues from all four campuses together. Prior to the fun and food, I gave a twenty-minute "state of the college" report from the new guy on the block before allowing for a twenty-minute period for questions. The very first question wasn't a question; rather, it was a five-minute comment from a veteran educator, who was considered a no-filtered iconoclast by some of his peers. The essence of his comment was, "It is very refreshing to finally have a president who is approachable and accessible."

His comment was greeted with a smattering of applause and an unbearable and immediate pit in my stomach. While his backhanded compliment might have been well-intentioned, it was an obvious slight to my predecessor and good friend, the college's founder, David B. Sutherland. I took a few deep breaths and responded, "Naturally, Dave and I are different personalities: Dave is an introvert with sharp wit, and I am obviously more gregarious and a bit over the extroversion line on the Myers-Briggs scale. But is there anyone here who *doesn't* appreciate the very notion that Dave Sutherland embedded a deep, unassailable integrity about educational quality within this place he loves so much? I appreciate that some of you like my style, but the best I can promise you is that I won't mess up what Dave has created."

I didn't have to fake anything; after all, it was all true. I simply tried to ensure I didn't abuse the commentator. Thunderous applause ensued, signalling it was time to eat, drink, and play.

Leaders with clarity of what they stand for, greet their mistakes with genuine and timely ownership and genuine apology, building, rather than diminishing, trust in their leadership. This inner and consistent coherence is always on standby to take issues of conflict that arise—large and tiny— and turn them into teachable moments to advance a leader's authenticity and organizational cultural progress.

Chapter Nine Takeaways

- **Mistakes offer an opportunity to reinforce values and increase learning:**
  Those in leadership positions will make unintentional mistakes or mistakes informed by a serious or even minor lack of judgment. Deeply felt and timely apologies for mistakes that also carry lessons learned going forward, will attract forgiveness and trust. Clarity regarding those core values can turn moments of tension and conflict into teachable moments to advance cultural change within an organization or the public trust of an electorate.

EXERCISE #9:

Recall a situation when you made a mistake in judgment or an unintentional error in your professional role or personal life. How easy—or difficult—was it for you to own up and apologize in a timely manner? Explain.

Your Notes

Chapter Ten
Say What?
The Critical Importance of Language

I ADMIT I'M A stickler for language; "say what you mean and mean what you say" works for me. On the simplest and most irritating level, the misuse of "imply" and "infer" drive me up the wall, as mentioned in the previous chapter; and, on a more serious level, language used by everyday leaders is often harmful when it comes to bringing about more effective and appropriate change—even if such harm is unintentional. The worst of all is when language is weaponized and informed by deliberate actions in order to mislead true intentions.

Okay, let's not worry about that simple stuff. I really do strive to ignore those who butcher grammar—who don't know when to use "I" or "me" as the object pronoun. In our fragile, bilingual country, I am trying to ignore Anglos who insist on pronouncing crêpe as "crape". Who cares? A local eatery nearby calls itself "The Crêpe Escape", and when I went into to explain their rhyme didn't work, they said, "Well, everyone pronounces it 'crape'." I stood down from my high horse and ordered a "crape", which was delicious. Enough said.

A few years back, the actor Woody Harrelson came to our place in Toronto to play poker. He was kind enough to bring what he described as "tofu cheesecake". Awful. Just awful. It would have tasted better if he had just called it "tofu pie"! A friend of mine recently posted a recipe for "vegetarian Bolognese". Sorry, but you simply cannot make a Bolognese without meat.

Anyway, enough food-related examples about truth in packaging; after all, being too picky in print here leaves my own grammatical imperfections wide open for hypocritical fodder.

Let us examine the often-unexamined use of language that is actually unhelpful to the cause of effective change leadership. For example, over the past several or so decades, we have heard our political class calling for policies that will help Ontario or Canada to "compete in the global economy". This clarion call for global economic leadership is not only the purview of Canadian pols. We hear it around the world. Sounds okay, right? Wrong. I find the word "compete" to be problematic. What, I don't like competition? Heck, yes I do, if confined to a tennis match or even a poker game. In 1988, then-Ontario Premier David Peterson's "Premier's Council on the Economy" released a report entitled *Competing in the New Global Economy*. Written by the late and great David Pecaut, it was a very compelling call to support the need to invest in our human capital. However, its inclusion of the word "competing" raises a question concerning an all-important missing critical policy companion question: if we *win* in the global economy, what will our relationship be with the international and domestic losers? Too picky? Too precious?

Well, perhaps, but we continue to live in a have/have not world—within and beyond our borders—that foments income disparity, racism, crime, and, at worst, terrorism. How about we aim to be *successful* in the global economy, defining 'success', in part, regarding how relationships within our countries and beyond, grow stronger, not weaker.

When Canadian Prime Minister Mulroney paved the way for free trade with the U.S. in 1988, he seemed to understand that there would be domestic "losers". His election campaign included the provision of transition funding for companies and sectors that would be hurt by the trade agreement. To my knowledge, no such funding was ever provided—and, in my view, every goal worthy of achievement needs to be examined for how it might affect the larger context. We should be asking, with far greater diligence, whether there could be any unintended consequences for others if we were to be successful in achieving something. For me, being successful in the global economy should carry a higher level of enlightened concern for sustaining gains through an understanding of how to understand and even support those impacted by our well-intended actions.

Here's an even subtler example of language that carries some baggage: when I hear the phrase "social and economic"—as in, *social and economic policy*—it raises some serious concerns regarding how we think about policymaking and choosing directions, as well as how we organize and plan to deliver on promised outcomes. In my view, one of the three words in this phrase is a problem: *and* serves as an indelible reminder of how we bifurcate our language and actions, including how we structure our decision-making processes. Is childcare an economic issue *or* is it a social issue? Yes, and yes. Is the economy a means or an end? Neo-liberals live and breathe the notion that a robust economy is an end, often defining "robust" according to narrow market indices. In my view, *a robust economy is a means toward achieving outcomes that are largely social* such as: an economy that reduces income inequality, provides adequate housing, clean air to breathe, clean water to drink, nutritious food to eat, high-quality non-profit childcare, and recreational opportunities for the many, rather than the few. It's an economy that squarely supports genuine reconciliation with Indigenous peoples and deals squarely with increasing opportunities for racialized people.

Then again, look at how our organizations—in particular, our governments—are organized. Economic ministries and social ministries are not only separated organizationally and geographically, they generally operate on a "never-the-brains-shall-meet" ethos as part of the policymaking process. Childcare is never discussed in Treasury ministries unless education ministers come begging for money they shouldn't have to beg for. This is all about a mindset that flows from the language we use.

When Ontario Premier Rae strengthened the Premier's Councils that Premier Peterson had established by dedicating deputy ministers to each of two councils, I was delighted to be asked to serve as Deputy Minister of the Premier's Council on

Health, Wellbeing, and Social Justice. When the Premier offered me the job, while I was very pleased, my enthusiasm didn't seem to get in the way of my very cheeky and somewhat disrespectful question: "Premier, given the purpose of the councils is to develop medium- and long-term policy goals, shouldn't we have just one council made up of external notables from business, labour, communities, social and health services, and social justice leaders?"

Mr. Rae's response: "So, do you want the job or not?"

"Sir, I'm so sorry... I was just thinking aloud."

Toward the end of his tenure, the Premier did collapse the economic and "social" council into one, but without enough time to realize the potential of coherent and integrated policymaking. As I noted earlier, Ontario's Premier Harris cancelled the council, along with the many massive across-the-board cuts on July 21, 1995—only a few months into his tenure. This was among the many "false economies" implemented by Mr. Harris.

Speaking of the "health" council, one of the reasons *my* council was named "Health, Wellbeing and Social Justice" was actually in pursuit of dealing with another language issue: when we refer to our "healthcare system" or "Ministry of Health", they are totally bogus descriptors: as I noted earlier we actually have an *illness* system and a Ministry of *Illness*!

A few years ago, I ran into one of my favourite Ontario politicians, Deb Matthews, who was holding the "health" file. Because we were alone, I greeted her with, "How's the Minister of Illness today?" She smiled a knowing smile.

By bringing together "health", "wellbeing", and "social justice", Premier Rae understood that we needed policies that dealt with healthy outcomes for people; he understood the so-called upstream determinants of health, such as childcare, early learning, housing, decent wages, and a cared-for environment, and the fact that they all contributed greatly to positive health outcomes—and that is exactly what this council focused on and developed, including a framework for early childhood education for Ontario.

Sometimes, however, the language challenge is driven by a deliberate attempt to obfuscate. In some cases, language is used to totally camouflage what is really intended—a pretense that what is really at play is the opposite of what is implied. As an example, former Premier Harris's Tenant Protection Act was hardly a bill that favoured fairness for tenants; rather, it was a seriously pro-landlord bill. Mr. Harris was a master at branding things with totally opposite intent in mind.

At other times, language is a Trojan Horse for an ideological end game. The phrase "politically correct" has been weaponized to attack those who actively seek redress for those who are disadvantaged through no fault of their own, standing up against any homophobic, racist, or sexist activity. It is a hurtful political dagger. This phrase is a shorthand and dismissive putdown, designed to make those who are still trying to find their legs as activists, a little more hesitant. And what about the use of SLAPP lawsuits (Strategic Lawsuit Against Public Participation) brought by the powerful in order to silence and intimidate critics and social activists under the assumption they can't handle the costs of a legal battle?

Back to one of former Ontario Premier Harris's favourite mantras: "They are nothing but a special interest group." The intent is to portray groups of people who commit to a common effort to deal with an important issue as "selfish" so that anyone who, for example, was part of the "community living" movement that supported the needs of those who have intellectual disabilities was categorized as part of a "special interest" group. This also applied to those who fought the severe cuts to health, social services, or environmental protection, who were all similarly portrayed as "narrow" and "selfish" with the "special interest" label. I naturally found it highly distasteful—perhaps because it seemed to work effectively for Harris' political base, as well as for many on the fence.

At the time, I recall recounting the work of Frenchman Alexis de Tocqueville and his mid-1800s treatise on *Democracy in America.* He observed what we might call today, "civil society", noting the importance of grassroots activities around common interests as a key component of a healthy democracy. He viewed "special interest" activity as the breeding ground for enabling informed democratic participation.

In today's Ontario, we have Mr. Harris's political cousin, Doug Ford, exercising his creative use of misleading bumper sticker communications, such as *Ontario, Open for Business.* Business leaders everywhere know that quality education, training, and government labour-upgrading programs are a top priority when making relocation and investment decisions; smart business leaders want an "all hands-on deck" creative and flexible workforce. They refer to it as "human capital"—the other side of the "human development" coin made possible through high-quality education. Mr. Ford has taken a sledgehammer to Ontario's education continuum, from pre-school and childcare, through to post-secondary education, and everything in-between.

Ford even changed the licence plate slogan to *Ontario—A Place to Grow*. Surprise: I love it. Why? It's simple. I'm an educator who believes in lifelong learning, and, as I noted, high-quality education is about the growth of human development—our most precious social/economic asset. In Ontario, we see, in plain sight, a remarkable hypocrisy illustrated by this gap between the new plate slogan and the government's devaluation of education.

Finally, good intentions regarding the use of language to connect with others can be tricky. In my case, I do love language, and have found that going out of one's way to say something in another's language, however modest, can generate an emotional connection. I was once invited to give a keynote address to American college presidents in San Antonio, Texas. Aware that there was a contingent of Hispanic-American leaders in the audience, I simply stated, in Spanish, that I was "very happy to be here". After my speech, there were approximately 15 colleagues lined up to chat. About ten were Hispanic-Americans who wanted to ask questions about leadership issues. In my view, I think I became more "accessible" to them simply because I spoke a few words in Spanish.

More recently, I've had a more challenging situation. For a number of years, my place of work—the Ontario Institute for Education—issued an electronic seasonal greeting, featuring perhaps 10–15 of our colleagues, offering greetings in their first language. One year, I suggested we ensure we had someone issue a greeting in an Indigenous language. Given that Indigenous languages were taken away as part of our horrific colonial history, none of our Indigenous faculty at the time could bring greetings in their grandparents' language. Hence, I offered a greeting in Ojibway, and received both kudos and serious ridicule for appropriating an Indigenous language. I had sought counsel from one of my Indigenous colleagues beforehand, who had simply noted that, if I was clear about who taught me "these words" and under what conditions, there would be no problem. In my short greeting, I did acknowledge the Elder in Ontario's far North, who had taught me this salutation.

A footnote to my language habit. I do love language but have become increasingly aware of the need to be careful about the where, when, and context of my use of another's language as a shortcut to gain respect. It can backfire. It can be taken, understandably, as well-intentioned but disquieting appropriation.

Let us turn to another language-related issue, one that cuts to the chase regarding issues of racism at worst and unconscious bias at best. As I recounted earlier on, I learned about the have/have not issues regarding White privilege and African Americans as a young baseball player. I noticed the different conditions of environment and equipment present in different parts of Chicago, including its South Side. It took some time for me to learn more directly about what it was, and still is like to be Black in America from one of my University of Michigan roommates. I will not use his name because I have been not been able to locate him and seek his permission to tell this story. I'll call him Robert. By way of background, like me, Robert was a student athlete. He was a superstar football player who went on to the NFL. I was a baseball player going nowhere. One night, Robert invited another star Michigan football player to dinner. When Marvin (name changed) showed up, Robert's dialect changed on a dime, matching Marvin's inner-city Detroit Black English with his own hometown version. When Marvin left, I asked Robert what had just unfolded—what I could only describe as bilingualism. He told me that an uncle advised him early on that, if he wanted to be successful in a White world, it was better to speak *their* language—White English. Regarding Robert and Marvin's so-called "inner city" language, sometimes known as Ebonics, African-American vernacular English is *not* slang, but rather a language with a well-formed set of rules of pronunciation, syntax, and grammar, capable of conveying complex logic and reasoning. Lesson learned back then.

Later in life, when I was a professor at McGill, I was asked to provide workshops on effective pedagogy to professors at various universities and colleges, including Coppin State College (now University) in Baltimore. This was an institution with mostly Black students and professors.

On my first day with a group of 25 African American professors, I asked each, in turn, to describe their main issues with teaching and learning. Halfway through the exercise, a professor of English with a mid-Atlantic accent worthy of Lord Laurence Olivier stated, "My students simply aren't motivated; only half come to class, and their awful English needs so much work."

Putting on a pleasant poker face, I called on the next colleague—also an English professor. He rekindled the memory of my roommate Robert's story. He said, as politely as he could, "Well, I guess I am lucky my students *are* showing up. My approach is a little different. I begin by noting the fact that inner-city Black is a fulsome language in all aspects, and that learning 'mainstream' American White English will be a helpful language to learn nevertheless." Full stop. Actually, his classes were bursting because of the number of students who transferred from Lord Olivier's class.

Have you ever heard people of White privilege refer to a Black person, famous or otherwise, as "articulate" or "well-spoken"? More specifically, 99% of the time, it's really about, "Wow, they speak White English." This unconscious bias is remarkably widespread, including among those who would furiously claim they are clearly anti-racist. Sure, this is not as difficult as those who commit acts of explicit racism, but this unconscious bias remains an obstacle preventing meaningful progress. The lighter the skin or the "Whiter" the language, the more opportunities open up. Not good. Not good at all. Thus, as part of our commitment to improving the language we use, how we take in messages from others with authentic language differences, is key to who is recruited to tables of influence.

Have you heard of those who claim to take a hard stance against racism equate such racial issues to their own discrimination for being overweight (or whatever else) as a child? Or, in the case of a former Canadian politician who recently compared racist hurt to the teasing he received for wearing glasses as a kid? You can't fake empathy with a weak and fast substitute for something so much deeper. We simply need to listen to the lived experience of others rather than waiting your turn for an "I understand your pain" response.

Here's another baseball story to illustrate the systemic challenges. In addition to my baseball journey as a player and coach (University of Toronto team), I was also a baseball writer. I wrote a weekly column with my son Jesse for two small town Ontario newspapers and was a stringer for United Press International (UPI) covering the Toronto Blue Jays home games: a deputy minister by day, sportswriter by night! As part of the UPI work, I got to know Blue Jays manager Cito Caston and Jays' President, Paul Beeston. After Cito led the Jays to back to back World Series wins, the University of Toronto awarded Cito with an honorary doctorate, and

Beeston suggested to Cito that I assist with the writing of his address. We spent hours chatting about his experience as a Black player in a game that, to this day, still carries the underbelly of racism. Cito was clear with me about his feelings about being called "a players' manager", well-liked by his team, while another high-profile White manager, with less overall success at the time, was called "the game's thinking manager." Cito's final convocation address text tamed down his emotions regarding the extreme racism he experienced over the course of his playing and managerial time. He stated it this way: *the fact that I am being honored with a doctorate in law, even gives me a leg up on Tony La Russa manager of the A's who only has a regular degree in law. Tony's a great guy and very smart; and while he's been named manager of the year and I haven't, I'm the one with a University of Toronto doctorate.* To be clear, in my view, it was difficult for Cito to express even this *soft* comparison. He just couldn't keep his emotions totally buried. Good for him. In today's baseball world, the subtleties of racist language still shows up if you analyze, for example, the language used by baseball scouts to discuss promising players: Black players are very often described in physical terms: "stud", "unbridled strength and speed"; while White players descriptions often include "understands the game."[15]

For me, I have been trying to expunge my unconscious biases since I was a child athlete, through to university and

---

[15] *How racial bias can seep into baseball scouting reports, Boston Globe,* June 2020.

beyond. My struggle continues today but experience helps—that is, friends sharing stories with lived experience at the heart of their narratives, or real-life witnessing of such biases. Making mistakes and getting the tough feedback also helps, as was the case when I was Deputy Minister of Education. I was asked by Ontario's former Premier Rae to develop and integrate an uber ministry that brought together pre-school, elementary, secondary, post-secondary education and training. In a major government re-organization, I actually replaced four deputies in 1993 to develop something very ambitious and special.

As an aside, I received a 1% raise for my efforts. I'm not a very good negotiator when it comes to these personal things. As part of my plan, I wanted to create an assistant ministerial portfolio that focused entirely on issues of equity and inclusion for *all* of Ontario's education and training offerings; it was the first portfolio of its kind in Canada at any level of government. As part of the broad consultation I conducted with various stakeholders, I asked the Black Educators' Working Group to review what I had in mind.

Six of their members sat with me to review the draft of what I labeled the *Access and Equity* portfolio. I was so pleased with their endorsement of its shape and intended activities. Until the group's chair, Bev Salmon, noted, "The only problem is the title of the portfolio. You need to include something about racism."

I responded with, "Good point, Bev, but I wanted to ensure we signaled a positive intent going forward."

It was then that Macarthur Hunter, a school principal, joined in with a little force. It turns out Mac and I knew each other from our days at Michigan, where he was a standout world-class track star. "Charles, here's the deal: you need to add 'anti-racism' to the title. You need to *name* it, and you need to understand that naming it *is* positive."

Everyone agreed, with each individual providing an explanation as for why it was an important positive step from a personal point of view. I felt embarrassed and defensive and it showed. After all, I really felt I was one of the enlightened White guys. But I tried hard to focus, listening intently to their reasoning. And then, I felt better. I was listening. I was seeking to understand. Look, it really was really hard for me to move beyond defensive. But after all, *what is right is more important than who is right*. An easy lesson to put on the page. But when it comes to over-embracing your experience, such as when you think your anti-racism journey or quest to support Indigenous peoples' aspirations for social and economic justice is perfectly formed, *then* you realize your journey of understanding movements like Black Lives Matter or understanding the full essence of Indigenous reconciliation, will *never* reach its conclusion. It's an ongoing process for me.

Anyway, an Assistant Deputy Minister for *Anti-Racism, Access, and Equity* was created. We were on our way—that is, until Premier Rae's successor, Premier Mike Harris, scrapped it all. It was the first portfolio of its kind in Canada, and it didn't last long and has not been put back since by all successor governments in Ontario. I continue to lament this short-sightedness.

How we discuss things, what and how we say things, how we decide to label our efforts, and how we decode both deliberate and unintentional cases of obfuscation, matters. Language is important, and leaders need to avoid the pitfalls of linguistic confusion. And we need to avoid the linguistic or experiential appropriation we see more often as our insecurities about how we handle important social movements grow. Simply put, *we need to strip bare intentionally and unintentionally harmful language that impedes human progress.*

Chapter Ten Takeaways

- **The importance of language that conveys clear meaning and intent:**
  We need to say what we mean and mean what we say in a consistent manner. It is also important to understand the larger context in which we use our communications to advance our priorities. We need to always ask if using certain words or phrases carry unintended consequences or raise other issues that need attention.

- **The importance of challenging language designed to impede human progress:**
  We are living in an age of bumper sticker communications and an ever-increasing use of misinformation or the insidious use of dis-information to intentionally mislead various publics. It is critical that all is done to expose the use of language that stands as an obstacle to accomplishing goals worthy of a better future for the many.

EXERCISE #10:

What are your language pet peeves? Have you ever unintentionally miscommunicated something at work or private world? How did you handle it? Can you describe a use of language designed to mislead that you found concerning?

Your Notes

Chapter Eleven
Lessons Learned from World War III

I HAD JUST FINISHED the penultimate draft of this manuscript when COVID-19's pandemic changed the world. We still have no clue what world will emerge. At this point, while it's important to begin re-imagining what should be, it's way too early to claim anything definite about anything. After all, it took a few generations to fully understand the ways in which WWII affected the global order and its underlying relationships. What I do know, however, is this: writing a book on leadership *without* calling some attention to how the virus crisis either reinforces lessons already noted or springs forth new ones for consideration, would be a mistake. So, here is my initial take.

First and foremost, there is enormous pressure on many societal "actors" to be right—to be "smart"—in the midst of this crisis. Including me! With good intentions, for example, we witness information from health experts who are in conflict with one another, or suffer from being too afraid to take the risk to be tough, knowing or thinking it is too soon to advise for certain regarding what the healthy things to do are. I've witnessed Canada's leading health journalist, Andre Picard, early on, write a column noting that "seniors' care settings are the new cruise ships" and that "we should remove our loved ones ASAP". Yikes. Informed by journalistic pressure or instincts to pull back a curtain, his column caused a bit of panic for many. My wife and I stayed up all night wondering and worrying if we should remove my mother-in law from her retirement home. It turned out that this very early warning was likely very good advice for those situations where what he suggested was actually feasible and appropriate. Indeed, he was bold; unafraid to apply his investigative nose for a chance at "truth". He was out-front of what has turned out to be a very sad situation regarding the unfortunate number of deaths in Quebec and Ontario's long-term care facilities.

What I have learned thus far, is that the COVID-19 information explosion requires serious reflection and *very* diligent filtering. While we receive these well-intentioned conjectures, no one has offered "the gospel" about how this will end; no one knows the social, economic, fiscal, educational, environmental, or governmental changes that will, or should, arise as a result. While it is important to start imagining what might happen—what *should* happen—we simply *do not know*, and yet it is clearly time to ask the right questions.

Sure, in the short run, we have received good information about the basics (i.e. what we should be doing personally, including serious isolation, effective handwashing, physical separation, etc.). I have also learned about other "details" such as the science says we need to stay away from Ibuprofen-related products since they make things worse if you have a COVID-instigated fever.

I admit it is difficult for me to see so many others ignore the basics—including friends, who think having large numbers of extended family members and friends over because "we can trust they are safe" qualifies as "isolation". Another friend thinks that wearing gloves to and from a grocery store is just fine, not understanding that gloves *are* "hands" that are carrying and spreading microbes. Don't forget the twenty-five- to thirty-five-year-olds who continue to party on in tight quarters oblivious to the danger to themselves and others.

Regarding what our new or revised world might be, however, I am guided by that personal vision of mine that we need to ensure the future is more just, safer, healthier, and more prosperous for the many, rather than for the elite few. Being clear about the *end game* is critical. Because of this, I hope that *the disruptive nature of this crisis can result in a pathway for a better future* for the many. But we will see. For me, many leadership lessons are being reinforced or are newly arising.

Let's take the lesson that *being overly risk-averse can be risky.* Ontario has some positive lessons to offer that I will get to later; however, many observers believe that Canada's largest province, Ontario, has lagged behind regarding the need for real tough isolation early on and throughout to date. It has been following the advice of its Chief Medical Officer of Health, which is fair enough on the surface. But then again, has he been lagging behind the curve he is trying to flatten? Was he too afraid to be tougher in a timelier manner? Hard to prove but many have suggested he step aside. It seems that British Columbia's Medical Officer of Health, Bonnie Henry, has distinguished herself when it comes to timing, clarity, empathy, and quiet confidence. Meanwhile, Theresa Tam, Canada's Chief Medical Officer of Public Health also told us what she knew and what she did not and has been proactive and bold as appropriate. Dr. Tam was recently criticized for noting early on that face coverings weren't necessary and, as things have evolved regarding experience, she, like so many others around the world, has changed her mind. Given the organic and unpredictable nature of this crisis, criticizing an evolved opinion from an authentic communicator, such as Dr. Tam, was a cheap shot offered by a *Globe and Mail* columnist trying to find something original to write. Stating an "old" lesson differently, *an effective leader cannot be afraid to be wrong, always secure enough to change a view based on evolving experience and evidence.*

The Ontario government's handling of education provides a useful lens for gleaning new leadership lessons and reinforcing others already discussed. First, it's important to note that prior to the virus outbreak, the government had made decisions that were considered by experts to be counter to the quality of education because of their funding cuts, increasing class sizes, and more. So, the base from which Ontario's Minister of Education began dealing with schooling during the pandemic was considered to be diminished. From the beginning of the pandemic in March, 2020, the Minister began frequent on-again/off-again communications about what should happen, keeping alive the notion that students might and should return to school at the end of April. Then middle of May. Then the end of May. It's good that more and more folks now know what the word "exponential" actually means. The virus continues to dole out that understanding. No doubt he was trying to be optimistic and reassuring. But in retrospect, was he riding the horse of false hope when he should have announced that distance learning would be in place until the end of the school year in June? There seems to be widespread agreement that, in March, he should have set in motion a process to begin imagining how best to plan for the possibility of school openings the Fall of 2020.

Unfortunately, the Minister has been perceived by many educators and education experts to ignore the leadership principles that *effective collaboration breeds creativity and commitment* and that *what is right is more important than who is right.* Denmark's successful approach to school openings is founded on the kind of collaboration and proper funding that is totally inclusive and perceived by many observers to be totally absent from our experience in Ontario.

Hiding behind the challenged claim that "we are following the best medical advice in the world," his school opening plans actually ignored the very best evidence regarding class sizes, social distancing, ventilated space, outdoor learning, mental health supports for students and teachers and the increasing evidence regarding young children and susceptibility to the virus and potential for asymptomatic carrying. A huge amount of pressure was placed on local school authorities to "get it done" without any substantial new funding. Right up until schools began opening in September, all of this fomented chaos and stress with almost daily tidbits of confusing announcements.

Did the Minister squander the two most important "resources" required to deal with the complexities of a crisis— time and collaboration? Regarding the precious commodity of time to prepare, as I noted earlier: *quality trumps speed.* Most observers in Canada and around the globe knew back at the beginning of the pandemic that there could only be three options for a return to school plan: stay at home remote learning; face to face in schools; and a hybrid combo of the two. *Not* rocket science, and yet Ontario's Minister seemed to have discovered, and proudly announced, these options late in the preparation game.

As well, at first, he announced that local school boards could decide what option(s) would be best for their circumstances with input from local public health leaders. Boards began their planning. Then the Minister changed his mind late in the process and directed an "in-school" approach: "get it done," he demanded. And if parents are worried, sure he noted, you can keep the kids at home for distance learning. I agree with the Minister that the best goal is to imagine all students back into a school-based environment. The issue is when, with what resources, can a safe return be possible.

The result, as I write this chapter, that Ontario's late in the game top down "directives", ignoring class size evidence, proper distancing and properly ventilated space has caused huge stress for parents, students, teachers, and their leaders. An increasingly large number of parents are keeping their kids at home given that they do not believe that the in-school supports required by the government have been provided. The irony is the Minister, quite correctly, touted the benefits of students being back in school with their peers. As I noted, good, of course. Then he created the conditions that too many parents felt were too unsafe to send their children to school. Instead of parents having the choice of a safe, high-quality school environment for their children, many feel they have no choice but to keep their kids at home. The pressure on parents, students, teachers and local education leaders have felt is palpable as the scrambling continues. This could have been avoided with better use of planning time, genuine collaboration with education's grassroots, and proper investment on the part of the government.

A quick comment about the need to ensure that *quality trumps speed.* You might understandably ponder that a crisis doesn't afford the luxury of taking too much time unless you can anticipate well in advance the kind of preparation required for something like the opening of schools noted in the Ontario case study. As leaders, we can't sit by while Rome burns with the *sudden onset* of a crisis. But many crises are often mis-handled because the key "actors" rush, helter-skelter, to hasty decisions. In sports, elite athletes often refer to how their performance is enhanced because the "game slows down" for them in tense situations. Increasingly, researchers who have studied this notion believe that this means the ability to stay calm while disregarding and blocking out the confusing white noise that abounds and focusing intently on the things that count, the things you can control. *Applied to crises in our world, it means slowing things down to go faster.* It means *starving the distractions and feeding the focus.*

Ontario's handling of school openings reinforces *the need to consult with everyone who has genuine expertise and will be the front-line implementers of a workable plan.* The implementation gap that distinguishes between good intentions and terrible actions can only be overcome if respectful collaborations among all the appropriate doers and thinkers have the time to do the appropriate creative and strategic problem-solving.

Another obvious lesson for me? This Minister, when going into the COVID-19 crisis, according to social media tracking was lacking in trust with teachers, students, experts and many parents due to his handling of various educational issues. His tone was perceived by many to be condescending. As I pointed out in Chapter Five, the power of evidence-based storytelling means that, *while the messages might be the right ones, we sometimes need different storytellers to fit the "audience" or situation*—and, as an example of this, I noted how we recruited storytellers with the right tone and authenticity to talk about the evidence regarding early learning.

In the case of the necessity of ensuring that the proper messages are developed, communicated, *and heard*, the critical ingredient of self-knowledge to complement thyself (Chapter Three) seems to have been missing. If a leader knows that whatever he or she says is being ignored, the enlightened leader—the secure leader—should provide a substitute storyteller to ensure the messages are heard. If the quality of self-knowledge and personal security was at play, perhaps the Minister or Premier would have asked someone else to take over to assist with communications—a calm, matter-of-fact and more "trusted" person—to fill in. Remember, *what is right is more important than who is right.* The notion that we sometimes have to get over ourselves and realize that we might not be the most effective storyteller is a tough lesson to learn and apply. I know; I have struggled with this myself. Feedback from honest and direct colleagues has helped me learn this difficult lesson.

As I reflect on how the current Ontario government has handled education before and during the pandemic, it seems like there are only two assessments possible. Either the government lacks competence regarding its handling of publicly funded education—both before and during the pandemic as many observers have pointed out, or its actions reflect a Trojan Horse that carries the ideological endgame of privatization. As Noam Chomsky famously mused: *That's the standard technique of privatization: defund, make sure things don't work, people get angry, you hand it over to private capital.* I am not a conspiracy theorist at heart, but I do pay close attention to behaviour when it comes to the things that matter to me.

By the time of this book's publication, there will be much to assess regarding the ups and likely downs of the implementation of school openings in Ontario and around the world. Not sure how it will all turn out.

My views on Ontario's Premier Doug Ford and his presence throughout COVID? Well, notwithstanding he was teleprompter-driven from day one, he was perceived to step up to the plate on several levels. His demeanor was calm and respectful, and the actions to support Ontario's diverse population were noteworthy and positive. The real enigma and irony is that, prior to the crisis, the Premier's mantra—*for the people*—was believed by many to be a shallow and cynical bumper sticker con-game: what his government did on almost every file—whether education, the environment, social services, income security, or legal aid—felt more like *screw the people* to me—typical of the recent right-wing populism that exploits weakness with false promises to gain trust.

Now, during the pandemic, the Premier's actions have come a little closer to displaying behaviour that is genuinely *for the people*—at least at the beginning of the pandemic. While I remain reluctant to totally trust the Premier's actions behind his words, many of my colleagues and friends give him more credit. And his poll numbers show it. Oh, the power of a crisis. Does it reveal things more clearly about who we really are—good, bad, or ugly? Yes. Many examples abound; locally, nationally, and globally. Can a crisis lead to a genuine epiphany and deeply impact change to one's beliefs? Has Ontario's Premier Doug Ford, for example, discovered what "good government" should actually mean? Does he now realize that cancelling demos and research on basic income and scrapping minimum wage increases was wrong? Over a year ago, he announced huge cuts to public health in Ontario. Does he now think it was wrong, given the extraordinary pressure on Ontario's public health capacity?

In my view, there is no doubt regarding how well Premier Ford's *words* regarding redefining what his mantra, *for the people,* means during the COVID-9 period. Early on, his tone, empathy, and content relating to helping those in need was often spot-on. So, will he ever admit that he has had a fundamental and disruptive personal change to his beliefs on the road to Damascus? That remains to be seen.

Recently, Ford has shown vein-popping indignation in relation to the conditions of Ontario's long-term care facilities, scenes of death, and the horrific conditions that caused them. I guess I might give him more credit for a rebirth if he apologized for the cuts he made last year—cuts that totally eviscerated the long-term care facilities' inspection capabilities. It is this that also feeds into that larger question about the future: who is this guy, really? To his credit, as noted, Premier Ford has exceeded expectations regarding nice teleprompter messages which reinforces a basic notion I have learned from observing politicians and leaders in other fields: leaders actually compete against expectations. In this case, the expectations regarding how Mr. Ford would handle this crisis were likely quite different—even diametrically opposite—from his earlier performance

CHARLES E. PASCAL

The major issue facing Ontario and so many other jurisdictions is that, beyond the daily pressures, there has been disorganization and a lack of focused leadership in ensuring testing and tracking COVID occurrences. In addition to this, some believe that Ontario's default priority is what's good for the business community. So, with Ontario's COVID-19 numbers heading in the wrong direction, did he take his foot off the gas in allowing businesses to begin opening too soon? At a time when concerns about school openings are at a feverish level, Ontario's premier has opened our bars. #SchoolsNotBars is trending big time on Twitter as people worry about the government's priorities. The very idea of prematurely opening bars, where two drinks can turn six feet into six inches, is worrisome at best. What is in full sight for me is the war within the Premier about appealing to his narrower base versus what is best for the many. With his popularity doubled as a result of his pandemic persona, will he call a premature snap election to capitalize accordingly? If he does and if he goes on to win, what premier will show up? What will *for the people* mean then? Has the crisis in this instance truly transformed deeply held beliefs or will sheep's clothing begin to show it wear?

For me, while some are trying to predict the new realities of a devastatingly unpredictable future, it seems to me that some of the answers might lie all around us. Or at least the right questions are beginning to appear. Recently, I, like others, have frequently noted that necessity is the parent of invention. A good deal of innovative thinking and actions are taking place that likely should have occurred before (and without!) the pandemic.

A myriad of notions are, indeed, arising in all quarters, from ideas about a more relevant and effective educational/learning environment, income disparity, and public health reform, to small business models in need of transformation. Does anyone really think that the restaurant business will return to "normal"? And what about the role of government? Has the notion of "good government" taken on a deeper meaning? Has the crisis reinforced the very notion that trust, honesty, and transparent and accurate information are public goods? I'm not sure, but there are innovative "actions" and thinking taking place all around us that we need to capture for that better future. One of my favorite lessons already discussed comes to mind: *catch people and organizations doing things right.*

Regarding my education passion, core to my leadership journey, is the fact that there is no way we should revert to the old normal; too many now know what some have known before. So many questions arise: How can we ensure our pre-school through post-secondary education becomes a platform for mental health and wellbeing, as opposed to a non-system that's part of the problem? How can we develop a creative problem-solving approach that supports the development of our students into future change-making leaders? What is required to truly develop distance/remote learning capabilities for *all* students and *all* teachers and professors so that quality of learning is central? How can we develop new and effective collaborative relationships between parents and educators in order to properly support the students they "share"? How can we ensure that education is a truly effective force against racism, homophobia, sexism, and LGBTQ bias?

This last question calls to mind the only time the COVID-19 crisis took root on the "second page" during the spring of 2020, supplanted by the protests against—yet again—the murder of a Black man, George Floyd, killed by American police in plain sight. And only a few months later, we witnessed Jacob Blake being shot seven times in the back by another White cop. And the haphazard killing of Breonna Taylor! If we flash back to Toronto's Yonge Street Riot in early May 1992, it is important to note that the riots did not come from an absence of warning signs—at least for those who were paying attention. It started with a rally, organized by the Black Action Defence Committee, protesting the acquittal of four white Los Angeles cops who were video-taped beating up African American, Rodney King. At the same time of this acquittal, another reason for taking to the streets arose in Toronto when a White Toronto officer shot and killed a 22-year-old Black man.

Community activists and scholars alike had described the great justice divide affecting the Black community, and, only one month after the riot on Toronto's main street, Stephen Lewis—an advisor to Premier Bob Rae at the time—tabled his report.

Two things will stun anyone who reads the report: one, it set a speed record, since Lewis crammed an incredible amount of consultation into a month and produced 37 pages of advice to the Premier; and second, the remarkable force and quality of Lewis's recommendations. Sadly, many of them remain timely today, but Premier Rae wasted zero time in directing his ministers and deputy ministers to implement recommendations related to several key ministries.

As Deputy Minister of Education, my marching orders were clear: develop and implement an anti-racism strategy for Ontario's education system. The good news is that we made remarkable progress in a short time under former Minister Dave Cooke's superb leadership with an effective process and a framework for action. The bad news? With implementation well underway, Mr. Rae's successor, Mike Harris, scrapped the entire plan and process.

Unfortunately, successive governments have never come close to reinstating this short-lived comprehensive plan. Has the time come to go back to the future in an effort to ensure that education becomes a pre-eminent and sustainable driver for change? Of course, the Yonge Street Riot *was* a crisis. It should have sparked a long-term commitment to ensuring that education in Ontario became a beacon for supporting the dignity and opportunity for all its people. Canadians love to read our global clippings about fairness and respect for diversity. "We're better than the U.S." is not a bumper sticker to be proud of.

Lessons galore arise from this "case" surrounding the need to ensure that evidence needs to trump ideology; that we need to develop strategies that overcome short-termism and figure out ways to develop non-partisan approaches. The Yonge Street Riot showed how quickly great ideas, developed by a widespread and public collaboration—as well as the political will of Premier Rae to move into action mode—can make a difference. And yet it didn't: it was all scrapped by a subsequent narrow-minded government that labeled hurtful nonsense as "common sense"—and so, here we are, 30 years later, with a "pandemic" of systemic racism in plain sight. Is the outrage pervasive enough across the societal continuum to ensure demonstrated progress? It feels like it. Do I worry that, just like the progress we thought would unfold regarding justice and fairness for Indigenous peoples as a result of our Truth and Reconciliation Commission (TRC), that the current high-minded commitments to ensure *this moment is for real,* will fade? A bit, but the Black Lives Matter movement has given rise to a further depth of confidence for its leaders, its members, and, importantly, a fast-growing cohort of allies necessary to sustain small and propel large steps to our better future. I do believe this is *the moment* that will carry forward progress for all racialized peoples, including revisiting and acting on the TRC's Calls to Action. The work we did on education and racism 30 years ago was the single most meaningful thing I was privileged to deal with as a public servant. Its lack of sustained commitment is my most painful to relive, considering what it could have meant. Which is why this *moment* is so personally important. Never too late.

One of the early pandemic clarion calls for inclusion was *we're all in this together.* Well, however well-intentioned that mantra was, the pandemic has clearly noted for those whose privileged lives come with blinders, that when it comes to those who are disadvantaged through no fault of their own, they have not been well-served by education, health and social services, the justice system, and more. We *should* be *all in this together, but we are not,* and that should be a defining goal going forward.

So, what about the COVID-19 pandemic legacy? Can we hope for something better? While the *crisis* is causing people to think differently, I am not so much of a Pollyanna to think that the 1%ers and most corporate leaders will shed the greed that is indelibly etched into their DNA. The more hopeful question is: has there been enough truly transformational experience in the electorates that determine which governments take power, to make a difference? What about the millennials and post-millennials? Has narrowly focused and unhelpful government actions politized enough new voters to understand the power of their "block"? I hope so. Governments have policy levers that can alter what public and private organizations do when it comes to acting *for the people.* We will see. I know that many with whom I have spoken about this do think I am beyond Pollyanna.

And the doomsday scenario? The notion that things will become so dour regarding personal insecurity that people will take on a vigilante approach to securing much more than a neighbor's supply of toilet paper. Without question, leadership of a new and pervasive quality must be in great demand if we are to survive. I suppose that being realistic about the worst possible future provides opportunities to anticipate and prevent it.

This recent quote by the well-regarded Indian author Suzanna Arundhati Roy says it best:

> *Historically, pandemics have forced humans to break with the past and imagine their world anew. This one is no different. It is a portal, a gateway between one world and the next. We can choose to walk through it, dragging the carcasses of our prejudice and hatred, our avarice, our data banks and dead ideas, our dead rivers and smoky skies behind us. Or we can walk through lightly, with little luggage, ready to imagine another world.*[16]

---

[16] Roy, Arundhati, 2020.

Chapter Eleven Takeaways

- **A crisis provides opportunities for personal and professional growth**

EXERCISE #11:

From your perspective, who, in the public domain, has performed really well during the pandemic crisis? How and why? What have you learned about leadership from this person? On a personal level, how have you faired during this difficult time. What have you learned about you?

Your Notes

Chapter Twelve
Embracing the Power of Optimism

GIVEN THE SHEER NATURE of the personal and professional challenges of COVID-19, the advantages of having an optimistic approach to everything seems to have lost a bit of power for even those who live in that neighborhood of Pollyanna—myself included.

For as long as I can remember, I have been an extreme optimist; however, in these past few years, reality has moved me a bit further away from being a totally knee-jerk cheerleader. Indeed, while I am old enough to vividly recall air raid drills in elementary school in Chicago— and, later on, enduring the threat felt around me regarding the Cuban missile crisis—I have never felt less safe; never felt the world was is such peril, as I do today. The sheer amount of negativity and immoral abrogation of true leadership apparent today, so evident in the U.S and beyond over the past number of years, chips away at the most optimistic DNA. I felt this way before COVID-19!

In addition to the pedestal-like position of my youth, my optimism was also fueled by my early success as a student, athlete, and, latterly, a chance to lead, with some success, in various and diverse situations. Always buttressed and complemented by the talents of so many others (*never* a one-man band), I became confident that all problems—even ones that appeared intractable—could be solved. Thinking and acting strategically, going deep on core obstacles with what seems like a natural systems brain, bringing empathy and respect for alternative views, and learning with and from smarter collaborators, usually worked for me—and it still does. As I noted earlier, while I have received credit for various accomplishments, I will always try to share the kudos with those countless others who were and are key to all I do. All of this has created an even deeper optimism about effectively wading through the waves of negativity that continuously ebb and flow around us.

Lately, however, I do admit I am less sure of myself and less able to determine how I can make things—*anything*—better, other than simply focusing on being a better partner, dad, and granddad—the worthiest of endeavors for sure. But this doesn't stifle thoughts of "changing the world". I still think that the lesson of *doing fewer things better rather than all things less well* is useful in determining what baby steps and opportunities exist to avoid either burnout or unhelpful delusion of effort. The lesson I noted earlier—the *power of visionary incrementalism,* a gift arising from my encounter with Tommy Douglas—also applies. Being clear about the longer-term vision is key and choosing a few things that carry hopeful possibilities for meaningful change to do well, remains critical for me. My impatience to get things "done" is, of course, exacerbated by less time ahead than that road in the rear-view mirror. My optimism needs to be nurtured by hope for post-millennial leadership coming down the pike. In the meantime, surrounding myself with positive and constructive people is more important than ever.

A word or more about our current context:

Well before the virus (will we be marking time with BV and AV?) hit the world, the U.S. Senate farce of an impeachment hearing regarding the most obstructionist president in American history, had concluded. Interestingly, even though I am a political junkie, I did not watch a single second of that Senate hearing; instead, I made a healthy choice to avoid watching what has been described as an immoral abrogation of the responsibilities given to Congressional members to uphold their constitutional commitment to impartially examine the facts. I have learned the hard way to do what I can to avoid spending time with those who misrepresent evidence, who are mean, and who wish to take advantage of vulnerable people. Unlike my wife and others, I do not constantly watch non-stop COVID-19 updates; instead, I try to stay focused on the core expectations on how to stay safe and healthy, how to best support my family, friends, and colleagues, and how I might maintain positive ways of staying connected with people with meaning. Avoiding negativity is the healthier choice; hence, I do try to avoid hanging around gloom-and-doomers, and, more critically, those whose motives and behavior seem destructive or grossly self-serving.

Saying this, when it comes to social media—Twitter in particular—I fail miserably: I simply can't help trying to expose those whom I believe are imbued with narcissism and a destructive world view that is about supporting the elite few. As you might guess from the previous chapter, Ontario's Minister of Education has been a recent target of mine. I cannot seem to ignore his obvious over-the-top, self-serving ambition. I have even taken Twitter holidays in an attempt to ignore this most destructive Ontario Minister of Education I've witnessed over the past 40 years. Recently, I finally blocked him, leaving it to others to call him out. That felt very liberating. But I still get riled up while he continues to mis-represent what he and his government are doing regarding public education in Ontario.

Enough ink for him. The fact that former Ontario Finance Minister, Greg Sorbara, is such a close friend speaks volumes. While Greg can be a political bulldog when the game of politics calls upon him, he is one of the most optimistic and generous people I have ever met when it comes to openness to people's foibles—especially mine! Regarding surrounding yourself with good people, people for whom trust is an absolute, built up over decades, it's not an accident that I play on-line poker with my card buddies twice a day most days. This is pure Covidian relief: laughing, teasing, bluffing, and arguing about the issues of the day, as we have for over twenty-five years.

Online book clubs, online bridge with three friends, and Zoom-style cocktail hours are helping many people get through. Being part of the meaningful social protests that abound today provides a binding and morally purposeful sense of belonging. Simpler things are powerful sources of joy, fuel the need for calm, things that don't cost money. Playing catch with my wife and daughter. Just connecting with my grandkids in various ways. The most special are social distance gatherings in a park. Daily meditation with my wife and relaxation exercises by myself help a lot, as does walking more. And while I have actually discovered I enjoy more alone time than I used to, hanging out with folks where reciprocal love and respect rules, is the best elixir to top up my optimism deficit when it's down a quart.

But trying to effect change these days, with so many foes or impediments to deal with, even within our own organizations, is damn hard. Legendary baseball manager Casey Stengel was once asked about his key to successful leadership. "The secret is to keep the twenty guys who hate you away from the four guys who are undecided." I have observed that otherwise-effective leaders can become obsessed with ensuring that *everyone* is on-board with a new idea; that, even though every effort has been made to ensure bottom–up input and discussions, and 90% are ready to go, huge and wasted energy is placed on winning over the 10% of firm naysayers. I have learned this lesson the hard way: *politely ignore those who are chronically against everything and focus on those on the fence.* While I have tried to be an effective democratic and inclusive leader, I have learned that focusing on the grouchy and entrenched naysayer will lead to a loss of support from those who wish to move forward and those on the fence. And it saps one's energy. These chronically entrenched antagonists represent a *state of affairs*, something that just *is*. You can solve a problem, but insanity is around the corner for those who try to solve a state of affairs. For me, I have spent far too much energy trying to please everyone... and I mean *everyone*. It remains a challenge.

As leaders, it's never been more important that we ensure that, whatever we do and wherever we do it, we must also advance enlightened notions of equity and fairness, informed by a true commitment to anti-oppression. How do we do this? First and foremost, it's about how we, as leaders, behave and talk. It's about the decisions we make about hiring and about professional development. We have to be Gandhi-like; embodying the changes that are contrary to the prevailing winds of cynical and hurtful behaviour of those who wish to keep the disadvantaged, disadvantaged; those who believe that an unfettered libertarian marketplace is better than publicly led healthcare and education; those who prey on the vulnerable as they promise populist solutions that actually make their followers' lives more difficult. As noted throughout these chapters, we have to be better listeners and actively seek deeper understanding in an effort to allow ourselves to grow to become more effective and worthy models of something better. I know that there are very decent people who have very different world views about how best to deal with things like poverty. Although challenging, I continue to try to listen in an ongoing effort to develop new coalitions to deal with very difficult complex issues. As Shakespeare noted in The Tempest: *Misery acquaints a man with strange bedfellows.* When I can connect in a meaningful way with a thought *adversary* and move to a higher place of collaboration, wow, what a boost to my optimism that real change *is* possible.

We do, indeed, need to retain, or regain, a sense of optimism fueled by keeping company with the like-minded while continuing to respect and learn from those captured by alternative world views. This is hard work and requires the energy of the next generation of change agents, with new ideas and the tenacity to effectively disrupt an unhelpful status quo. As I noted at outset, the lessons offered from my long-distance leadership journey are for those who follow, to take, adapt, leave aside, or replace. For me, I will try to retain my optimism informed by an ever-expanding cohort of neighbours committed to those shared values that uplift the many, reinforced by small and medium successes regarding the ideas and policies that move us forward. That daily meditation also helps calm the negativity nerves.

Chapter Twelve Takeaways

- **Seek to be positive and optimistic to maintain a commitment to change:**
  Whether one is an optimist or not, life provides moments of small and large challenges that test our resolve to keep moving forward in intentional and meaningful ways. We need to ensure we create what works for us to keep our outlook positive through relationships that nurture us and what we decide to do or not do in our daily lives.

EXERCISE #12:

Are you naturally optimistic or pessimistic about how you go about your work and how you live your daily life? What are the best sources of support for you when you need to feel more confident and hopeful about your ability to make a difference in your work and/or private life?

Your Notes

Chapter Thirteen
Honourable Mentions

WHILE MY BIG TAKEAWAY lessons concerning leadership have been noted in the previous chapters, there are so many other things I have learned that deserve honourable mentions. The fact is, due to my daily *Inside Out* reflective practice that focuses on the ways in which I can improve my own leadership, new ways of seeing a better-informed way of "doing leadership" arise. What did I learn from my yesterday? What did some public figure do that I should emulate or avoid like the plague? And what lessons provide hope from our plague-like experience with the virus? This chapter is simply a quick-fire attempt to table a few more of these hard-earned lessons.

Throughout this brief, personal, and continuous journey of leadership development, I have emphasized the value of collaboration, bottom–up participation, and deeper listening to those with diverse views—all of this being in service of developing quality outcomes that are "owned" and understood by all required to support the effective implementation of great ideas. I have noted the challenges of avoiding the implementation gap through effective processes, noting that the *process is the product*. This leads me to my summarizing of all of this a little differently: *quality trumps speed* as I have noted. Moving too quickly to implementing a new, promising idea in a top–down fashion generates major wasteful energy and efforts, particularly when it comes to dealing with the fallout of misunderstandings and/or disruption that impacts personal situations or the aspirations of others.

In this sense, implementation speed kills; instead, taking time for genuine approaches for input and discussion increases not only the quality of the idea, but also both its implementation plan and the demonstrated levels of commitment to the task. That said, caution needs to be exercised in regard to how long a process of developing implementation ownership should be permitted to go on: there comes a time when getting on with it sets in. The *need to avoid consultation fatigue* leads me to amend my lesson accordingly: *quality trumps speed—but don't take forever.*

Another implementation lesson deals with the documents that guide the plans for getting the right things accomplished. Whether it's a new curriculum launched by a government or a strategic plan developed by an organization, I strongly believe that they should always be communicated as a "draft", reinforcing that implementation over time after the experience of "doing", will bring minor—or even major— necessary tweaking to the surface. My lesson? *Embrace the beauty of the draft*. Indeed, it is my preference that these documents carry the "draft" stamp. Whether or not this is the course of action decided upon, in one way or another, it is really important to convey that plans are organic. When I was a deputy minister, I actually tried to suggest we use "working draft" for a new policy or curriculum, to convey this sentiment, but I was overruled by my ministry colleagues and my political leadership. They believed my approach was a naïve signal that we weren't really sure of our intentions. Remember that university president who told me about the strategic plan *he* "develop*ed*", the suffix noting it was fixed in cement?

Onto another common issue that continues to draw my attention: there is a kind of structural superficiality often associated with whether or not the responsibility for a change within an organization or a jurisdiction should be centrally *or* de-centrally led. Ah... The false dichotomy of the central versus decentral debates! We need to extract "versus" from the equation and instead travel deeper and wiser regarding what needs to be centralized, and what should and *can* be decentralized to achieve the results we need. The most salient version of these discussions over the past decades is embedded in Canada's fragile federation. For example, while we have the Canada Health Act, is healthcare equally provided across the nation? In 2004, Prime Minister Paul Martin negotiated his "fix healthcare for a generation" Health Accord with the provinces and territories—including a $41 billion (CAD) transfer to the provinces over 10 years. It was clear that the provinces and territories would be in the best position to know how best to use this new money based on local needs; one province might wish to deal with re-engineering its approach to joint replacements to reduce wait times, another focusing on primary care improvements. That was the idea.

"Provinces know best. Thanks for the cash, Paul," was the refrain from provincial premiers. Unfortunately, the "transfer" of these resources came with zero accountability to report on both plans before and after receiving the money, and the notion of providing transparent information about progress with the use of this new money just wasn't on. The very fact that a fed/prov partnership in which the senior government provides resources to the junior jurisdiction with no strings attached was—and continues to be—a problem.

I once gave a keynote entitled *What Does it Mean to be a Child in Canada?*, noting the disparities regarding the provision of supports to children from province to province. Where a child lives makes a difference. On the devastating side of all this is the unfairness for the First Nations children, as noted earlier.

As discussed, as I alluded to earlier, we also got closer to a national set of principles in regard to a national early learning and child care approach under Prime Minister Martin's tenure, during which his very able Minister, Ken Dryden, achieved a signed agreement among all the provinces and territories. While the plan included the local distribution of money, the agreement called for clear expectations that local initiatives had to adhere to four principles: Quality; Universal; Accessible; and Developmental (QUAD). In this case, the plan included the establishment of a tracking and reporting system in order to measure the implementation of these principles. Kudos to Mr. Martin and Mr. Dryden.

It was a thoughtful example of the balance between a nationally led approach with clear principles and resource provision, combined with the decentralized provision of services—and a soupçon of accountability. Excellent, except that, during Mr. Martin's successor's first several weeks in Office, Stephen Harper scrapped it, along with two other *accords*: Kyoto (environment) and Kelowna (Indigenous land rights).

Increasingly, we witness stronger regional differences regarding power-sharing and emotionally charged concerns with current fiscal arrangements; the political environment is replete with too much extremism, and, while a national conversation in Canada about ensuring the right central-decentral balance would be ideal, elections are ill-suited moments to have a truly "adult conversation".

Perhaps it is time for an independent process of renewing and updating our federal balance—a modern version of the Canadian Rowell-Sirois Commission created to explore federal-provincial relations and fiscal federalism in the late 1930s. However, it is my thought that this idea should inform the content of another book—one that I am ill-equipped to write. There is no doubt that COVID-19's fundamental assault on our economic basics should give rise to something dramatically different from our BV times; there is also no doubt that there will be some process for thinking about a new norm when it comes to all things economic. Think about the total post-WWII reconstruction that took place.

While I have only used the context in which the decentralizing train seems to have left the Canadian station as the proxy for the balance question, the same quest for this balance applies within all organizations. Earlier, I spoke of the problems with "offices of..." solutions to things like ensuring equity within an organization, or offices of mental health and the like. I noted that we need to ensure the right roles and balance regarding who is responsible for what. It seems to me that a centrally located "office of..." needs to lead to the development of clear principles and processes that are widely shared with "local" leaders—chairs, directors, and other front-line leaders. Remember, *the process is the product*, and an effective process also informs the initial need for these front-line leaders to be trained regarding their responsibilities in implementing a new policy or program.

Unless the reasons for establishing an anti-oppression office, for example, are embedded into the performance objectives of front-line managers, organizational cultural change will not evolve. We need centrally led initiatives regarding what is clearly expected—along with informed locally led implementation—together with centrally tracked results across the organization to guide continuous improvement. This clearly established balance of roles and accountability would produce the changes we seek.

As you may recall, I noted that when I became a college president, I shared a few leadership principles with my new colleagues within the college community. You might recall that one of them was *participation breeds creativity and commitment.* After about a year, we made it clear through our behaviour that we really *did* believe in collaborative approaches—and it worked: our budget process evolved into an integrating one that expected each budget unit leader (department chairs, for example) to involve all of their colleagues in a process of doing an environmental scan of future opportunities and threats, as well as how they might affect their short-, medium-, and long-term education and training goals and resource needs. This is also another example of *the process is the product* that ensured that front-line leaders fully involved (and documented) their colleagues' participation (including support staff) and further ensured that budgeting process *taught* strategic thinking, beyond typically narrow annual requests for more money.

It worked. Very well, in fact. Our level of collaboration also included seeking student input, as well as input from others who had formal responsibilities including our faculty and support staff unions.

We established a large and representative budget committee to finalize the budget priorities for board consideration. Eventually, we started using the *concept of co-determination*, underlying that our intention was to work through the process so that we reached a high level of agreement about our very best conclusions for the health of the college's future. We wanted to stay clear of low-common-denominator compromises that could dominate efforts at democratic leadership.

We also clarified that, while we deeply valued our partnerships and commitment to co-determination, final decisions regarding certain major decisions (for example, final budget approval, program cancellations, new hires, etc.) legally resided with the Board. And, while the Board did sometimes adjust to the advice provided to them, it was relatively rare considering the thorough and open nature of the process. Nevertheless, the reasons for any changes were clearly provided to the budget committee and the college community at large. It's easy to throw around notions of collaboration or partnership, but it's harder still to implement these ideas of distributed shared power through actual behaviour that really counts. Essential to democratic leadership is the need to be clear about the nature of partnerships.

Too often the notions of *partnership* or *collaboration,* lack clarity regarding expectations of their practical applications. When Premier Rae appointed me Deputy Minister of the Premier's Council on Health, Wellbeing, and Social Justice, I reported directly to him in his role of Chair of the Council. As I noted earlier, the Council itself was a high-level partnership table, bringing together a remarkable and diverse group of experts and practitioners. As I became comfortable with Mr. Rae, I felt more at ease with providing him with unsolicited advice—not just what was expected. At the time, his newly elected NDP government—as well as virtually all of its ministers—were communicating widely that their election was an almost revolutionary opportunity to share power; to be an effective partner with all of Ontario's constituents and organizations; to become the best partnering government in history. As the first NDP government ever to take power at Queen's Park (Ontario's place of government), this kind of social democratic messaging seemed to come naturally, and yet it all reminded me of the mistake I had made in my role as a rookie college president. My core values regarding things like collaboration *before* the rank and file actually started to feel the change, creating a disconnect between my rhetoric and reality for too many. Sure, I learned to be clear that my words were aspirational, that things would take time, but what was also key was the need to paint a clearer picture regarding what would be different over time.

So, I became uneasy that the gap between the Rae government's espoused beliefs about partnership and implied notions of co-determination was increasingly creating an implementation and trust chasm. With this in mind, I wrote an essay entitled *So You Want to Be My Partner*, the initial intention of which was that it would be for the Premier's eyes only, but that he might share this tongue-in-cheek, yet pointed, tome with his Cabinet. Okay, call me naïve; this unpublished piece remains on the shelf, and, to date, I have not received any feedback from the former Premier, although a non-response is deafening feedback, I suppose. In my intro to the paper, I noted the following:

I am uncertain about whether or not the many people in your government who stake claim to an interest in partnership mean the same things.

(To lighten things up at the beginning, I inserted a wonderful dialogue extracted from the wonderful British comedy, *Yes, Minister.)*

Bernard asked us, "What's wrong with Open Government?" I could hardly believe my ears.

Arnold pointed out, with great clarity, that Open Government is a contradiction in terms. You can be open, or you can have government.

Bernard claims that the citizens of a democracy have a right to know. We explained that, in fact, they have a right to be ignorant. Knowledge only means complicity and guilt. Ignorance has a certain dignity.

Bernard then said, "The Minister wants Open Government." I remarked that one just does not give people what they want, if it's not good for them; one does not, for example, give whisky to an alcoholic.

Arnold rightly added that, if people do not know what you're doing, they don't know what you're doing wrong.

More seriously, I inserted a quote from the late and highly regarded former Federal Deputy Minister, Arthur Kroeger:

There is an inherent tendency for governments to approach consultation with something less than a fully open mind. More often than we care to admit, what is presented as consultation is, in reality, an exercise in trying to get the public to see that we already have the right answer.

The essence of my paper was to reinforce a key lesson that continues to have meaning due to its absence in too many public and private places: *it is essential to clearly define and understand up-front, the roles and responsibilities of various and all participants in consultations and partnerships.* Whether intentional or unintentional, too many organizational leaders throw around superficial expectations about partnerships without being clear on the nature of a collaboration. Clarification is essential. Is it a co-determining partnership? A senior/junior relationship? Advisory? Far too often, many so-called consultations seem to align with Arthur Kroeger's description.

Another quick-fire lesson that perhaps I should have embedded in the earlier chapters about communications. Just didn't seem to fit. It's the lesson of *no surprises.* It is critically important not to put people we depend on—and those who depend on us—off guard by surprising them with information they should have known about. This is also about ensuring that people you depend on continue to trust you. When I spoke earlier about Premier Rae's incredible self-government *treaty* with the Chiefs of Ontario, it came as a complete surprise to me as the deputy minister who had a major role to play with Indigenous child welfare leaders. I heard about this at the same time as the Premier announced it at a press conference and had to pretend I knew all about it when my phone started ringing five minutes after the public event. Another time, during the early 90s—a time of austerity that required major cutbacks—as a deputy with only barebones left to cut—we eliminated a $200k per year grant to Gambler's Anonymous. We had already cut about $1.5 billion (CAD) out of our $12 billion (CAD) budget in social services. Fine. Except three days later, the government of Ontario announced they were establishing casinos to raise revenue. Naturally, Gamblers Anonymous noted very publicly the remarkable hypocrisy of cutting what would be more necessary with casinos coming down the pike. I was directed to call them and offer to triple their original grant. It would have been nice to have had a heads up.

Okay, enough pointing the finger at a former boss. When I was a college president, we became very good at ensuring that any good news arising from a board meeting—things like the approval of a new wing of a building or new program or the impending visit of a dignitary—quickly became a news item on local television, radio, or the daily newspaper. Great reputational enhancement for our work. Except that I was constantly getting complaints from colleagues within the college that they were hearing about the good news from the media—and often from neighbours—unaware of what had been announced publicly. Easy fix. So once we learned that we were surprising our own folks, our Director of Communications simply took the draft news release that she had prepared for immediate release—pending the Board's decisions—and turned it into an internal note that was faxed immediately to all unit heads following the meeting. As leaders, *we need to practice the no surprises rule by knowing who needs to know what and when, to ensure people we count on are not blindsided.*

Moving on to another issue, I've spent a good deal of time over the years trying to understand the best ways to assess the quality of various services: from pre-school education through to post-secondary; from grassroots social services to "illness" interventions. As an example of this, I have shadowed people charged with visiting early years' settings to assess the quality of supports for young children. The best of these quality experts not only know what they are looking for, but also *why*. They have deeply internalized what excellent pedagogy looks like; those subtle efforts of an early childhood educator to guide, not direct, children's curiosity-driven, play-based learning. They *know* at a deep level why various characteristics of an early learning environment make a difference to a child's development, because their preparation was informed by an effective reflective training experience. On the other hand, I have witnessed those with clipboard checklists superficially noting the frequencies of certain behaviours. Importantly, I have observed the quality of feedback these different assessors provide to those they have observed. In this regard, the difference between those who understand the *why* of what they are evaluating compared to those who have been given a pro-forma checklist, is startling.

Indeed, the process of developing an approach to solving a particular problem or improving a service must deeply involve those who will be at the front-line of change, if we want to promote genuine progress.

There are pre-packaged, off-the-shelf programs for training in just about everything. Unfortunately, those who are asked to implement them had nothing to do with their development. Many of these packaged programs—including a well-known so-called "parent training" offering—are bereft of independent R&D, and, indeed, for those programs that do provide research "results", the research is often funded by the program's designer/owner. Do not trust so-called research supported by those who have financial gain connected to the purchase of their product; instead, follow the money to determine if any training offering has legitimate and independent research behind it.

One final concern that fights for a place on my Top 10 Pet Peeves: the boiler plate approach to solving problems that well-known uber-consulting companies employ. Far too often, I have observed off-the-shelf final reports for extremely expensive consulting efforts wondering how often these reports have actually improved results or the operational effectiveness of an organization. Making money in an overly efficient manner drives so many of these consulting firms. Effective bottom–up participation—going deep on analysing organizational cultures—takes time and money. The lesson here? *Beware of large prestigious consulting firms who create the illusion of rigorous analysis while actually doing the minimum to make a boiler plate final report look relevant to a particular client's needs or wants.* Oh my, can't wait to see what response I might get from this lesson.

Other notions concerning what I can learn to inform my own leadership continue to abound on an almost-daily basis. As I note in the final chapter, *the beat goes on.*

Chapter Thirteen — What's *Your* Takeaway?

EXERCISE #13:

Okay, getting close to the end. I have no doubt that the lessons I have noted throughout these pages are far from comprehensive. My experience and lessons hopefully overlap significantly with your experience and leadership interests. However, before moving to the final chapter, I would like you to answer a question: what is a key leadership lesson that is important to you that I have not mentioned, something *I* can learn from?

Your Notes

Chapter Fourteen
The Beat Goes On

AS I STATED AT the beginning of this leadership journey, that the many lessons I have learned— the many I *continue* to learn—flow from *my* experience. I truly hope that many—or even just a few—of my lessons resonate with you and your own journey. My wish is that my lessons, as well as those I have appropriated from others, as stated with intended redundancy throughout, stimulate your own thinking and accordingly challenge you to lead in different, unique and, naturally, more effective ways.

Of course, the big lessons for me claim a place in chapter titles:

- *Feedback is the Breakfast of Champions.* The critical importance of personal accountability and growth through diverse sources of feedback.
- *Complement Thyself.* Know who you are; know your assets; know who and what you need to complement your leadership!
- *Being Right is Not a Strategy.* Paying active attention to the views of others and building understanding before "seeking to be understood".
- *The Power of Evidence-Based Storytelling.* Effective change requires sound evidence, communicated with stories told by diverse and respected "tellers".

- *Ditch the Media Blame Game.* Better understand the possibilities/limitations of media sources to communicate more effectively.
- *Improvement is the Enemy of Change.* The critical importance of systems-change actions that deal with underlying obstacles for true change to happen.
- *Choosing and Achieving World-Changing Outcomes.* The importance of a long-term vision, informed by clear goals, informed by moral purpose.
- *The Graceful Power of Apology and the Opportunity of Mistakes.* Taking advantage of the teachable moments of errors to grow and reinforce core values.
- *Say What? The Critical Importance of Language.* Clearing away the smokescreen of misinformation and intentional disinformation.
- *Lessons Learned from World War III.* The worst crisis of our lifetime provides lessons about what we can do better.
- *Embracing the Power of Optimism.* Hanging out with the hopeful while eschewing negativity in the face of chaos.

Other far superior leaders and writers put what I try to communicate in simpler but more powerful ways. I am reminded of the last president of Czechoslovakia and the Czech Republic's first president, the remarkable Vaclav Havel. In 1990, he addressed the U.S. Congress, noting that *the salvation of this human world lies nowhere else than in the human heart, in the human power to reflect, in human meekness and in human responsibility*[17]. In a single sentence, this famous writer/leader captured what this much lesser scribe took pages to express: the importance of looking *within* through reflection, the importance of humility as a driver of learning from others and a commitment to something beyond ourselves.

In the previous chapter, I noted a few other "quick-fire" lessons, as well as new ones that always crop up for me. Furthermore, embedded in the chapters throughout are a few others that have become personal mantras for me. *Doing fewer things better rather than all things less well* is so important regarding setting priorities; it is critical to emphasize the need to choose those few things that can make the biggest difference and avoid wasting energy and resources trying to do way too much. Something else that is central to my leadership is my notion that *what is right is more important than who is right*. When a leader's too-frequent default is position power driven by the need to be "right", coupled with a healthy insecurity to boot, an organization loses tremendously creative capital that can be offered by others, regardless of position or hierarchy.

A first cousin of this important lesson for me is the *importance of catching people and organizations doing things right*. In my experience, one of the best sources of ideas for great public policy or practice improvement is finding

---

[17] Havel, V., 1990, available at https://www.vhlf.org/havel-quotes/speech-to-the-u-s-congress.

examples that shine a light on what's possible, then figuring out how to scale it up.

Two more of my frequently repeated lessons for anyone who will listen: *overcome the hardening of the* categories and *short-termism.* These are the twin diseases that will prevent effective change due to silo thinking and structures, as well as the failure to think beyond the immediacy of current circumstances and pressures.

I have often talked about the fact that the *process is the product.* Without effective transparent and inclusive processes that fully involve internal and external opportunities for meaningful participation, the outcomes will suffer in their shape and relevance along with lost opportunities for effective and sustained implementation.

Naturally, everyone has some very basic, clear notions when it comes to considering what great leadership looks like—and, given the beauty of simplicity, I guess I could have saved a good deal of time and spared some trees by writing a short article on the importance of:

- Emotional intelligence and naturally-present empathy,
- Thinking and acting strategically,
- Humility that drives ongoing learning, and
- Communicating clearly, ideas that matter.

Perhaps there is one additional leadership characteristic that deserves a place on the list of powerful simplicity:

I truly loved my 15 years at the Atkinson Charitable Foundation, informed by the remarkable Joseph E. Atkinson (who, as we have established, was one of Canada's most progressive 20th century thought leaders). I learned a great deal about the use of his *Toronto Star* newspaper as an unrelenting tool for change beginning in 1899. I also learned that he married a working journalist, Elmina Elliott, in 1892. As an accomplished professional journalist and thinker in her own right, her advice to Mr. Atkinson in the face of challenges on how to come down on a particular approach to a particular issue? She would pose, "What's the *kind* thing to do, Joe?"

When all is said and done, in emphasizing that my lessons and values are, indeed, mine, the most important leadership lessons for you to apply must be yours. In the first chapter, I asked you to write down your own leadership principles and values, determining what you stand for and developing a way of holding yourself accountable with things like a daily or weekly reflective diary. You might also consider a 360 process that provides those around you with an opportunity to give you the gift of constructive feedback in a safe manner. This can increase your self-knowledge, the key engine for personal growth. As part of this process of determining *your values,* I asked you to write down the people who have inspired you the most, and why. This was intended for you to make explicit what you value regarding effective leadership. Did you write down your thoughts about good leadership? How did *you* do, *vis-a-vis* my experience? How did *I* do in comparison with your own experience? Let me know, please. Remember, feedback is the breakfast of champions!

Once again, if you gain nothing from my stroll through

my leadership memory lane other than the power of regular personal reflection regarding your values and how they play out in your behaviour, then I will feel really content that writing this has been worthwhile.

Regarding keeping our conversations going, I noted in Chapter One that my website will provide a "meeting place" for sharing new ideas about applying our lessons and stories that bring these ideas into clear focus. http://charlespascal.com

As we move to recess, my favourite school subject, I remain driven by my mantra that **we need to do all we can to ensure the future is more just, safer, healthier, and prosperous for the many, rather than for the elite few**. At this stage of my journey, it felt absolutely necessary to share what I *think* I know from my experience. Annoying or not, it's also a time in my life when people start asking me the tombstone question: what's your journey's epitaph? Notwithstanding the fact that cremation will prevent me from taking up too much space, my epitaph is simply: *I tried.*

I said at the beginning that I have found so much inspiration from my family and friends. I also told the story of an amazing opportunity to get to know my most inspiring public leader, Tommy Douglas—the father of our cherished Canadian universal healthcare system. I share Tommy's love of Alfred Lord Tennyson's famous poem, *Ulysses*. Here's an excerpt we both seem to cherish:

The lights begin to twinkle from the rocks:
The long day wanes: the slow moon climbs: the deep
Moans round with many voices. Come, my friends,
'T is not too late to seek a newer world.

Acknowledgements

I am very fortunate for the many relationships I have had with real-deal leaders who have afforded me a front row seat to learn from their gifts; their demonstrated ability to push for changes that make a difference. Most of them have found their way into this leadership memoir.

I have also been incredibly fortunate to have traveled with many wonderful peer academics at the universities of Michigan, McGill and Toronto, who have understood the power of evidence to change the world. I have had dozens of amazing colleagues who have been so generous with their time and intellect in support of my journey as a scholar and teacher.

A big thank you to Hayley Paige and her team at Notebook Publishing whose guidance and tough loving care was so central to the outcome. As I have noted, the *process is the product,* and working with Hayley and her colleagues has been very special.

I have acknowledged in Chapter One the importance of my early years and the indelible influence of my parents and grandparents. This initial journey of support has been richly sustained through the up-close presence of my brothers, Roger and Ross, and the many aunts, uncles, cousins and in-laws who have been part of a largesse of good fortune for me.

Finally, and holding down first place in my heart, my immediate clan. I refer to my children—Blaise, Jesse and Tai—in the book. Each of these wonderful people offers special gifts to my life. They, and my grandkids, try to make me a better dad and grandad in so many ways. I hope they keep trying. Finally, Tassie, my partner of more than 40 years, has been both my rock and my compass, providing me with the confidence to take chances, the commitment to do better, and the vision to take on little and bigger things that matter.

Index

CPSIA information can be obtained
at www.ICGtesting.com
Printed in the USA
BVHW090800071220
595078BV00006B/62

9 781913 206444